日中印の真価を問う

Japan
China
India

世界経済危機をめぐって

Asia Giants in the Face of the Global Economic Crisis

林華生
■
浜勝彦
■
澁谷祐

編著

白帝社

まえがき

2008年9月に米国発金融危機が勃発した。この危機が猛スピードで世界金融危機や世界経済危機を誘発した。そして，G20の開催に象徴されるように，日米欧などの先進国とBRICsに代表される新興国が一体になって，世界規模の危機の対策に取り組んだ。これらの国々は対策の度合いや方策は違うが，基本的には大規模な財政出動による緊急経済対策が柱だった。

現在，世界各国の緊急経済対策が奏功し，世界経済危機は沈静化の方向に向かいつつある。しかし，"雇用なき景気回復"に見られるように，世界各国が高い失業率に直面している。特に欧米諸国は二桁の失業率に悩まされている。それだけではない。経済改革や金融セクターの改革，金融機構の監督機能の強化，世界規模の保護主義の台頭の防止などの対策がまだスムーズに展開されておらず，顕著な成果を挙げていない。その結果として，一部の新興国を除いて，世界各国の経済は深刻な不況と低迷状態が続いている。

しかし，新興国の中国やインドにおいては急速な経済成長は注目を浴びているが，いろいろな経済発展の歪みが露呈し顕著化している。中国においては，1978年以来実施してきた32年間の改革開放経済政策の「負の遺産」として，沿海部と内陸部の経済発展の不均衡，所得格差の拡大，環境汚染，汚職腐敗の蔓延，資産バブルの激化などが挙げられる。インドにおいては，1991年以来導入してきた20年間の「新経済政策」の「経済発展の必要悪」として，同じく環境汚染，所得格差の拡大，都市部と農村部の経済発展の不均衡が見られるほか，カースト制度，農業生産の疲弊，インド独特の混合経済の低生産性，巨大財閥による独占体制の顕在化などが挙げられる。

勿論，世界二大人口大国が長年の持続的な経済発展の過程の中で，上に述べた経済発展の歪みの発生や悪化は避けられない。しかし，これらの一連の歪みを適宜に正さなければ，社会的政治的不安になると同時にいずれ経済的停滞を引き起こすに違いない。現時点の中国やインドは新興国として世界経済の発展を牽引していると期待されている。世界経済発展の重荷にならないように有効なマクロ経済政策を実施してほしいものである。

日本においては，財政赤字（「国の借金」）は欧米諸国よりは深刻だが，総じて経済ファンダメンタルズは欧米諸国より良いのである。経済回復の兆しも見え始めているが，経済は依然低迷していて無気力である。デフレ経済救済，経済二番底の有効な政策が打ち出せない。近い将来，経済が健全な発展の軌道に

乗ることは期待できない。日本は欧米諸国と同様，世界経済発展を強力に牽引していく力が欠いているように見える。

現在，米国発金融危機や世界経済危機の原因，対策，再発防止の究明が重要な課題となっている。本書は日中印政治経済と米国政治経済との相互依存・相互補完関係，アジア諸国の経済発展と世界経済危機との関係，アジアの天然資源と安全保障と米国との関係等を重点的に解明しようと試みた。勿論,国別に，例えば日中印米の政治経済の実態分析や経済発展戦略等についての分析や解明も欠かせない。そこで，我々は日中印の第一線で活躍されている学者や研究者に原稿を依頼した。また米国やフィンランドの著名な学者や研究者にも原稿を依頼した。幸運にも各専門家から力作労作を寄せて頂いた。本書は中国語の論文を和訳して載せたが，英語の論文は原文のまま載せた。この誌面を借りて本書の執筆者に深く感謝申し上げる。尚本書はそれぞれの執筆者の個人的見解であり所属機関を代表するものではないことを申し添える。

早稲田大学アジア太平洋研究センター・東アジア地域研究部会と早稲田大学中華経済研究所は定期的に研究会を共催してきた。その研究成果の一部は，林華生，浜勝彦，澁谷祐編著『アジア経済発展のアキレス腱—資源枯渇と環境破壊—』（文真堂，2008年7月）として刊行された。今回はその第二部として，刊行される運びとなった。我々は早稲田大学アジア太平洋研究センターと早稲田大学中華経済研究所の財政的援助なしには，長年に亘って，研究会を共催することは出来なかった。また浜勝彦と澁谷祐両氏に研究会の運営に多大なる御協力を得た。特に澁谷氏においては本書の企画や出版に御尽力された。研究会のメンバーである王元氏が王少普論文を和訳した。厚くお礼申し上げる。

本書は早稲田大学総合研究機構から出版助成を頂いた。早稲田大学中華経済研究所は頂新国際集団の援助を受けて研究活動や出版活動を展開することができた。合わせてここに衷心より御礼申し上げる。尚出版に御尽力頂いた株式会社白帝社の山内広子さんには心から感謝申し上げる次第である。

林　華生
早稲田大学大学院アジア太平洋研究科教授
早稲田大学アジア太平洋研究センター教授
早稲田大学中華経済研究所所長

2010年2月　吉日

目　次

はじめに

第1部　世界経済危機とアジア

第1章　世界経済危機と日中印……………………………………… 8
　　　林華生　早稲田大学大学院アジア太平洋研究科教授, 早稲田大学中華経済研究所所長
第2章　世界経済危機と「東アジア共同体」…………………………… 26
　　　谷口　誠　桜美林大学北東アジア総合研究所特別顧問, 北東アジア研究交流ネットワーク代表幹事
第3章　世界経済危機と中日米三ヶ国関係…………………………… 42
　　　王少普　上海交通大学環太平洋研究センター教授, 日本研究センター主任教授
第4章　ポスト世界金融危機時代の新興国市場とグローバル企業の動向… 51
　　　木下俊彦　早稲田大学大学院アジア太平洋研究科客員教授

第2部　東アジアのエネルギー・安全保障と米新政権

第5章　東アジアのエネルギー安全保障とリスク…………………… 70
　　　澁谷　祐　早稲田大学アジア太平洋研究センター特別研究員
第6章　東アジアの安全保障と米新政権……………………………… 91
　　　美根慶樹　キヤノングローバル戦略研究所特別研究員

第3部　中印経済発展の課題と展望

第7章　中国改革開放30年の政策展開過程――その成果と課題 ………… 110
　　　浜　勝彦　創価大学名誉教授,（社）中国研究所理事長
第8章　インド型経済発展モデルとグローバル不況………………… 125
　　　清水　学　帝京大学経済学部教授

第4部　アジアの経済発展と世界経済危機——外国からの視点

第9章　アジア太平洋の地域統合の進展と世界金融危機(2008-2009年) … 146
　　　　ハンス C. ブロムクイスト　ハンケン経済経営学院（フィンランド）教授

Chapter 9　The Progress of Regional Integration in Asia-Pacific and the Global Financial Crisis of 2008－2009, Hans C. Blomqvist

第10章　インドと日本—新しい状況と機会……………………………… 165
　　　　H.S. プラバカル　ジャワハラル・ネルー大学国際問題研究所日本研究科准教授

Chapter 10　India-Japan: New Situation and New Opportunities, H.S. Prabhakar

第11章　大きすぎて助けられない世界の金融メルトダウン ………… 188
　　　　トーマス・ファーガソン　マサチューセッツ大学政治学部教授（ボストン）
　　　　ロバート・ジョンソン　ソロス財団マネージメント専務理事（共同執筆）

Chapter 11　Too Big To Bail: The "Paulson Put," U.S. Presidential Politics, and the Global Financial Meltdown, Thomas Ferguson and Robert Johnson

第12章　エピローグ—世界経済危機が日中印に与える衝撃 ………… 240
　　　　林華生　早稲田大学大学院アジア太平洋研究科教授、早稲田大学中華経済研究所所長

Chapter 12　Epilogue—Impacts of the Global Economic Crisis on Japan, China and India, Lim Hua Sing

主な略語一覧
執筆者略歴

第1部　世界経済危機とアジア

第1章　世界経済危機と日中印

林華生*

　日本は1991年3月にバブル経済が崩壊してから、"失われた20年"の間、一時的な経済回復の期間もあったが、基本的には、経済低迷が続いている。政府は多額の財政赤字を抱えているが、経済的ファンダメンタルズは欧米の先進国より悪くない。日本経済の世界経済における地位はまだ相当高い。日本はまだまだ米国経済の回復や世界経済の振興と発展に大きな貢献が期待できよう。一方、中国は過去32年間の経済発展の結果、今年GDPが日本を超える。中国はまた世界最大の外貨準備金保有国として世界に君臨する。インドは中国と同様、新興国として順調な経済発展が脚光を浴びるようになってきた。インドの一人当たりGDPはまだ小さいが、人口が多いこともありGDPは巨大である。インドはBRICsの一員として国際舞台で重要性を増していくに違いない。

　日中印はアジア太平洋においては当然のことだが、世界においてもその存在感と役割が日増しに重要となっている。日中印の2008年に起きた米国発金融危機ひいては世界経済危機との関わり、日中印の米国経済における地位と役割を分析すれば、これらアジア三大国の経済実力が窺える。本論は日中印の米国発金融危機後の米国経済と世界経済危機と関連して分析する。

1．米国発金融危機と世界経済危機

　大手投資銀行・証券会社のリーマン・ブラザーズの破綻が発端となった米国金融危機が、瞬く間に全世界に波及し、世界金融危機となり、世界経済危機となった。

　1997-98年のアジア金融危機は韓国の他に、発展途上国のアジア諸国、とりわけASEANを中心とする国々に発生した。今回2008年の金融危機が経済超大国のアメリカに端を発したことは世界を震撼させた。

　この100年に一度の危機は「津波」、「乱気流」とも呼ばれ、1930年代の世界経済恐慌と例えられた。1930年代の世界経済恐慌は、第二次世界大戦へと進展していったが、幸い今回の世界経済恐慌は先進国（日米欧など）と新興国（BRICsを中心として）の緊密な提携と協力により、沈静化の方向に向かいつつあるように見える。

---

*　早稲田大学大学院アジア太平洋研究科教授、早稲田大学中華経済研究所所長。

米国発の金融危機はもはやG7やG8で解決できるものではない。金融危機発生後の世界の対応は早く，金融危機後初めての世界会議，つまり金融危機への対処を話し合うG20緊急首脳会議は2008年11月14日ワシントンD.C,で開催された。その後も2009年4月2日ロンドン，9月24日ピッツバーグ，11月6日セントアンドリュースで開催され，先進国と新興国のそれぞれの大規模な財政出動と企業救済政策が打ち出され，内需拡大と国内経済の刺激により，世界経済がようやく緩やかな回復の兆しを見せ始めた。しかし，「雇用なき景気回復」に象徴されるように，世界各国の経済は未だに低迷し，失業状況もますます深刻化してきている。米国の失業率は危機前の8％前後から現在10％程度に悪化しており，日本の失業率は戦後最高の水準に達している。現在，EU27ヶ国中，16ヶ国が二桁の失業率であると報道されている。スペインのような17.4％（2009年4月）の高失業率の国もある。中国は経済発展の優等生であり，世界経済を牽引しているが，中国もまた深刻な失業問題に悩まされている。したがって，世界各国の経済はすでに底打ちになっていると楽観視されているが，油断はできない。

　米国は金融危機発生後，経済体質や企業体質は一向改善されていない。低貯蓄過剰消費社会，深刻な双子赤字の経済体質（後に詳細に分析する），金融セクターを中心とする企業の抜本的改革は行わない，長年の医療制度改革も成果が見られない，などである。日本は長年深刻な財政赤字を抱えている一方，デフレと円高に直面している。危機後の財政出動策による経済刺激は顕著な成果を上げていない。新たに政権を担った民主党政府は財政困窮で2009年8月の総選挙時にマニフェストで約束していた経済救済資金を調達できず，国債発行額を44兆円以下に抑えるという努力目標もあっさりと破られた。また，国内外（国内的には国家財政赤字の削減と国家予算の編成や雇用問題の改善，国際的には米軍普天間基地の移設問題など）の問題が山積しており，新政権としての役割をなかなか果たせないでいる。

　中国は今回の世界金融危機に際し，緊急な財政出動に乗り出した。中国は4兆元の財政出動により，内需拡大や国内経済刺激策が奏功し，2008年は8％の成長率を達成した。また，2009年には9.6％の成長率を達成したと推測されている。しかし，財政出動のかなりの部分が株や不動産市場に流入し，株・不動産バブルが発生している。中国政府はバブル経済を警戒し，対応策を出し始めているが，効果は未知である。一方，世界経済が低迷している中，輸出入貿易も激減してきたので，国内経済の発展に悪影響を及ぼしかねない。また，長年の所得格差問題，国営企業改革問題，沿海部と内陸部の発展格差問題，環

境汚染問題，官僚汚職問題なども国家政策として解決していかねばならない。

インドは日本や中国ほど世界経済危機に直撃されていない。インドの金融市場は日本や中国ほど発展しておらず，しかも欧米金融市場に開放されていないので，金融危機に直撃されていないと考えられる。インドは 2007 年より，5 年間で 3 千 500 億米ドルの資金を調達し，空港，港湾，都市高速鉄道，大規模発電所などのインフラ整備に取り組んできた。このように，インドは近年の積極的な外貨導入や，着実なインフラの整備により，経済が順調に発展しているように見える。さらに，インド経済は中国経済の輸出貿易による発展パターンとは違い，内需拡大や国内経済の刺激による経済発展戦略をとってきたので，2009 年も 6％程度の経済成長が見込まれている。しかし，インドの経済発展の潜在的力を過大評価してはならない。インドにおいては，遅れた社会的工業的インフラ建設がなかなか経済発展に追いつかない，農業生産の疲弊，多種族・多宗教・多言語による社会の多様性や煩雑性，カースト制度，混合経済の低生産性，巨大財閥による独占体制などがインド経済の飛躍的発展を阻害している。

2．日中印の経済強靭性をどう評価するか

日本は深刻な財政赤字問題を抱えているほか，輸出貿易も円高で深刻な打撃を受けている。しかし，日本の経済的ファンダメンタルズは欧米諸国ほど悪くない。しかも，円高を利用して，そして膨大な外貨準備金を利用して，主に対米投資（米企業の M&A，株や国債の購入）を展開している。日本資本の積極的な対米投資により，米国経済を支えている一面をも見逃してはいけない。例えば，表 1 に見るように，日本の外貨準備金は 1 兆 494 億ドル（2009 年末）に上っている。2009 年 6 月末までには，日本の米国債購入実績は 7 千 118 億ドルに上り，そして同年 10 月末までにはその金額が 7 千 465 億ドルに上った。米国経済における日本の影響力が窺える。

一方，中国とインドは新興国として，その発展ぶりが世界の注目を集めている。G20 における中国とインドの重要性はロシアやブラジルと同様，ますます重要となってきた。勿論，中国の 1 人当たり GDP は米国と日本のそれぞれの 11.6％と 15.8％に過ぎない。インドの一人当たり GDP は米国と日本のそれぞれの 5.9％と 8.0％に過ぎない。しかし中印は顕著な，しかも迅速な経済発展が新興国の中のリーダー格となっている。また，表 1 に見るように，中国は世界最大の外貨準備金を持っており（2 兆 3 千 991 億ドル），米国債購入実績は 2009 年 6 月末の時点においては，すでに 7 千 764 億ドルに上り，同年

10月末には8千億ドル前後で推移している。発展途上国の中国が経済大国の米国の国債を最も保有していることは甚だ異常であるといわざるを得ないだろう。
　他方，インドは"貧しい大国"であるが，"世界最大の民主主義国家"でもある。2009年12月には2千873億7千400万ドルの外貨準備金を保有している。米国の833億7千500万ドルの3.4倍である。また，インドは2009年5月末には388億ドルに上る米国債を保有している。
　以上述べたように，日中印は大量の米国債を保有している。その総額は何と1兆5千270億ドルに上り，驚く数字である。日中印は米国経済と密接な関係にあることを物語っている。米国債の基盤は日中印に支えられていると言っても過言ではない。特に日中両国（加えてイギリス）が米国債や株を購入しなければ，米国の金融体制は成り立たない。また米国債や株が放出されれば，直ちに米国に金融危機が起こり，米国の金融体制，ひいては世界の金融体制が崩壊するであろう。
　とは言え，米国債や株を大量に抱えている日中印は米国金融体制の崩壊を期待していない。金利の高い，安定的な米国債と高い株価は基本的には日中印にとって有利なのである。他方，後で述べるが，日中両国は外貨準備高のうち，米国通貨ドルの保有率が非常に高いので，日中は米ドルの切り下げを望まない。日本は堅調な日本円を期待しない，中国は堅調な人民元を期待しない最大の原因の一つはつまり弱い米ドルを期待しないからである。米ドルが急激に弱くならないように，日中両政府は常に円売りドル買いと元売りドル買いを繰り返してきた。米ドルの急激な下落はつまり日中の富（外貨準備金）の損失に繋がる。日中が米景気に左右されないように，外貨準備金の米ドルの比重を減らし，通貨のバスケット制の方向へ持っていくことが重要な課題である。
　世界の経済状況は良くない。日本経済も低迷している。しかし，日本の銀行金融機関・証券会社・中央政府は資金を抱えている。常に金利の高い米国債や株に投資を回す。一方，中印経済も厳しいが中印は新興国の優等生である。特に世界一の外貨準備金を保有している中国は，手っ取り早く米国債や株を購入する。しかし中長期的に見れば，米国債や株の大量購入による米国経済依存体質から方向調整や脱皮する方策を考えなければならない。
　インドの経済発展水準は中国より20年くらい遅れている。中国の経済発展水準は日本より50年くらい遅れている。とすれば，インドは日本よりも70年ぐらい遅れていると考えられる。端的に，インドの外貨準備金を日中と比べれば，弱体である。したがって，インドが米国債や株を大量購入し，対米経済

表1　日中印米の経済指標

	面積	人口	GDP	1人当たりGDP	外貨準備	米国債購入実績
日本	37万7911.01km²	1億2758万人（2009年10月）	4.290兆ドル（2007年）	33,600ドル（2007年）	1兆494億ドル（2009年末）	7,118億ドル（2009年6月末）
中国	約960万km²（日本の約25倍）	約13億2800万人（2009年7月）	4.400兆ドル（2007年）	5,300ドル（2007年）	2兆3,991億ドル（2009年末）	7,764億ドル（2009年6月末）
インド	328.73万km²（日本の約8.7倍）	11億3560万人（2007年）	2.989兆ドル（2007年）	2,700ドル（2007年）	2,873億7,400万米ドル（2009年12月）	388億ドル（2009年5月末）
米国	962.8万km²（日本の約25倍）	3億718万人（2009年10月）	13.84兆ドル（2007年）	45,800ドル（2007年）	833億7,500万ドル（2009年7月）	——

出所：The CIA World Factbook 2009（Skyhorse Publishing, Inc. New York），外務省ホームページ，日本経済新聞などより作成。

支配するとは考えられない。インドは大量の海外債務や借款を抱えながら，限られた財源を活用して，社会的工業的インフラの建設による景気刺激や内需拡大による国内経済発展を図った方が良いと思われる。

3．債務大国――米国の財政赤字と貿易赤字

米国の名目GDP金額は14兆4千414億ドル（2009年11月，以下同じ），日本は4兆9千107億ドル，中国は4兆3千274億ドルである。明らかに米国が世界一の経済大国である。しかし，別の角度から考えると，米国は債務国であり，大きな負債を抱えている世界最大の債務国でもある。2009年度の米国の財政赤字は過去最大だった前年度の約3倍の約1兆4千億ドルであることは特に注目されよう。

レーガン政権（1981―89年）が発足して間もなく，1981年2月に米国経済の再建計画において，(1) 政府支出の削減，(2) 大幅な減税，(3) 規制緩和（deregulation）政策と (4) 安定した金融政策が実施された。その結果，国内の経済発展を促進したが，米国の「双子の赤字」（財政赤字と貿易赤字）を引き起こした。

ブッシュ政権（1989―93年）はレーガン政権の「負の遺産」を引き継いだだけでなく，基本的にはレーガン政権の経済政策をそのまま踏襲。増税しないまま，財政再建及び政府支出の削減を実現した。その結果，「双子の赤字」は解決できなかった。

クリントン政権（1993―2001年）は特に1998年から，(1) 財政赤字の削

表2　米国の財政収支（1979 － 2009）（単位：10億米ドル）

年	収　入	支　出	収　支
1979	463.3	504	▲ 40.7
1980	517.1	590.9	▲ 73.8
1981	599.3	678.2	▲ 79.0
1982	617.8	745.7	▲ 128.0
1983	600.6	808.4	▲ 207.8
1984	666.5	851.9	▲ 185.4
1985	734.1	946.4	▲ 212.3
1986	769.2	990.4	▲ 221.2
1987	854.4	1,004.1	▲ 149.7
1988	909.3	1,064.5	▲ 155.2
1989	991.2	1,143.8	▲ 152.6
1990	1,032.0	1,253.1	▲ 221.0
1991	1,055.0	1,324.3	▲ 269.2
1992	1,091.3	1,381.6	▲ 290.3
1993	1,154.5	1,409.5	▲ 255.1
1994	1,258.7	1,461.9	▲ 203.2
1995	1,351.9	1,515.9	▲ 164.0
1996	1,453.2	1,560.6	▲ 107.4
1997	1,579.4	1,601.3	▲ 21.9
1998	1,722.0	1,652.7	69.3
1999	1,827.6	1,702.0	125.6
2000	2,025.5	1,789.2	236.2
2001	1,991.4	1,863.2	128.2
2002	1,853.4	2,011.2	▲ 157.8
2003	1,782.5	2,160.1	▲ 377.6
2004	1,880.3	2,293.0	▲ 412.7
2005	2,153.9	2,472.2	▲ 318.3
2006	2,406.3	2,655.4	▲ 248.2
2007	2,568.2	2,728.9	▲ 160.7
2008	2,524.3	2,982.8	▲ 458.5
2009	2,156.7	3,997.8	▲ 1,841.2

出所：Office of Management and Budget より作成。

減，(2) 政府部門の規制緩和と職員のリストラを通じて効率化のアップ，(3) 投資を促進し生産性の向上を重視した。国防支出（1990年の冷戦終結）と公共医療保障を削減，高額所得者の個人所得税の税率，最高法人の税率及びガソリン税収を高めた。加えて，IT革命は生産力を向上させ，新産業の発展を促進した。その結果，米国の好景気が作り上げられ，米国の「双子の赤字」は一時的に解消された。

　ジョージ・W・ブッシュ政権（2001―2009年1月まで，オバマ政権は

表3 米国の国際貿易収支 (1989 − 2008)

(単位:10億米ドル)

年	輸出	輸入	収支
1989	363.8	473.2	▲109.4
1990	393.8	494.8	▲101
1991	421.9	488.2	▲66.3
1992	448.2	532.7	▲84.5
1993	465.1	580.7	▲115.6
1994	512.6	663.3	▲150.7
1995	584.7	743.5	▲158.8
1996	625.1	795.3	▲170.2
1997	689.2	869.7	▲180.5
1998	682.1	911.9	▲229.8
1999	695.8	1024.6	▲328.8
2000	781.9	1218.0	▲436.1
2001	729.1	1141.0	▲411.9
2002	693.1	1161.4	▲468.3
2003	724.8	1257.1	▲532.3
2004	814.9	1469.7	▲654.8
2005	901.1	1673.5	▲772.4
2006	1026.0	1853.9	▲827.9
2007	1148.2	1957.0	▲808.8
2008	1287.4	2103.6	▲816.2

出所:U.S Census Bureau Foreign Division より作成。

2009年1月20日より)は以下の経済政策を推進した。(1) 国防予算を増加する (2008年の国防支出は6千246億ドル,前年同期比4.1%増。ちなみに2008年におけるイラク・アフガニスタン戦争に1千920億ドルを拠出した。2009年2月時点での見積額国防予算は6千512億ドルに上る),(2) 国防費以外の支出については,なるべく現状を維持,(3) エネルギーと運送(高速道路建設などの補助)の費用を増加,(4) 教育と地域開発の費用を減らす。2007年,米国の財政赤字は2,441億ドルだった。ブッシュ計画では,2008年の財政赤字を2千393億ドルに減らすはずだった。しかし,米国の財政赤字は年々増えている。2010年度の会計年度予算教書によれば,2013年会計年度の財政赤字は5千330億ドルまで圧縮するとしている。

　レーガン政権から現在のオバマ政権にかけて,クリントン政権(1993 ― 2001年)期間中の1998 ― 2001年を除き,米国は一貫して「財政赤字」に苦悶している。(表2参照)。そして,2008年の米国の財政赤字は4千585億ドルとなり,2009年には1兆8千412億ドルと膨らんだ。2009年の財政赤字拡大の主因は総額1千500億ドルの景気対策,法人税の減収,国防費等の歳出

増によるものであった。

　一方，米国は輸入大国と消費大国として，主に日本，中国，インドそして世界各国から製品を輸入している。そのため，米国は常に貿易赤字である（表3参照）。

　日本，中国，インドは米国に対し，常に莫大な貿易黒字を保有している（表4，5，6参照）。2008年には，日本，中国，インドの米国に対する貿易黒字はそれぞれ767.7億ドル，2千848.6億ドル，82.6億ドルである。これら三カ国の対米貿易黒字は3千698.9億ドルと上り，同年の米国の国際貿易総赤字の8千162億ドルの45.3％（2007年は45.6％）を占めるに至った。特に，中国だけでも，米国の国際貿易総赤字の34.9％（2007年は34.0％）を占めている。このように，米国は長期に亘り，財政赤字と貿易赤字が増え続け，世界最大の債務国になった。

表4　米日貿易（2004 − 2008）（単位：100万米ドル）

	輸　出	輸　入	収　支
2004年	54,400	133,339	▲ 78,939
2005年	55,409.6	141,950	▲ 86,540.4
2006年	59,649.3	152,244	▲ 92,594.7
2007年	62,664.9	149,423	▲ 86,758.1
2008年	66,579.2	143,352	▲ 76,772.8

出所：IMFより作成。

表5　米中貿易（2004 − 2008）（単位：100万米ドル）

	輸　出	輸　入	収　支
2004年	34,721.0	210,526.0	▲ 175,805
2005年	41,836.7	259,838.0	▲ 218,001.3
2006年	55,224.0	305,788.0	▲ 250,564
2007年	65,238.4	340,118.0	▲ 274,879.6
2008年	71,457.0	356,319.0	▲ 284,862

出所：IMFより作成。

表6　米印貿易（2004 − 2008）（単位：100万米ドル）

	輸　出	輸　入	収　支
2004年	6,095.0	16,436.7	▲ 10,341.7
2005年	7,957.9	19,875.1	▲ 11,917.2
2006年	10,091.3	22,992.7	▲ 12,901.4
2007年	17,592.4	25,113.6	▲ 7,521.2
2008年	18,666.4	26,931.5	▲ 8,265.1

出所：IMFより作成。

4．日本と中国が米国の二大債権国

「双子の赤字」を解消するために，米国は経済発展を通じて国家収入を増やす一方，米ドル紙幣の印刷を増やしたり，政府の公債を発行したりせざるを得ない。

米ドルは国際基軸通貨として世界中で利用されている。特に，米ドルの世界各国の外貨準備高に占める比率は非常に高い。図1に示すように，世界各国の外貨準備高の主な通貨は，米ドルが64.8%，ユーロが14.6%，日本円が4.5%，英ポンドが4.4%，スイスフランが0.7%，その他が11%である。IMF（国際通貨基金）加盟国の外貨準備高に占める比率は，米ドルが66.3%，ユーロが24.8%，日本円が3.4%，スイスフランが0.2%，その他が1.3%である（図2参照）。

中国と日本は世界一と二の外貨準備大国である。中国の外貨準備金は基本的には，海外企業による直接投資，国際貿易黒字，政府の為替介入による米通貨の大量購入，投機資金として中国国内に流入等によるものと考えられる。日本の場合も，外貨準備金の貯め方も大体中国と同じである。

日中の外貨準備金における米国通貨の比率は相当高い。中国の外貨準備金の構成は米ドルが65%，ユーロが20%，日本円が10%，その他が5%である。一方，日本の外貨準備金の構成は米ドルが87%，ユーロが12%，その他が1%である。

米国経済の不況は米ドルの切り下げをもたらした。中国と日本の通貨が切り上げることは，日中両国の経済に非常に悪い影響を及ぼす。日中両国はリスク

図1　外貨準備に占める比率

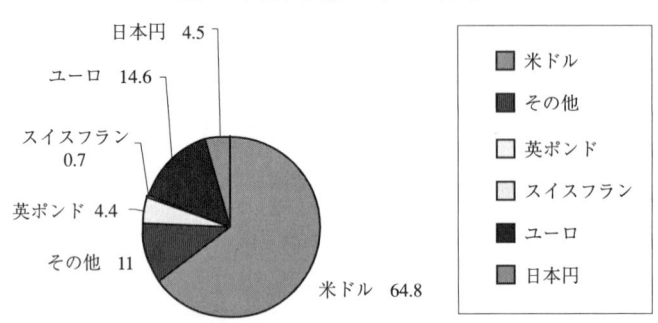

出所：『日本経済新聞』，2004年7月4日

図2　IMF各加盟国の外貨準備に占める比率

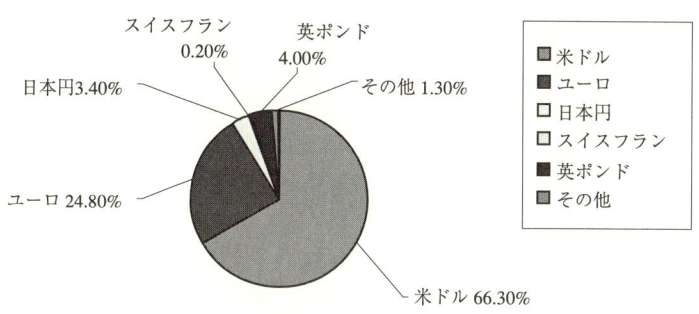

出所：『日本経済新聞』，2006年8月18日

を分散するため，"バスケット通貨制"に真剣に取り組まねばならないのである。

　また，中国と日本は米国国債の二大購買国であり，それぞれが発行済み米国債を13％と19％保有している。日中両国（特に日本）は銀行の利息が低いため，大量の資金が米国の国債市場に流出した。同時に，前述したように，日中両国は多額の対米貿易黒字を保有している。米国との貿易摩擦を削減ないし防止するために，日中両国は貿易黒字で米国の国債と債券を購買している。

　中国の経済成長率は発展途上国の先頭に立っており，貯蓄率の最も高い国でもある。一方，日本は先進工業国の中で最も貯蓄率の高い国である。両国の貯蓄率と大量の貿易黒字は米国の国債，証券及び債券にとっての資金の源泉である。

　これで分るように，日中両国（加えてイギリスとドイツ）は米国にとって，極めて重要な債権国である。日本は先進国であり，米国の同盟国でもあり，日本が米国の主な債権国であることは不思議ではないが，改革開放以来30年の発展途上国である中国が一挙に世界一の外貨準備保有国及び米国の極めて重要な債権国になったことは新しい目で見るべきであろう。

5．政府系ファンドと国民金融資産の役割

　現在，世界での1日の外国為替取引は3兆ドルを超える。その中でドルの関与する取引は9割を占め，ユーロの取引は4割弱と推定される。このことはドルが国際基軸通貨として広く運用されていることを物語っている。

米国経済は外国の資金の流入によって支えられている。米国の多額の貿易赤字と財政赤字（双子の赤字）は外国資金によって賄われている。言うまでもなく，米国は世界中に投資しており，米国企業は世界中に進出している。米国内において産業空洞化が発生していない最大の原因は外国資本や企業の補填によるものである，と考えられる。まさに，"米国の国際収支を見ると，2006年の経常収支赤字は8千億ドルと巨額であるが，1兆8千億ドルの資本流入が経常黒字を賄うだけでなく，米国の1兆ドルの海外投資を可能にしている"（坂本正弘"米国軸の資金循環不変"，『日本経済新聞』，2008年2月20日）。

　近年，外国ファンドの中で，OPEC産油国を中心とするオイルマネーと政府系ファンドの比重が高まりつつ，その存在感と動向が非常に注目されている。原油価格は，1985年の1バレルあたり18ドルが2008年7月11日には147ドルに急騰した。原油価格の急騰は需要と供給のアンバランスに起因するが，投機資金（ホットマネー）による投機的活動も無視できない。中近東諸国を中心とする産油国は原油価格の急騰により，資金が潤沢である。その資金を運用するため，世界各国にイスラム・バンクを設立すると同時に，政府系ファンドを設立するようになった。現在，世界の政府系ファンドは約40有り，保有資産は合計2兆5千億ドルとヘッジファンドを上回ると推定される。政府系ファンドは中東産油国に集中しているが，ノルウェー，シンガポール，中国，ロシアの政府系ファンドも投機市場において重要である（表7参照）。政府系ファンドは積極的に海外不動産の購入等に乗り出している。2008年，ニュー

表7　主な政府系ファンド（SWF）※

国	名称	資産規模（億ドル）	資金源
アラブ首長国連邦（UAE）	アブダビ投資庁	9,000	石油
	ムバダラ開発	170	石油
シンガポール	シンガポール政府投資公社	3,300	外貨準備
	テマセク・ホールディングス	1,080	外貨準備など
ノルウェー	政府年金基金	3,600	石油，ガス
サウジアラビア	サウジ通貨庁	3,000	石油
中　国	中国投資有限責任公司	2,000	外貨準備
	中国中央匯金投資公司	1,000	外貨準備など
クウェート	クウェート投資庁	2,500	石油
ロシア	政府安定化基金	1,500	石油
香　港	香港金融管理局	1,400	外貨準備など
米　国	アラスカ州永久準備基金	400	原油
オーストラリア	将来基金	400	財政黒字
ニュージーランド	公的年金基金	100	政府出資

※Sovereign Wealth Fund
出所：各種資料より作成。

ヨークを代表する高層ビルであるクライスラービルを，アラブ首長国連邦（UAE）の政府系ファンド「アブダビ投資評議会（ADIC）」が約8億ドルで買収した。クライスラービルは，エンパイアステートビルと並んでマンハッタンの観光名所で，ニューヨークの象徴でもある。その他，カタールとクウェートの政府系ファンドが2008年5月に米投資会社と共同で，GMビルを買収した。

中国政府は，外貨準備を利用して，中国投資有限責任公司（CIC，2千億ドル）と中央匯金投資公司（CHICL，1千億ドル）を設立した。資金面ではアラブ首長国連邦，運用実績においてはノルウェー，シンガポール，クウェートには及ばないが，精力的に資金運用を展開している。将来，一層の外貨準備を利用し，増資による資金運用の展開が考えられる。また，米国債や社債だけでなく，先進国の通貨の売買，工業資源の開発や農産物の確保，世界各地の企業のM&Aなどに乗り出すと考えられよう。

一方，中国の四大銀行（中国銀行，中国商工銀行，中国建設銀行，中国農業銀行。貸出総額が中国全体の貸出総額に占める割合は約60％に達している）や中国国家開発銀行の国内流動資金量が潤沢の上，人民元切り上げを見込んで流入する大量の投機資金が急増（1兆7千500億ドルに上るという驚異的試算さえある）しているため，資金が市場に過剰供給されている。その上，中国政府はバブル経済を抑制するため，マクロコントロールによる銀行の融資の制限を行った。また，貿易黒字の増加により，外貨準備が膨らんだ。そして中国の対外援助や対外投資が促されるようになった。

日本の場合はどうか。2009年12月末の財政赤字（「国の借金」）は871兆円（国民一人あたり約683万円の借金となる計算）に上る。政府はその巨額な赤字の解決策を二つ考えている。一つは消費税の引き上げによる歳入の増加である。もう一つはいわゆる"霞ヶ関埋蔵金"（主な特別会計の積立金〔埋蔵金〕残高は以下の通りである。厚生保険134兆3千972億円，財政融資資金26兆4千1億円，外国為替資金15兆5千524億円，国債整理基金11兆4千169億円，労働保険11兆2千668億円）の活用である。しかしこれら二つの解決策は簡単には施行できないだろう。この巨額な財政赤字をすぐに解決することは困難だが，低迷し続けてきた日本経済を活性化させ，少しずつ減らしてゆくことが肝要である。日本経済の活性化は国民金融資産の運用に掛かると見てよかろう。日本の国民金融資産は1千536兆円（預貯金，債券，株式）にも上ると推定される。国民は金融機関や証券会社を通じて対外投資を行っている。一方，民間企業の海外資産による収益が増えると同時に，国際貿易による黒字の拡大も外貨準備を膨らませる。しかし，日本においては，基本的には中

表8 英バークレイズの追加増資への出資者

	出資額（億ポンド）	比率（％）
三井住友銀行	5	2.1
カタール投資庁	17.64	7.7
チャレンジャー（カタール首相一族の保有企業）	5.33	2.3
テマセク（シンガポール）	2	2.9
中国国家開発銀行	1.36	3.1
その他の投資家	13.36	—

注：1ポンド＝約212円。三井住友銀行以外の出資額，増資後の持ち株比率は最大値。
出所：『日本経済新聞』，2008年6月26日。

央政府による政府系ファンドは設立されていない。つまり，日本は投資を民間金融機関や企業に委ねる傾向が強い。したがって，日本の海外投資活動はほとんど民間金融機関や企業によって展開されている。

米国はサブプライムローン（信用力の低い個人や低所得者向けの融資）問題で，米国の銀行や金融証券会社が問題の処理に手間取り，米国発の金融危機へと発展した。日欧の銀行や金融証券会社も莫大な損失を蒙った。

今，世界中の銀行や金融証券会社が再編を強いられている。一つ顕著な現象は，欧米金融機関の莫大な損失による再編に，世界中の政府系ファンドや日本の金融機関の積極的な参入であろう（表8参照）。

米大手銀行シティグループはサブプライムローンに関連した証券化事業などに失敗し，460億ドル程度（米国の外貨準備高は833億7千500万ドル〔2009年7月〕，ビル・ゲイツ氏の個人資産は500億ドル（2009年9月フォーブスより）と推定される）の損失を計上したという。

シティグループはリストラ策を断行した際，日本をアジア事業の中核と見なし，今後日本の個人資産が証券分野に更にシフトすると期待し，シティグループの日本証券部門（旧日興コーディアルグループ）を売却しないとの決定を下した。このことは端的に，日本は米国の国債や社債の大きな買い手であると同時に，サブプライムローンの崩壊で苦境に立たされている米国金融機関の証券分野に，日本の個人金融資産がさらに活用されると見受けられよう。

米地方銀行で住宅ローン大手のインディマック・バンコープ（資産規模は320億ドル，預金量は190億ドル）が破綻（2008年7月11日）し，金融市場にさらに衝撃を与えた。やや早い話だが，世界中の政府系ファンドや金融機関が米国を中心とする欧米の証券市場への一層の参入や合併と買収（**M&A**）の動きが出てくることが考えられよう。潤沢な資金を保有している中国政府や政府系ファンドと，多額な個人金融資産を抱えている日本は，米国市場への一

層の介入によって，米国経済を一層支えて行くと思われる。

6．米中の経済関係と人民元の切り上げ

　米国は対中国の貿易赤字を是正するために，近年，米国をはじめ西側諸国は中国政府に人民元の切り上げを迫っている。一方，中国経済の順調な発展に伴い，人民元が堅調　になったため，中国政府も徐々に人民元の切り上げを施行している。

　中国政府は人民元と米ドルを固定為替レートにしているわけではない。人民元は変動している。米ドルと人民元の為替レートは1ドル=8.27人民元を挟んで小幅に推移していた。しかし，2005年7月21日，人民元は11年ぶりに調整され始めた。人民元は2%切り上げ，1ドル=8.27人民元から1ドル=8.11人民元へと切り上がった。近年，人民元の切り上げが続き，現在，1ドル=7人民元割れで，人民元は約18%切り上がった。日米の関係者と経済学者は，中国製品が国際市場で高い競争力を有するのは人民元が過小評価されているからである，と主張する。人民元は価値を正しく評価されるべきで，人民元をなるべく早く切り上げるべきであり，さらに40%の切り上げをするべきだと提言した。

　2007年度，日本の対中国の輸出貿易額は初めて対米国の輸出貿易額を超えた。同年，日本の対中国の貿易赤字は10兆8千249億円に達した（100円=1ドル）。日本は人民元の切り上げが日本の貿易バランスを改善できるとは思っていない。2006年に米国の対中国の貿易赤字は1千443億ドル，中国の貿易黒字総額の83.1%を占めた。したがって，米国は人民元の切り上げを通じて，中国の対米黒字を削減し，米国の対中国の貿易赤字額を減らしていきたいと考えている。

　2006年の米中間の貿易額は，1979年に米中が外交関係を正式に樹立した時の106倍に相当する（年平均増加率は18.9%）。明らかに米国の国内市場は中国の輸出に大きく依存している。実際，多くの西側の関係者と経済学者が予測したように，人民元の切り上げは，中国製品の日本をはじめ西側諸国への輸出に対して，大きな影響を与えていない。そのため，西側諸国，特に米国にとっては適切な人民元の切り上げが米国及び欧州諸国の貿易赤字を大幅に改善できるとは期待できない。

　また，人民元を大幅に切り上げたら，中国で生産している日米欧のメーカー（日本の中国進出企業は約2万5千社），及び日米欧の中国製品の消費者は真っ先に損を被るはずである。実際，2006年末，米国の対中投資額は累計で（実

績ベース）540億ドルに達した。品質が良くて安価な中国製品は米国の消費者のニーズに応えている。中国側は対米の貿易黒字で米国の国債と債券を購買したと主張した。

　実は，中国政府は人民元の大幅な切り上げを望んではいない。西側諸国は外交を通じて何度も人民元を大幅に切り上げるように中国に圧力をかけている。人民元の切り上げは結局有効にコントロールされるべきである。

　1980年代半ばの日本は，米国をはじめ西側諸国の圧力を受けて，日本円を大幅に切り上げた。その結果，米ドルと日本円の為替レートは1985年秋のG5前の1ドル=242円から1995年4月の1ドル=79円へと切り上がった。10年間に300%も切り上げた。これは日本経済に災いの元を残し，世界の通貨体制及び金融体制を乱した。

　日本円の対米ドルの大幅な変動は特に，日本にマクロ的コントロールを失わせた。日本のバブル経済が1991年に崩壊して以来，20年が経過しようとしている。ところが，日本経済はまだ過去10年の日本円の切り上げによる後遺症から抜け出せずに，持続的な経済の発展の軌道に完全に乗れていないのである。

　中国にとって，これは一つの教訓である。実際，中国では現在すでにある程度のバブル経済になっており，土地不動産の値段が急騰し，株式市場は強気である。サブプライムローン問題が発生し，米国経済が不況を引き起こしたため，株の急落は中国にも波及し，一時的に中国の株も急落したが，すぐに回復した。政府は有効なマクロ的コントロールによって，銀行の貸し出しを制限し，不動産の急騰をコントロールしている。このほか，人民元の急速な切り上げは現在の深刻なインフレを抑えている。特に，国内外の農作物と食糧の値段が高騰した背景の下，堅調な人民元は輸入貿易を促進している。中国政府は人民元の切り上げのメリットとデメリットを十分に認識しており，人民元の急な切り上げを考えてはいないだろう。

　中国政府は2008年の経済成長率8%を達成し（十分な雇用機会を作るために），同時に，消費者物価指数（CPI）を4.8%以下にコントロールした。バブル経済と深刻なインフレ，米国をはじめ世界不況の中で，中国は極めて困難な持続的な経済成長を見事に実現した。

　中国経済は，2008年8月に開催された北京五輪や2010年5月に開催される予定の上海万博による経済効果はあるものの，中国経済全体に及ぼす悪影響は限定的ではあるが，南部大雪災害（2008年2月），四川大地震（2008年5月），大寒波（2010年1月）などの自然災害が，農産物の価格高騰がインフレ

に拍車をかけている。また，慢性的な水不足，旱魃や洪水，燃料代替品生産による農産物の転作，減産等により，世界規模のインフレはスタグフレーションを引き起こしている。そこで，中国のマクロ経済コントロールによる消費者物価指数を抑制することがますます困難になってくると言わざるを得ないだろう。

7．中国の経済戦略の模索

　米中関係が日増しに重要となってきている。米国は世界規模の出来事を米中主導で解決するため，G2の構想を提起した。中国も真剣に検討したが，結局米国の提案に乗ることを放棄した。これは正しい決断だが，米中関係はますます緊密になったことは否定できない。

　中国は大量の外貨準備高と貿易黒字をもって，大量の米国の国債と債券・株を購入した。一方では，流動資金で海外投資を行う。他方では，米中の経済摩擦と貿易摩擦を緩和する。中国にとって，このような措置は高い利益を実現できるが，大きなリスクにも直面している。

　実際，「オイルマネー」（oil money）と「イスラムファンド」（Islamic fund）が世界で大規模に動いているように，大量の外貨準備で為替レートの大幅な変動を抑え，米国などの国々の国債と債券・株を購買することは現在の金融市場の重要な取引と投資投機行為の一つである。現在，中国は30%～40%の外貨準備で米国の国債を購入している。

　このほか，政府系ファンドを設立し海外で投資を行うことは重要なビジネスの一つである。中東諸国，ノルウェー及びシンガポールにおいては，政府系ファンドがますます重要な役割を果たしている。中国政府は，2千億ドルで中国投資有限責任会社と中国中央匯金投資公司を設立し，次々に海外投資を行っている（例えば，サブプライムローンで莫大な損失を出した米国の証券会社であるモルガン・スタンレーに50億ドルを投資した）。ところが，経験や人材の不足，市場に詳しくないため，大きな損失を出した。中国は米国をはじめとする市場経済の特徴や運用についてさらに理解し，把握すべきであろう。

　世界一の外貨準備高を保有している中国は，リスク分散や国内経済建設のための運用を真剣に考えねばならないであろう。米国債や社債と株の大量購入はハイリターンもあるが，ハイリスクも考えねばならない。そもそも中国経済を米国経済の変動に左右される仕組みになっていることは得策ではない。ハイリターンを求め，ハイリスクを分散するために，中国は米国以外の国債や債券と株を購入する努力をせねばならないだろう。と同時に，中国通貨を"バスケット通貨"と一層リンクして強化していかねばならない。一方，中国は外貨準備

高を利用し，国内における環境保全，貧富格差の是正，医療制度の充実，教育設備の拡充，社会的インフラの建設等に国内資本をもっと活用せねばならないだろう。つまり，国内経済の発展による国民全体の生活保障や生活水準のレベルアップに重点を置くべきである。

前述した中国南部大雪災害や四川大地震，この二大災害を教訓に，社会的インフラ（学校，病院，福祉施設等）と工業的インフラ（道路，橋梁，発電所，港湾，ダム等）の充実が緊急な課題となろう。膨張した外貨準備高（1兆8千億ドル2008年6月末現在。そして1時間に2千万ドル増えつつあると推定される）を適宜に社会的・工業的インフラに充当することが急務である。上記二大災害が正に"地方の貧困"を露呈した。これを機に，"地方の救済と復興"を抜本的に対策した方が賢明である。そして中国南部や四川のみならず，中国全土の地方の建設や発展が中国政府にとって長期的な課題であり，人力と金銭を大量に注入することが不可欠である。

結　論

本論文は日中印と米国との経済関係について分析した。米国経済体制，とりわけ金融体制の脆弱性を分析し，日中印経済に依存する側面を点検し吟味した。米国発金融危機，ひいては世界経済危機は収束の方向に向かっているが，"雇用なき景気回復"に象徴されているように，世界経済は押しなべて低迷している。

日本においては，デフレと高い失業率に悩まされているが，欧米諸国ほど経済状況は悪くない。円高で輸出産業は疲弊しているが，中央政府が投資会社を持っていないので，銀行金融証券会社や大手企業が対外投資を増加することによって，難局を打開しようとしている。日本は中国に次いで，米国債や株の購入によって，対米経済影響力を増している。米国経済の対日依存がますます重要となっていくに違いない。

中国は経済新興国であり，経済大国である。現段階，そして将来ますます日米経済関係よりも米中経済関係が重要となっていくに違いない。米国は日本よりも，対中国重視が顕在化しつつある。これは本論文が中国経済や米中経済関係を幾分重点的に分析した理由である。

インドの経済力はまだ貧弱である。米国経済や世界経済に対する影響は日中ほどではない。インドは中国と同じく新興国であるが，アジアの大国である。インドはまた日本と同様，米国と同じ価値観を持っている。米印経済関係はインド経済の安定成長によって，ますます重要となっていくに違いない。

日中印の米国経済関与（国際貿易の緊密化，米国債や株の大量購入等）によって，日中印と米国経済との相互補完性や相互依存度が増していく。日中印が米国経済に依存するよりも，米国経済が日中印に依存する新しい枠組みがすでに形成されていると主張したい。

　斜陽国の日本と新興国の中印は米国発金融危機を救えなかった。しかし，米国経済の再建や回復には日中印に頼るところが大きい。歯止めの利かない消費大国米国は，潤沢な外貨準備金と高貯蓄率を誇る日中印に支えられている。日中印が米国経済との関与度がますます重要となっていくに違いない。

第2章　世界経済危機と「東アジア共同体」

谷口　誠*

1．世界経済危機の背景

　米国のサブプライムローンに端を発した今回の金融危機は，現在のグローバル化時代においては米国だけにとどまらず，急速に世界的規模の経済危機に発展した。100年に1度の危機といわれる今回の危機は，欧州，アジアを含め，世界経済に大きなダメージを与えた。米国を始め主要各国が緊急に対応策をとったため，世界経済は現在一時のパニック状態を脱し，やや小康を得ているように見えるが，その後遺症は大きく，世界経済がいつ再び成長軌道に戻るのか，その見通しをたてるのは容易ではない。先般開かれたラクイラG8サミット（イタリア）においても，安定し，よく機能する国際通貨システムを促進することが確認されはしたが，今回のような経済危機の再発を防止するための基本的対策が議論されたとは考えられない。

　私は，今回の危機は，現在の資本主義経済があまりにも米国型の市場経済至上主義に陥り，さらに金融資本が極端な形で世界経済を支配するに任せてきた結果，起こりうるべくして起こったものであり，また，この体制が変わらない限り，将来いつでも起こる危険性があると考えている。今回の危機の徴候は，注意していれば，すでに2006年頃から現れはじめていたことが分かる。そしてこの危機の発生は，単に米国だけの責任にとどまらず，米国の住宅ブームに便乗し，巨額の利益を得ようとして投資した欧州その他アジア諸国金融資本の責任も無視できない。

　今回の危機を，1929年に始まった1930年代の米国発の経済恐慌と比較することが適当かどうかは別として，今回の危機も1930年代の経済恐慌も，ともに米国の土地，住宅等の不動産への投機による株式の暴落に端を発した金融危機であったことは共通している。さらに今回の危機は，最近の米国経済を支えてきた住宅ブームの終焉と，住宅ローンなどを原資産とした証券化商品バブルの崩壊から生じた，より複雑な金融危機であるといえる。1930年代の経済恐慌は，フランクリン・ルーズベルト大統領のニューディール政策による多額の公共投資をもってしても，経済回復に約10年の年月を要し，世界経済に与

---

*　桜美林大学北東アジア総合研究所特別顧問，北東アジア研究交流ネットワーク（NEASE-NET）代表幹事。

えた影響も大きく，その結果1930年代の世界経済は保護主義に陥り，第2次世界大戦突入への導火線となったとされている。一方今回の危機が起きたのはグローバル化の時代であったため，その伝播のスピードは1930年代の危機とは比較にならない程早く，その対応の遅れは，極めて大きなダメージをもたらしたと考えられるが，その反面，現在は1930年代に比較し，マクロ経済政策と国際金融面での国際協力が進んでおり，1930年代の経済恐慌時ほどの悲劇が起きたとは考えられない。

2．オバマ政権は経済危機を克服できるか

オバマ大統領は，経済危機からの脱出策として，第2ニューディールともいえる7千870億ドルの大規模公共投資（環境，医療，教育等）による雇用拡大を目指す政策を打ち出しており，その他の財政支出1千680億ドルを加えると，米国のGDPの6.6％の大規模なものとなる。第2ニューディール政策が効力を発揮し，米国経済の回復，さらに今回の危機により大きなダメージを受けた世界経済が一日も早く回復軌道に乗ることを期待するが，現状ではその見通しは決して容易なものではない。今回の危機は，伝統的なケインズ的手法による公共投資が必要ではあるが，それのみで解決できるものではない。

今次経済危機に際し，オバマ政権に求められるビッグ・チェンジは，米国自身が米国型市場経済至上主義の意識改革を行ない，より健全な市場経済を基盤とした金融市場を構築することである。しかしオバマ政権の経済政策を支えるライトナー財務長官もラリー・サマーズ国家経済協議会（NEC）議長も，共にウォールストリートと強いつながりを持つ人たちである。果たしてオバマ政権が，米国型資本主義の原点ともいうべきウォールストリートの投資家達のマインドを変えることができるであろうか。

3．ブレトンウッズ体制（特にIMF）の改革の必要

一方，グローバル化の下で，欧州，アジア，ラテンアメリカなど，すでに世界経済全般に及んだ今回の危機のダメージは，米国一国の努力では解決できず，国際協力なくしては解決は目指せない。そのためには，世界の通貨，金融の安定に責任があるIMFの機能強化，特に監視機能の強化が必要となるが，これまでも世界の各地域で通貨危機が起こった際には，いつもIMFのより多角的な監視機能の強化の必要性が叫ばれ，議論されてきたにもかかわらず，一向に改善は見られていない。

オバマ政権の景気刺激策が効を奏し，2，3年で米国経済が回復すれば，米

国をはじめ世界の各国も今回の世界経済危機の痛みを忘れてしまい，そうなれば，IMFをはじめとし，OECDなど金融の自由化を推進してきた国際機関のイデオロギーや体制も変わることはないであろう。IMFはこれまで何度も深刻な通貨危機を経験してきたが，本来与えられている「通貨の安定」と「監視（surveillance）」という機能を十分に果してこなかったどころか，1997年に起こったアジア通貨危機においては，処方箋の適用の誤りにより，かえって危機を悪化させた。そして今回の世界金融危機に際しても，IMFがいかなる対策を講じたのか分らなかったし，IMFの顔が見えてこなかった。金融工学を駆使し，すさまじいスピードで進化する現在の金融資本の動きには，IMFの専門家もついて行かれないのであろうが，IMFのシステムそのものが，ウォールストリート，米財務省と三位一体化してしまっているようにも見える。

　今回危機に際し，フランスのサルコジ大統領，さらに英国のブラウン首相がIMFの改革を訴えたが，改革への国際的な流れを呼ぶことはなかった。日本の麻生首相（当時）は2008年10月の第一回金融サミットにおいて，IMF強化策としてIMFへの最大1000億ドルの資金供与を発表したが，これは今回危機の責任者として孤立しつつある米国と，資金不足に悩むIMFを喜ばせはしたものの，IMFの改革を条件としたものではなかった。しかもこの資金は，金融危機に陥ったアイスランドと東欧諸国の救済に使われただけであった。私はこの機会にこそ，欧米，特に米国に最大の投票権を与え，日本を始め中国，インド等新興国にはその経済力に見合った投票権が与えられていない，ブレトンウッズ体制のマイナスの遺産ともいうべきIMFシステム[1]の改革を，強く訴えるべきであったと思う。中国の胡錦濤国家主席が，2009年4月ロンドンで開催されたG20サミットにおいて，中国のクォータの増額と特別引出し権（SDR）の積極的活用という改革への具体的提案をし，またこれに先立つ3月23日には，中国人民銀行の周小川総裁が「国際通貨体制改革に関する考察」と題する論文を発表するなど，中国が最近積極的にIMFの改革を訴えていることは注目される。このような中国の要求を受け，これまでIMFのクォータ改革には消極的であった米国も柔軟に対応し，IMFも途上国のクォータの枠を5％増す決定を行った。5％という枠の拡大幅はけっして大きくは無いが，

---

1) IMFは加重投票制をとっており，拠出額に応じて投票権が決定される。現在主要国の拠出額のシェアは，米国17.09%，日本6.13%，ドイツ5.99%，英国，フランスがともに4.94%，中国3.72%，インド1.91%，韓国1.35%となっている。このように拠出額のシェアに応じ，米国の投票権は16.77%と高いので，重要事項の決定に当たっては事実上の拒否権を持っている。日本の投票権は6.02%，中国は3.66%に過ぎない。国連における日本の分担金シェアが16%であるのに対し，IMFにおけるシェアは極めて低く定められている点に注目したい。

これがブレトンウッズ体制の改革への道を開くことを期待したい。

現在の IMF のシステムがうまく機能しているとは言いがたい。そもそも IMF は，1971年のニクソンショックにより，金・ドル本位制が機能しなくなり，ドル本位制に切り替えられたとき，ブレトンウッズ体制も崩壊したはずである。しかしそれだからといって，現 IMF に代わる組織を創設できるかというと，米国が簡単に応ずるわけがない。結局，米国は基本的には基軸通貨としてのドル体制の維持に努め，多少の改革を行ったとしても米国主導型の IMF システムを崩すことはないであろう。そうであれば世界経済はまた違った形の経済危機を招来する危険性がある。今回は住宅など不動産への投機から発生したが，現在の米国型金融資本主義が続く限り，このような経済危機は，いかなる商品への投機からも生ずる危険性があり，また，将来いつでも起こる可能性がある。例えば将来のビジネスといわれるエコ・ビジネスに関連し，温暖化防止のための排出権取引が利益を生み出すビジネスとして金融資本の投機の対象となれば，環境の名を借りた経済危機が起こる危険性もあろう。

かかる状況の下では，各国及び各地域は，それぞれが今回のようなダメージを受けないよう自衛の手段を講ぜざるを得ない。1930年代には，保護主義が蔓延し，これが第2次世界大戦に繋がったといわれているが，21世紀におけるグローバル化した世界が，その過ちを再び犯そうとするとは考えられない。私は，世界が米国を責めるよりも，むしろ国力が相対的に低下したとはいえ，依然として米国に政治的にも経済的にも依存し，米国の一極支配を助長してきたことに責任を感じるべきだと考えている。

オバマ政権には，前政権とは違った戦略をとることを期待したいが，今回の経済危機を経験した世界は，米国の一極支配から脱するためにも，従来の先進主要国主体の G8 体制に，BRICs などこれからの世界の政治，経済の運営に責任のあるメンバーを加え，より多様化した世界へと移行する必要がある。そのためには，G8 体制に BRICs などを加えた G20 体制の重要性が増してこよう。

また，今回のような金融危機に際しては，今まで注目を浴びてこなかったが，世界の主要国の中央銀行などが参加し，中央銀行間の協力促進により世界の金融システムの安定化を図っている国際決済銀行（BIS）[2] の機能強化も検討されるべきであろう。さらにグローバリゼーションの下で頻繁に移動す

---

2) BIS（Bank for International Settlements）は1930年に設立された中央銀行および通貨当局をメンバーとする組織で，本部はスイスのバーゼルにある。加盟国は主要先進国のみならず，中国，インド，ブラジル，サウジアラビア等の主要途上国を含み，50数カ国に達している。

る多額の外国為替への投機を抑制する手段として小額の課税を行うトービン税（Tobin Tax）の導入も検討されるべきだと考えている。私がOECDにいた1990年代，OECDでは，トービン税はタブー視されていた。

このような状況の下でEUは，色々な問題を抱えているとはいえ，今回の経済危機を経験し，ますます地域統合の質を高めていくものと見られる。

では，われわれ日本の位置するアジアはどのような対応をすべきなのか，本稿においてはこの点を中心に議論を進めてみたい。

4. 世界経済危機のアジア経済への影響

1997年のアジア通貨危機により痛い経験をしたはずのアジアではあるが，当初は今回の米国のサブプライムローン問題を，対岸の火事としてしか見ていなかったきらいがある。米国サブプライムローンは，前述のとおりすでに2006年頃には問題化しており，日本を含め中国など，単に米国経済のみならず，世界経済，特に米国市場に貿易，投資面で大きく依存しているアジア主要国は，この問題にもっと強い警戒心を持つべきであった。

この米国発の金融危機の第一波は，主としてヨーロッパなどの，金融市場の自由化の進んだ先進国経済を直撃し，日本をはじめアジア経済は，当初それほどの被害を受けなかった。しかし，米国の実体経済が急激に悪化するに伴い，金融危機の第二波が日本，中国，韓国をはじめアジアの実体経済を襲い，次第に大きな影響が出始めた。

日本においても，米国の3大自動車会社同様，日本の誇るトヨタをはじめとする3大自動車会社が生産調整に追い込まれ，他にも日立，東芝，ソニーなどの主要企業が人員整理を余儀なくされた。そして一挙に多くの人達が解雇され，住む家を失い，厳寒の中を路頭に迷うことになった。これは市場経済に慣れ親しんできたわれわれにとっても大きなショックであった。日本には，十数年前にすでに不動産投資によるバブルが弾け，大手銀行が巨額の不良債権を抱え，その処理に政府が公的資金を投入したという苦い経験があったため，米国のサブプライムローンにはあまり手を出さず，金融機関のダメージが比較的軽微であったことは救いであった。にもかかわらず日本経済が，その実体経済において，先進国のなかで最も大きなダメージを受けたのは何故であったのだろうか。これは日本経済が健全な発展を遂げるためにも，十分に検証されるべき問題である。後述のとおり，日本のGDPに占める輸出依存度は16%（2008年度）と，アジア主要国のなかで，決して高くは無い。しかしながら私は，第1に日本の輸出主要産品が，自動車，鉄鋼，家電などの耐久消費財に集中して

いること，第2に米国市場への依存度が高いこと（日本の輸出の20.4%）が主な原因であると分析している。したがって日本経済が将来より健全な発展を遂げるためには，輸出製品の多様化（サービス貿易を含む）と輸出市場の多様化，そして内需の拡大を目指さねばならない。

2008年末にはアジア諸国も急激な株価下落を経験した（日本41%，中国63%，韓国32%，インド19%，インドネシア55%，シンガポール52%，タイ46%）。そして，実質成長率も下落し始めた。

日本の経済成長率について，日銀は，2008年12月に行った経済見通しでは，2008年度の実質国内総生産（GDP）の成長率をマイナス0.8%，2009年度はゼロ成長としていたが，2009年1月22日には，2008年度成長率をマイナス1.8%，2009年度成長見通しをマイナス2.0%（IMFはマイナス6.2%）に下方修正した。今後の見通しも極めて不透明であり，戦後最悪の状況にあるとの悲観論が漂う中で，2009年1-3月の実質成長率は，前期比4.0%減，年率換算で15.2%減という戦後最大の減少となり，日本は今回の世界経済危機により，主要先進国の中で最も急激な落ち込みを示した。さらに失業率は5.2%にのぼり，日本としては最悪の雇用問題を抱えることになった。日本は15兆円の財政投融資など，GDPの3.3%に当たる大規模公共投資を行うことになったが，これにより2009年後半から2010年度にかけて景気の回復を期待したい。

中国の経済成長率は，過去20数年にわたって年平均10%以上の高成長を遂げ，中国政府もごく最近まで自信満々であったが，2008年度の国内総生産の実質成長率は9%と6年ぶりに10%を割った。中国政府は，2009年度の目標成長率を8.0%としているが，IMFの予想では6.5%となっている。しかし中国は，いち早く2010年までに約4兆元（約59兆円）の景気刺激策を実施することを決定しており，このような大規模な景気刺激策（GDPの6%台）の効果が発揮され，開発の遅れている中・西部にも力を入れて内需を拡大できれば，目標とする8%あるいはそれを上回る成長率を達成できるのではないかと考えられる。

韓国は，2007年には株高，通貨高のバブル状況にあったが，2008年末より世界経済の景気鈍化の影響を受けて株式市場を中心に資金が流出し，通貨，株価が大幅に下落した。その救済策として，2008年10月30日，日本と米国による通貨スワップ協定に続き，12月12日には日本と中国による通貨スワップ拡大が決定した。2009年4月のIMFによる韓国経済の成長見通しはマイナス4.0%であったが，最近の韓国政府の発表によれば，韓国経済は回復の基調に

あり，2009年度のGDP実質成長率はマイナス1.6%と上方修正された。

5．あまりにも米国経済に依存し，危機意識のなかったアジア

これまでのアジア経済の発展のパターンを見ると，日本を始め，ASEAN，人口大国である中国，また韓国も，内需の拡大よりも外国市場，特に米国市場への輸出により急速な発展を遂げており，これがアジア経済を成功に導いたことは否定できない。例えば，アジアの主要国の2008年度の輸出依存度（輸出額／GDP）は，中国38%，韓国45%，インドネシア27%，マレーシア113%，フィリピン39%，シンガポール187%，タイ66%，ベトナム66%と高く，日本は16%，インドも16%と比較的低い。一般的には輸出依存度の高い国ほど，今回のような世界的経済危機の影響を受け易く，したがってアジアの実体経済上のダメージは大きいものと見られる。さらに今回問題なのは，アジアの多くの国の輸出先が米国，EU，日本に集中していることである。特に米国には，2007年度には日本20.4%，中国19.1%，マレーシア15.6%，フィリピン13.0%，タイ12.6%，ベトナム22.4%，カンボジア60.1%，インド15.0%，パキスタン20.0%となっており，これらの米国市場への輸出依存度の高い国へのダメージは大きいものと見られる。

また，アジアの外貨準備額は高く，2009年度には中国2兆1千326億ドル，日本1兆423億ドル，インド2千719億ドル，韓国2千542億ドル，シンガポール1千763億ドルと世界の上位ランキングを独占しているが，問題は，中国がその外貨準備額の21.5%を，日本が19.2%を米国国債に投資していることである。2008年10月には，海外からの米国国債への全投資額の約半分がアジアからの投資により占められている。このようなアジアの貿易と投資パターンは，輸出（特に米国市場）により稼いだ外貨を，米国に投資していることを示すものである。日本，中国をはじめ，アジア諸国にとって，米国国債への投資は最も安全だという，神話に近い信仰があるように見受けられるが，今回の米国の金融危機による米国経済への信頼の低下は，米国国債の価値を大幅に目減りさせることになった。

ところが日本も中国も（特に中国は），今回の金融危機後もさらに米国国債を買い増そうとしている。これは，買い増すことにより，米国経済の回復を早め，損害を少なくしようとするためなのか，または経済危機に悩む米国への外交的配慮ないしは恩を売るためなのか，それとも米国に勝る，多額の外貨準備を投資すべきマーケットをまだ見出せないのか，その何れの要素も当てはまるように見える。

今回の米国発の金融危機は，アジアのこのような米国市場への依存体質への強い警告と受け止めるべきだと考えるが，果たして日本，中国を始め，アジア諸国が，そのような認識を持っているであろうか。

6．経済危機は「アジア共同体」成立への突破口となりうるか
　そもそも「東アジア共同体」構想は，1997年にタイに始まったアジア通貨危機を契機として生まれたものであり，危機回避のために必要に迫られて，ASEANのイニシアティブの下にASEAN＋3（日・中・韓）による協議体制が立ち上がったという背景がある。したがって歴史的にも，EU（欧州連合）のように，まずヨーロッパ統合への理念とビジョンがあり，シューマン・プラン[3]のような戦略の下に60年に及ぶ歴史を積み重ねて出来たものとは，全く発生の次元が違うといってもよい。しかし今回の経済危機は世界規模にわたり，米国もEUも自身の経済回復に精一杯で，他を省みる余裕が無い。そのような危機に際してこそ，「東アジア共同体」のもとでの協力体制が必要となってくる。

　「東アジア共同体」構想は，20億人に達する人口規模はいうに及ばず，経済規模からいえば，日本，韓国といった先進国経済と，NIEs（新興工業化経済群）を主体としたASEAN，さらに躍進する経済大国である中国を加えると，EU，NAFTA（北米自由貿易協定）に伍しても，決して引けをとらず，中国，ASEANなどの経済成長率より見ても「東アジア共同体」が成立すれば，EU，NAFTAをはるかに凌駕する可能性は十分あると考えられる。

　しかし，「東アジア共同体」の政治的・歴史的基盤は脆弱である。ASEANは，1967年の成立以来，政治的にも経済的にも地域統合を果たしてきたが，東アジアの大国である日本，中国，韓国の間には，未だに歴史認識の相違から来る政治的，社会的対立という溝が埋められていない。ここに「東アジア共同体」を立ち上げることの難しさがある。2000年頃より始まった「東アジア共同体」設立交渉が，最近は全く進展していないが，その最大の理由は，これまで「東アジア共同体」設立の交渉は，ASEANを母体として行われてきたが，東アジアの3経済大国である，日・中・韓の間で本格的交渉が行われてきたとはいえないことである。日・中・韓は，それぞれASEANとの間にFTA（自由貿易協定）とEPA（経済連携協定）を締結する交渉を進め，これらは既

---

3) 1950年5月9日，フランス外相シューマンは，フランスとドイツの全石炭・鉄鋼生産を共同の最高機関の下に置く，ヨーロッパの石炭・鉄鋼生産のプール化構想を発表した。この構想を基に欧州石炭鉄鋼共同体（ECSC）が生まれ，現在のEUに発展した。

に締結されたが，肝心の日・中・韓の間には，まだ何も締結されていない。日本と韓国，中国と韓国との間では，FTA と EPA の交渉が行われているが，最も貿易量の大きい日本と中国の間には，交渉の兆しすら見えない。これでは，「東アジア共同体」といっても極めて歪な形の共同体としかいいようが無い。

「東アジア共同体」交渉の初期においては，ASEAN が重要な役割を果たしてきたが，交渉が大詰めを迎えるに従い，日・中・韓，特に日本と中国の覇権争いが始まり，その結果，これまで共同体交渉においては一枚岩であった ASEAN が分裂をきたし，交渉は頓挫してしまった。その責任は日本と中国の双方にあるが，日本の責任は特に大きい。

ではこのように頓挫した「東アジア共同体」交渉を生き返らせ，実効性のある「東アジア共同体」を構築するにはどうすればよいのであろうか。そのためには，日・中・韓 3 カ国が，今回の世界経済危機が自国のみならずアジア経済全体にもたらす深刻なダメージを十分に認識し，今後も起こりうる危機の影響を回避すべく，「東アジア共同体」の構築に向けて本格的に協力する以外に解決策はない。その意味で，2008 年 12 月 13 日，北九州において，今回の世界金融危機への対応を協議すべく急遽日・中・韓 3 カ国首脳会議が開催されたことは，高く評価される。このような 3 カ国首脳会議がより頻繁に開かれることにより，「東アジア共同体」への道がより開かれることを期待したい。

7．経済危機を乗り越え，「東アジア共同体」へ
(1)「東アジア共同体」の原点に立ち戻れ—「アジア通貨基金」の再構築

今回の経済危機へのアジアの対応を考えるとき，1997 年 7 月に起こったアジア通貨危機の際，日本がとった迅速かつ効果的な対策を思い起こす必要がある。日本は直ちに新宮沢構想による救済措置を実施し，アジア通貨基金（AMF）構想を打ち出した。アジア通貨基金構想は，米国のラリー・サマーズ財務長官（当時）の反対に会い挫折したが，2000 年 5 月 ASEAN の提唱により，タイのチェンマイで開催された第 2 回 ASEAN＋3 蔵相会議において，チェンマイ・イニシアティブとして採択され，既存の通貨スワップ網を強化し，すべての ASEAN 加盟国に拡充されることになった。これは通貨危機を経験した ASEAN が，再び通貨危機が起こるのを回避しようとして取った対策であったが，この構想の基礎になったのは，日本が提案した AMF 構想であり，これをきっかけとした通貨協力から「東アジア共同体」構想が生まれたことはすでに述べたとおりである。演繹的にいえば，日本が提案した AMF 構想は「東アジア共同体」構想の産みの親ともいえる。折角このような素晴らしいアイディア

を出しながら，米国を説得できない外交力の弱さとリーダーシップの無さは，オバマ政権下の対米外交とアジア外交においても，克服すべき課題であろう。因みに AMF 構想に当初反対していたラリー・サマーズ財務長官（当時）は，アジア通貨危機が拡大し，事態が深刻化するに及び，AMF 構想に反対した非を認めた。彼がオバマ政権において，米国の経済政策の統帥役とも言えるホワイトハウスの NEC 議長に就任したことは前述の通りである。

　このような経緯から見て，日本は今回の極めて深刻な経済危機にあたり，対米配慮から，アジア通貨危機の蔓延を阻止できなかった前回の失敗を肝に銘じ，自国のみならず，アジアの経済回復のために，単に経済協力だけではなく，日本の持てる知的貢献を行うべきである。そのためには，「東アジア共同体」の原点に立ち戻り，まずチェンマイ・イニシアティブの多角化と拡大により積極的に貢献すべきである。現在スワップ枠は 1 千 200 億ドルまで拡大されているが，2008 年 12 月 13 日の日・中・韓 3 カ国首脳会議において，今回の経済危機の深刻な影響を受け，ウォン安に陥っている韓国に対し，日本と中国がそれぞれ 300 億ドルのスワップ枠の拡大を決定したことは評価される。また 2009 年 1 月 30 日，麻生首相（当時）はダボス会議において，経済危機が深刻化するアジア諸国への 170 億ドル以上の資金援助をおこなうことを表明した。これらの資金が有効に活用され，日本の貢献がアジアにおける共同体意識の醸成に活かされることを期待したい。

（2）アジア債券市場の育成

　1997 年の通貨危機を経験したアジアは，反省点の一つとして，海外の短期資金に頼りすぎたことを挙げ，より長期の資金を導入するため，日本，中国，韓国，ASEAN 各国，オーストラリア，ニュージーランドなどの財務省，中央銀行などが協議を重ねた結果，2005 年，アジア債券市場（Asia Bond Market）が設立され，業務を開始した。この構想も，2002 年 12 月 17 日チェンマイでの ASEAN ＋ 3 の非公式セッションにおいて日本が提案したものであり，アジアの債券市場の発展を通じて，アジアの貯蓄をアジア域内で有効に活用し，域内で投資に結び付けようというものであった。それまでアジアは輸出により稼いだ多額の外貨を，アジア域内で活用せず域外に投資し，リスクの高い域外からの短資を借り入れており，それがアジア通貨危機の一原因ともなっていた。したがってアジア債券市場の設立には，未発達なアジアの金融市場のインフラ強化のためにも期待が寄せられていた。

　しかしその後の活動を見ると，期待されたほどの進展は遂げていない。本来日本は，「アジア債券市場」の活動に，より活発に取り組むべきであるが，日

本はバブル崩壊後、その活動に積極性を失いつつあるように見える。AMF構想といい，アジア債券市場構想といい，折角の良い構想を進進させられないのは，対米配慮，さらに未だに強いドルへの依存体質，円を国際化することへの不安などから脱却できないからであろう。日本もアジアも今回の経済危機により，過剰な対米依存体質，対ドル依存体質がいかに大きな危険を伴うか，思い知ったはずである。これを機に，思い切った発想の転換を図らなければならない。

(3)「アジア投資銀行」の設立

2005年5月バンコクで開かれた国連アジア太平洋経済社会委員会（ESCAP）の年次総会において「アジア投資銀行」の設立提案が出された。これに対し，米国と日本が猛反対し，採決は見送られた。日本の反対の理由は，1966年に設立された「アジア開発銀行（ADB）」が，年間60億ドルのインフラ開発融資を行っており，新しく「アジア投資銀行」を設立することは，ADBの業務と重複するということであった。

しかしADBは，原則として加盟国の政府にのみ融資しており，民間企業のプロジェクトには融資できないので，アジア投資銀行の融資が必ずしもADBの融資と重複するとは限らない。しかも急成長を遂げているアジアでは，インフラ建設資金を必要としているが，1997年のアジア通貨危機以来，民間資金の流入は急減している。「アジア投資銀行」構想は，ヨーロッパの経験に基づいており，ヨーロッパには「ヨーロッパ開発銀行」とは別に，「ヨーロッパ投資銀行」がある。

世銀系のADBでは，世銀と同様，加重投票制を取っているので，出資額が大きい米国と日本は，大きな発言権を持っており，特に日本は歴代ADBの総裁を務めているが，国連の提案している「アジア投資銀行」は，国連式の一国一票システムにより運営されることになるので，多額の拠出をしたからといって，大きな発言権が与えられるわけではない。たしかにアジアにあまりにも多くの国際機関や基金が設立されることには問題があるが，「東アジア共同体」のASEAN＋3の場で「アジア投資銀行」の設立につき議論された際，12カ国が賛成し，反対したのは日本一国だけであったことから見ても，アジア投資銀行の設立がアジアにおいて望まれていることが分かる。日本は米国への配慮のみに終始するのではなく，今回の経済危機に際してのアジアへの協力の一環として，他のアジア諸国とも十分に協力すべきである。

(4) アジア共通通貨制度の設立

アジア共通通貨問題は，アジアにおいても長い間の懸案であった。特に先の

アジア通貨危機以降，ドルだけに依存せず，円，元，ウォンなど，アジア各国の通貨，ユーロ，オーストラリアドルなどによるバスケット方式による共通通貨制度の設立が議論されてきた。特に ADB が，アジア通貨単位（ACU）の研究を進めてきたことは評価される。

しかし日本の財務当局は，基本的には未だドル依存体質を抜け出せず，円を国際通貨として活用することには消極的である。円の地位が国際的に高かった時代ですら，円を国際金融市場の荒波に曝したくないという気持ちが強く，その体質が現在も変わっているとはいえない。

私は 1960 年代の後半の数年を，国連 ESCAP の前身である ECAFE（アジア極東経済委員会）に勤務していたが，その頃 ECAFE 事務局は，エール大学のロバート・トリフィン教授と協力し，アジア決済同盟（Asia Clearing Union）構想を打ち出した。この構想は当時の日本経済の発展に伴い，円を決済通貨として ECAFE 域内の貿易を拡大しようとしたもので，多くの ECAFE メンバー国の支持を得ていたが，当時の大蔵省の反対に会い，日の目を見なかった。

先般麻生前首相が，アジア金融市場の安定と発展のため，「危機の際，各国に『円』を融通できるようにする」と表明したが，これは外貨不足に陥った国に日本円を緊急に貸し出す措置であり，これまで日本が消極的であった「円の国際化」に繋がるものとして歓迎される。

一方中国も，アジアの共通通貨制度については研究を進めており，元も強くなりつつあるが，現在のところバスケット方式といえども，元をアジアの中で活用することには消極的である。しかし ASEAN など近隣諸国との貿易取引については，一部元建てでの決済を始めており，これも「人民元通貨圏」の育成に発展する可能性がある。

私は 2009 年 5 月 25－26 両日，中国吉林大学で開催された「グローバル金融危機下における東アジア通貨金融協力」と題する日中学術シンポジウムに出席する機会を得たが，そこでの印象は，一般的には，中国側参加者の中には，中国経済が近く日本経済を追い抜き，米国に次ぐ第 2 の経済大国になるであろうという最近の中国経済の躍進を反映して，元の将来についてもかなり自信を持って発言する学者が多かったこと，また米国と中国が G2 と呼ばれるようになったことを率直に喜んでいる学者も多かったということであった。また，この 20 年間に，中国では首相が 3 人交代しただけなのに，日本では 14 人もの首相が交代するなど，政治的に不安定であり，また日本経済も不安定なので，円は元のパートナーとして組む相手として好ましくないが，その点，オ

バマ政権のほうが政治的に安定しており、たとえドルの価値が下落したとしても、元が組むべきパートナーは依然としてドルであるとの発言もあった。

その一方で、中国側の通貨金融の専門家の中には、中国経済は規模が大きくなったとはいえ、未だ通貨金融のインフラ面と国際的経験に乏しいので、元の国際化には慎重であるべきで、自国通貨の安定を第一義的に考えるべきであるとの意見もあった。しかし会議全体の流れとしては、中国も次第に経済力に見合った元の国際化に向けて進まざるを得なくなるであろうとの認識はあった。私は、このような日中間の専門家による意見の交換から生まれる提言が、両国政府の政策に反映され、「円の国際化」と「元の国際化」が相互に競合することなく進んでいけば、それは単にアジア経済の内需拡大に貢献するだけではなく、「円」と「元」を中心とするアジアの共通通貨制度の設立への道が拓かれるであろうと期待している。

今回の経済危機は、アジアの大国である日・中・韓の3カ国の金融当局に、ドル依存体質の改善を迫るものである。日本としてはこの機を逃さず、これまでの保守的体質を改め、ADBを中心としてアジアの共通通貨制度の実現に向け、イニシアティブを取るべきである。

(5) アジア経済の内需拡大と「東アジア共同体」

今回の経済危機の影響がアジア経済のなかにはっきり表れてくるに従い、アジア主要国も、米国経済への依存体質を抜け出し、アジア域内の金融市場の整備と拡大、さらにこれを基盤とした域内貿易、投資の拡大に向かわねばならないことを自覚させられることになるが、それは今回の経済危機の苦いレッスンをプラスに変え、アジアの経済規模、人口規模をアジアの利点として十分に活かし、アジアが一丸となって内需の拡大に向かうよいチャンスと見ることもできる。内需の拡大は、今後のアジアの発展の鍵となるであろう。

2009年5月21日東京で開かれた日本経済新聞社主催の第15回国際交流会議「アジアの未来」において、麻生首相（当時）は、2020年までにアジア各国のGDPを倍増させる「アジア経済倍増構想」を発表し、日本がODAや貿易保険などで計670億ドルの支援をすることを打ち出した。この構想が有効に実現されれば、アジア域内の内需拡大に大きく貢献すると期待され、日本の発展にとっても重要なプロジェクトとなるであろう。

またアジア経済の充実を、単に経済圏の形成にとどめず、社会面、文化面へも広げていくことで、共同体意識を醸成すれば、「東アジア」、さらには「アジア共同体」の構築につながるであろう。

8．鳩山首相の「東アジア共同体」構想への期待

　2009年の総選挙において民主党が圧倒的勝利をおさめると、鳩山由紀夫新首相は、日本の国家目標として、「東アジア共同体」の創設を揚げ、さらにドル通貨基軸を脱し、アジアの共通通貨の実現、そして安全保障の問題にまで言及した。1990年代より「東アジア共同体」構想を描き、その実現を望んでいる私にとって、日本が新政権の下で積極的に「東アジア共同体」創設にむけたイニシアティブを取ることができれば、大変嬉しいことである。鳩山首相も認めるとおり、その実現は決して容易ではないであろうが、私は「東アジア共同体」の成立にこそ、これからの日本が生きていく道があると思う。

　日本にとって日米関係がこれからも重要であることは疑いの余地がない。しかし大国化する中国といかに付き合っていくかは、日本にとって死活の問題となるであろう。米国にとっても中国との関係は、日米関係を超えて重要となるであろう。したがって日本にとり、これまでのような米国一辺倒の時代は終わり、日本は複雑化し、変化する日・米・中関係の狭間の中で発展し、日本としてのアイデンティティーを高め、日本の安全保障を確保するために、より自主的な国家戦略を進めなければならない。米国に対しても、真の同盟関係を維持し発展させるためには、日本はいうべきことははっきりといわねばならない。

　前述の鳩山氏の「東アジア共同体」構想が2009年8月27日付ニューヨークタイムズに掲載されると、直ちに米国の日本研究者や政府関係者より、日米関係を損なうものとして、強い牽制と警告が発せられた。また日本の中でも、鳩山首相の「東アジア共同体」構想は、日米同盟の存続を危うくするとの意見や新聞広告も出された。同年11月14日来日中のオバマ大統領は、米国の新しい対アジア戦略について東京で講演し、米国はアジア太平洋国家であり、「東アジア共同体」構想には大きな関心を抱いているので、構想の段階から関与したいと述べた。これを受け日本では、米国をどのような形で「東アジア共同体」に含めるべきかといった議論が盛んに行われるようになった。私は、米国の「東アジア共同体」への関心は尊重すべきではあるが、「東アジア共同体」のオリジナルメンバーは、小泉元首相が2004年9月国連総会演説で明言したとおり、ASEAN10＋3（日，中，韓）を基盤とすべきであり、東アジアに属さない国を最初からメンバーに加えることには慎重であるべきだと考えている。「東アジア共同体」と銘打つ限り、東アジアに属する国をコアとしてスタートすべきであろう。ASEAN＋3でも纏まりにくいもいのを、最初から open regionalism と称してメンバーを拡大したり、functionalism と称して問題別にメンバーを変えていくのが日本の「東アジア共同体」構想であるなら

ば，これは「共同体」と名付けるべきではない。それはまさに「東アジア共同体」のAPEC化を招くことになろう。

　日本は新しい日米関係を築くためにも，粘り強い説得を通じ，「東アジア共同体」を構築することがアジアに発展と安定をもたらし，それが長期的には，米国にとってもプラスになるということを米国に認識させるよう，働きかけねばならない。米国に対し今までのようにYesマンであり続けることは，米国の日本蔑視につながる。

　一方大国化する中国に対しても，いたずらにライバル意識を持つべきではなく，「東アジア共同体」のコ・リーダーとして，より緊密な対話を進め，いうべきことは明確に伝えるべきである。そのためには，まず日中間を結ぶ太い人脈を作る必要がある。また中国は，経済的には発展しつつあるが，量的に拡大しても質的には実に多くの克服すべき問題を抱えている。そのうちの第1は環境問題，第2は高齢化問題である。これら2つの問題は，日本が高度成長の過程で経験し，幾多の試練を経て克服し，また今も改善に努めている問題である。これらの問題について真剣に中国にアドバイスできる国は，日本をおいてないであろう。中国もこれらの問題につき，日本から真摯に学ぶべきである。日本がこれらの問題につき，利害を超えて協力し，中国も日本に学ぶことにより，質的にも大国にふさわしい国に発展することは，日本のみならずアジアの発展と安定に寄与することになり，そこにこそ「東アジア共同体」を創設する意義がある。

9．新しい世界経済秩序の構築に向けて

　アジアが今回の経済危機を契機とし，また今後も起こるであろう危機から共に身を守るためにも，共同体意識を持ち，共同体の構築に向かい前進することができるならば，アジアは規模の大きい域内の内需拡大のチャンスを活かし，経済を活性化し，経済を回復の軌道に乗せることができるであろう。アジアにおける経済規模の大きな共同体の結成は，グローバル化時代におけるアジアの存在感と発言力を増すことになる。

　現在の世界経済秩序は主として欧米，特に米国が支配するブレトンウッズ体制のIMF，世界銀行によって形作られており，そのため日本を含めアジアの投票権が，その経済力に比して不当に弱いことは前述のとおりである。今回の経済危機を契機に，IMF，世界銀行の現行システムも変わらざるを得ないが，現状では基本的改革は望めず，糊塗策としての小改革に終わる可能性が大である。しかしアジアが共同体を結成することにより，日本，中国，さらにイン

ド，ASEAN が一致して，アジアとしてのアイデンティティーを高めるならば，アジアの発言力は強まり，アジアは欧州，北米と共に世界経済の三極構造の一翼を担うことが出来るであろう。そうすることによりアジアは，経済危機後の世界が求める，よりバランスのとれた新しい経済秩序の構築に大きく貢献できると確信している。

第3章　世界経済危機と中日米三ヶ国関係

王少普*

　世界経済危機は中日米の三ヶ国関係に重要な影響を与え，新しい課題と新しい協力関係の期待を示した。三ヶ国政策の方向性にかんがみ，協力の必要度は増し世界の潮流と三ヶ国の利益に合致する。さらに三ヶ国はコミュニケーションと相互信頼を強めるべきだ。三ヶ国の関係をバランスの取れた方向へ発展させ，かつ安定的，協力的，開放的な「トライアングル関係」を促進させることは，世界経済危機の克服，東アジア及びアジア太平洋地域の多角的協力の発展とアジア太平洋地域をはじめ世界の平和安定と繁栄の実現にとって重要な意義をもつ。

　世界の多極化と経済グローバリゼーションの衝撃の下，米国を中心とする戦後の世界秩序が大きく変貌した。世界経済危機はこの傾向を明示しつつ，国際関係に対して重要な影響を与えた。本文は世界経済危機の中米日三ヶ国関係に与える影響について重点的に検討したい。

1．人類的重要課題は三ヶ国間協力の意欲を強化する

　冷戦後において工業化の過度的な開発活動は人類社会と自然世界の矛盾を累積させ，ついに爆発の臨界点に達した。同時に経済のグローバリゼーションと世界の多極化が拍車をかけた。かかる変化は人類共通のリスクとともに共同利益の増加をもたらしたので，一国単独で問題を解決出来なくなった。例えば，石油等の化石エネルギーの枯渇や地球温暖化問題などである。

　経済規模において世界一位から三位までをそれぞれ占める中日米の三ヶ国は，石油消費量において世界の上位三位を占め，さらに CO_2 排出量においてはそれぞれ第一，第二，第五位を占め，諸問題に対して重大な責任を負うと同時に，その結果に対して特に敏感になっている。かかる状況は，石油価格問題等について同様の要請を迫っている。更に重要なことは，もし三ヶ国が世界的リスクに対して協力しないなら，三ヶ国と世界に対して巨大災禍をもたらす危険があるということである。

　世界金融経済危機の中，前掲の諸問題解決は，中日米の三ヶ国にとって新し

---

*　上海交通大学環太平洋研究センター教授，日本研究センター主任教授。

い意義を持つ。三ヶ国は経済困難を克服するため産業構造の調整と市場拡大の必要がある。「省エネルギー及び汚染物質排出削減」の緊急課題の解決は大きな商機を提供し，三ヶ国はこれらの問題において競争相手でもあるが，三ヶ国それぞれ独自な特徴を有しているので，三ヶ国協力はとくに重要である。2009年11月にオバマ米大統領は日本において「日本はこの問題で先頭に立ってきた。この重要な世界的目標を達成する上で，日本国民と重要なパートナーとなることを楽しみにしている」と演説した[1]。引き続きオバマ大統領は，訪中時の演説の中で「エネルギーの最大消費者と生産者である米国と中国両国が協力しなければ，この問題を解決することは不可能である」と指摘した[2]。

2．経済構造における中日米の相互支援体制を形成し，世界経済のバランスを取り戻すための協力が必要

経済グローバリゼーションは各国間の相互依頼関係を強化させた。三ヶ国の巨大経済規模と特別な経済モデルは経済・金融界において相互支援の特別の構造を構築した。即ち1980年代のレーガン政権時代の「新自由主義」のいわゆる「新米国モデル」は，「国家最小化，市場最大化」を告知し市場の調整力を強調した。「新米国モデル」において「決定権は短期利益を追求する企業経営者がにぎり，金融市場から資本調達を可能にした」[3]。「新米国モデル」，米ドルの覇権的地位と過剰消費の文化伝統が相結合し，独特な「債務型成長モデル」を形成した。

中国モデルは基本的に輸出指向型モデルである。改革開放の初期に中国は開発資金の不足問題を解決するため，さまざまな優遇措置をもって（特に廉価良質の労働力を使って）外国資本を導入した。この結果，大量の外国直接投資が中国市場に流入した。同時に，国内消費能力の増加と市場育成に相当時間が必要であるため，中国の対外貿易依存度は非常に高い水準に達した。中米両国は互いに第二位の貿易パートナーであり，日本は中国の第三位の貿易パートナー，かつ中国は日本にとって第一位の貿易パートナーで，中国は「世界の工場」となった。

日本はハイエンド製造業の国家であり，日本の輸出製品の特徴は高い附加価値である。現在日本は高度成長期と比べ，内需型に移行したが，対外貿易依存度は依然として高い。日本は生産コストを抑えるため労働集約型・資本集約型

---

1) 2009年11月14日，オバマ米大統領が東京で米国のアジア政策について行った演説。
2) 2009年11月17日『中米共同声明』
3) David Coates著，耿修林等訳，『資本主義のモデル』中国江蘇人民出版社，2001年版，12頁。

産業を中国へ移出した。日本は，中国を世界市場向けの生産基地化戦略を追求したので，対中国直接投資は明らかに輸出指向の伏線になった。投資貿易の相関性試算によれば，1994 — 2005 年の 11 年間，日本の対中国直接投資額と中国の対米輸出額との間の相関度は 0.88 を示した。日本は 2001 年以降，アジア向け輸出半製品の数量を大幅に拡大した。一方，アジア各国，特に中国は，米欧向け輸出製品の数量を拡大した。日本の電器，機械と運輸設備等のメーカーは対中投資と生産規模を常に拡大した。日本産の最終製品は先進国家・地域向けに輸出したため，日本の対中投資は中米貿易の場合に比べてあきらかに貿易創出効果（Trade Creation Effect）を発揮した。

このため，日本の経済学者・若杉隆平は以下のように指摘した。「日本，米国と中国または東アジアの間において貿易トライアングルが形成された。この貿易トライアングルは米国を最終市場とし，日本から輸出するか，あるいは当地で生産するかである。日本から米国向けの輸出は大きな成長がないように見えるが，日本の中国への輸出が絶えず成長しており，中国から米国への輸出も大幅に成長した」[4]。

中日両国とも対米貿易額は黒字だが，特に中国は黒字額が巨大である。同時にドルは基軸通貨であるため米国の資本収支は巨額赤字を計上せざるを得ない構造である。一方，アジアの輸出国は自国通貨の対ドル長期安定化のため外貨蓄積額を運用して米国債を購入せざるを得ない構造である。統計によれば，米国債残高は 2008 年 9 月現在，10 兆ドルを超過し，2009 年 11 月 16 日現在さらに 12 兆 310 億ドルに増加した。米国債保有額は中国が世界第一位の 7 千 989 億米ドルを保有し，日本が第二位の 7 千 515 億米ドルを保有した。

「新米国モデル」は世界経済の高度成長を支えたが，米国政府の監視機能不足と米国金融資本の利益至上主義の性格から，そのバランスが崩れ，世界の金融経済は重大な危機的状況に追い込まれた。この危機から完全脱出するためには，世界経済のバランスを再建しなければならない。世界経済の主要構成員である三ヶ国は特に重要な責任を負い，三ヶ国は協力して貿易保護主義を防止する必要がある。

3．アジア太平洋地域の経済統合を支持し，東アジア共同体論において協調する

世界金融経済危機は東アジア共同体論を加熱させた。東アジア共同体論は三ヶ国関係と密接にかかわっている。東アジア共同体は一種の統合概念である

---

[4] FROM RIETI NO.76

ので，いくつかの段階に分けて見る必要がある。現段階において東アジア経済共同体，即ち東アジア自由貿易地帯に限定できる。世界金融経済危機は東アジア自由貿易地帯の発展に新たなモメンタムを提供した。

米国は「債務型モデル」から「輸出型モデル」に転換を試みアジア市場進出に意欲的である。日本は米国向けの直接・間接的な輸出額を大幅に減少した。日本は不況から脱却するため国内需要をアジア域内需要に統合する「内外一体化政策」と呼ぶべき政策を展開した。中国は対米輸出の減少と同時に貿易摩擦が増えた。中国の対アジア地域の需要は増加した。東アジア自由貿易地帯のプロセスを早めることはアジア市場の拡大にプラスになるだろう。

中日米の三ヶ国において東アジア共同体論に対する賛否両論のいずれについても進展が見られた。

中国側の提案は，「10＋1」（ASEAN 10ヶ国に，中国，日本，韓国等それぞれが加わる）を基礎とし，「10＋3」（ASEAN 10ヶ国に中国，日本と韓国の三ヶ国が加わる）を主要なパイプとしつつ，東アジアサミットを重要な戦略論壇（フォーラム）として東アジア共同体のプロセスを推進していくというもの。同時に，アジア太平洋地域経済の統合化を支持し，米国がアジア太平洋国家として建設的な役割を発揮することを歓迎する。

日本側の提案は，東アジア共同体は「10＋6」（「10＋3」＋インド，オーストラリアとニュージーランド）を骨子としている。岡田外相は，米国は正式な加盟国としない形で創設を目指す考えを表明したが，鳩山首相は東アジア共同体から米国を排除すべきではないと表明した。しかし鳩山首相は岡田外相の考えを明確に否定したわけではない。日本はアジア太平洋地域経済の統合化を支持しつつ，日米同盟をアジア太平洋地域の平和安定と繁栄の基礎であるとの態度である。

米国は自ら太平洋国家を任じ，東アジア共同体から排除されれば反対すると主張した。米国は一連の行動を起こした。例えば，「東南アジア友好協力条約」加盟（29ヶ国加盟，2009年11月現在）と「環太平洋パートナーシップ協定」（TPP）への参加を表明し，環太平洋自由貿易協定を積極的に推進すること等である。同時に米国はアジア太平洋地域経済の統合実現を主張した。

東アジア共同体論について中日米の間にそれぞれの要求は異なるが，共通するところも多い。三ヶ国が東アジア共同体論の矛盾を如何に協調するかは，三ヶ国関係のみならず，東アジア・アジア太平洋地域経済の統合やアジア太平洋情勢・国際秩序に関係する。三ヶ国はともにアジア太平洋地域経済の統合を支持していることが基礎である。三ヶ国提案をならべれば三つの段階的目標を

設定することが考えられる。第一段階は「10＋3」を主要なパイプとして東アジア共同体建設を推進する。第二段階は「10＋6」に拡大する。第三段階はアジア太平洋自由貿易地帯に拡大する。総じて段階設定によって目標を区分するが，同時に区分を絶対化すべきではない。地域の特殊利益を優先すると同時に，地域間の共同利益を順次に拡大して行くことこそ，東アジア及びアジア太平洋地域における協力関係を積極的かつ適切に推進することができる。

4．世界の多極化は各国の外交関係に重要な変化をもたらし，中日米関係を相対的バランスの取れた方向へと発展させる

　経済のグローバリゼーションは国家間関係を，冷戦期の敵味方の二分化から，味方でありながらライバルでもあるという関係に発展させた。世界の多極化は，特に世界経済危機の影響によって各国の利益を一層多元化させることに寄与した。このような情況の下，各国政府は対外関係の「バランス」化のために配慮せざるを得なくなる。中日米関係の発展にもこのような傾向が見られた。

（1）オバマ政権のアジア政策は日米同盟を基礎とするものから，対中外交を重点とする方向に向かっている

　2009年11月のオバマ大統領の訪日を契機に，米国はアジア政策の調整に着手した。オバマ氏のアジア政策を概観すれば，以下のような特徴を四点挙げることができる。

　その一，オバマ大統領のアジア政策は米国の世界戦略の中で，ポスト冷戦時代において前例のない地位を占めた。世界危機と中国等のアジア新興国家の高度成長の結果，アジアの重要性が一層明確になった。オバマ大統領は，歴代大統領と比べ，いっそうアジアに目を向け，米国は太平洋国家であることを表明し，太平洋は米国とアジアの間の障害ではなく，両方を結ぶ帯であると主張した。

　その二，アジア・パートナーシップをさらに発展させること。米国世界戦略におけるアジアの地位の上昇，米国が挑戦すべき課題数の増加とアジア諸国の共通利益の発展にかんがみ，米国とアジア諸国は広く協力関係を確立すべきである。同大統領は，伝統的同盟国とならび新しいアジア・パートナーシップを希望した。同大統領は日米同盟を堅持し深化させると同時に，特に中国との協力の必要性と重要性を強調した。中国の高度発展は世界発展の源泉であり，米国は中国を封じ込める意図はなく，中国が国際的な舞台でより大きな役割を果たすことを歓迎すると指摘した[5]。

その三，積極的にアジア市場を開拓し，アジア太平洋の地域協力を重視すること。米国は経済危機から脱出するため経済発展の新戦略を確定した。その骨子は，貯蓄増強，歳出削減，金融改革，長期財政赤字・債務削減などであり，製造業重視と輸出増加路線を明示した。そのため積極的にアジア市場を開拓する必要がある。同大統領は，アジア諸国の対外貿易依存度の減少，内需拡大とアジア太平洋地域の多国間協力等について米国のイニシアティブを表明した。

その四，さらなる寛容的な文化態度を示し，米国的価値観の旗印を高く掲げること。米国的価値観を堅持することは米国の政治家の一貫した基本選択である。米国の優勢は相対的に弱まり，新米国・モデルが挑戦をうける今，米国的価値観を堅持することは新たな現実的な意義を有している。同大統領は，アジア太平洋地域が多元文化の地域であることを認めると同時に，固有の文化と経済の発展などの理由をもって行われる人権侵害に対して強く反対した。

オバマ大統領はそのアジア政策のなかから対中・対日政策を編み出した。対中政策の基本内容は二点ある。その一は，二国間の戦略的互恵パートナーシップの構築・深化させること。その二は，21世紀における全面的・積極的な中米関係の建設と実際行動におけるパートナーシップ関係を樹立することである。次に対日政策の基本内容について二点あり，一つは，日米同盟は依然として米国のアジア政策の基軸であり，日米同盟を堅持し深化させること。そして二つは，米日協力の内容を拡大させることである。

米国は，クリントン政権時代において，北米を基礎にアジア太平洋向けの扇形の輻射構造を構築する戦略構想を提起した。即ちこの扇形構造とは，日米同盟を基軸とし，米国と韓国，ASEAN，オーストラリア，ニュージーランドなどの国家（地域）相手に二国間の同盟関係を扇骨とし，APECを扇面とすることである。その目標は米国を中心とする新太平洋共同体を構築することである。この戦略構想は同盟関係と多国間協力との連携を強調した。オバマ大統領は変化しつつある地域・世界情勢の中においてこの方向をさらに前進させている。オバマ大統領は，アジアにおける日米同盟を基礎としつつ，対中協力を重点としながら同盟関係と多国間協力を整合するアジア政策の方向を打ち出した。

（2）鳩山政権の外交政策は米国とアジアの間のバランスを取ることを強調

同時に日本の民主党政権も対米政策の調整を主張した。これは，主に以下の二方面から見られる。

---

5) 2009年11月14日，オバマ米大統領が東京で米国のアジア政策について行った演説。

その一，日本政府は米国との「対等」的関係を求めること。冷戦後，ソ連の解体によって戦後最大の安全保障上の脅威が消えたため日本国内に自主意識が台頭した。この状況のもと小沢一郎民主党幹事長は先頭に立って，日本を「普通の国家」にするスローガンを打ち出した。このスローガンは戦後ヤルタ体制が日本に加えた制限を打破することを主眼とするものであるが，米日関係の主従関係を変化させる狙いが含まれる。米国を震源とする世界経済危機によって米国優勢が相対的に弱まり，日本の要求が強まった。日本の民主党は「(日米)緊密で対等」の関係と主張している。いわゆる「対等」とは，日本の国益と国民の願望を前提として対米関係を処理するという主張である。鳩山内閣はインド洋給油問題と普天間飛行場移設等の問題を抱えなかなか米国と妥協できないが，これらの問題は日本の国益と米国に対する「対等」の要求がどの程度実現できるかに関係している。

その二，日本政府は以前にもまして外交上の「バランス」に苦心している。日米同盟から来る制限は，日本の外交に単一方向性をもたらし，日本政府が「東南アジア友好協力条約」に参加を渋る原因もここにある。しかし，中国などアジア諸国の高度発展によって国際情勢に未曾有の変化が発生した。米国だけに依存することは日本の安全保障・経済運営上リスクがある。世界金融経済の危機の現在においてはなおさらだ。例えば，経済上，中国は日本にとって一番の貿易パートナーとなったが，日本の対中投資の相当の部分は中国を生産基地としており，その製品は最終的に米国向けに輸出される。米国の金融危機のため日本経済は相当被害を受けた。米国は今回危機を契機に，「債務型成長モデル」から「輸出型成長モデル」に転換すると提唱した。米国の政策転換は，日米はいずれも製造業のハイエンドに位置するため，必然的に相関領域において競争関係を刺激するだろう。このような情況の下，日本は経済「統合」と「アジア市場を内需市場とする」等のスローガンを打ち出した。ある有力機関の統計によれば，日本製造業の国別の将来投資先見通しについて，第一位，二位と三位はそれぞれ中国，インド，ベトナムの順となっている。即ち，日本外交は，これまでの米国中心から離れ，アジアとの間においてバランスを求める方向に転じることを意味するであろう。鳩山首相は，中日韓の三ヶ国首脳会議において，「日本が米国に頼りすぎる」と発言したがまさに言い当てている。岡田外相は米国が東アジア共同体の正式メンバーになるべきではないと主張した。

（3）中国外交は三ヶ国関係を安定的，協力的，開放的方向へと発展させようとしている

　日米同盟は冷戦期の産物である。長い間中国がその主要な仮想敵国の一つとなった。冷戦後日米同盟の役割に変化が起きたが，対中国戦略予防の確立と保持が，依然としてその戦略的目標の重要内容である。現在，米国はアジアで日米同盟を基礎とし，対中協力を重点とし，同盟関係と多角協力を整合する方向を打ち出した。日本も次第に米国とアジアの間にバランスを求めている。これらの変化に対し中国は大変歓迎している。

　中米関係について，胡錦濤主席は以下のように指摘した。

　　国際形勢は絶えず深刻且つ複雑に変化している。新情勢のもと人類平和と発展に関わる重大問題について中米両国は広汎の共通利益と協力拡大の可能性を有しつつ重要な共同責任を負っている。新時代における中米関係の戦略性と地球規模の性格が日増しに顕著になった[6]。

中日関係について，胡錦濤主席は次のとおり指摘した。

　　国際情勢は深刻且つ複雑変化している。中日両国が有している共通利益と課題が増している。両国関係は一層の高いレベルと広い空間に向けて発展する重要な機会に直面している。中国は日本と共に，両国人民の根本的利益に着眼し，世界発展の潮流に順応し，中日間の戦略的互恵関係を持続し，かつ深く前進させようと願っている[7]。

　中米関係は中日関係に比べ世界性を有しているが，中国は中米関係と中日関係を共に戦略的レベルにおいて運営努力している。同時に，中国は引き続き，独立自主の平和外交方針を堅持し，「平和勢力側に立つ立場は不動」，非同盟とし，世界各国と良好な関係に向け努力をする。中日米関係を世界潮流に順応させ，安定的，協力的，開放的な方向に発展させるため努力し，積極的な役割を発揮すべきである。

　世界の経済危機は中日米の三ヶ国関係に重要な影響を与えた。現在の三ヶ国政策の方向性にかんがみ，協力の必要性度は増し世界のトレンドと三ヶ国の利益は合致している。三ヶ国はさらにコミュニケーションと相互信頼を強めるべ

6）2009年11月17日，胡錦濤中国国家主席が北京でオバマ米大統領会見した時の発言。
7）2009年9月21日，胡錦濤中国国家主席がニューヨークで鳩山由紀夫日本首相と会見した時の発言。

きだ。三ヶ国の関係をバランスの取れた方向へ発展し、かつ安定的,協力的,開放的な「トライアングル関係」の形成を促進させることは,世界経済危機を克服し,東アジア及びアジア太平洋地域の多角的協力の発展を促進し,アジア太平洋のみならず世界の平和安定と繁栄の実現にとって重要な意義をもつ。

(訳者:王元　早稲田大学アジア太平洋研究センター特別研究員　学術博士)

第4章 ポスト世界金融危機時代の新興国市場と
　　　　グローバル企業の動向

木下俊彦*

はじめに

　世界金融危機後，先進国と中国，インドなどの新興国のGDPや貿易金額のワールド・シェアは大きく変化した。実際のところ，新興国がV字型に近い経済回復を見せているのと比べて，先進国経済は回復基調にあるものの，2番底の可能性さえ残っている。かくして，相互の力関係にも激変が起こりつつある。「リーマン・ショック」以前は，G8で実質的に処理方針が決められていた世界規模の重要経済問題は，以降，G8に代わってG20が問題解決のための主要な議論の場となった。先進国は，人口・国土大国で，急成長を遂げる中国，インド，ブラジルなどによる地球環境対策や国際通貨体制などの既成秩序の改変要求に苦渋の選択を迫られている。そして，新興国が新市場創設やグローバル資本の受け皿として世界の主導的役割を果たしつつある。もちろん，1人あたり所得や絶対貧困者数などからいって，中国やインドが途上国であることには変わりないが，人口，国土面積，高度知的水準保有者数，穀物収量，保有外貨準備高，対内・対外直接投資額，軍事力など総合力からいって，中国やインドはもはや通常の「第3世界」の国とはいえず，特別の仕分けが必要になっている。とはいえ，先進国にとって，異なる政治体制下になる中国と民主主義ルールが通じるインドの位置づけは同じではない。にもかかわらず，ほとんどすべての国が経済大国・中国との平和的共存を希望している。

　そういう複雑な状況を考慮すれば，米国のオバマ大統領が，中国に戦略提携関係のグレードアップを意味する「米中2極（G2）構想」を提案した理由も理解できる。米国が，欧州，日本，インド，ロシアなどを差し置いて，中国にG2提案をした理由は，中国に「世界の責任あるステークホルダー」としての役割（義務）を期待してのことであった。この提案に対して，中国の温家宝首相は，グローバルな問題を米中だけ決めるのはおかしいなどという建前論で体よく断ったが，多くの国際問題で米国と引き続き協調していきたいと回答している（木下 [2009]）。しかし，現地メディアの調査でも，中国の大手企業や国民の多数は，すでに自国は「経済大国」だとの意識を持っており，自国の

---

* 早稲田大学大学院アジア太平洋研究科客員教授。

「内政問題」に価値観の異なる米国や欧州からあれこれ非難を受けたくないという強い「ナショナリズム」の波動が強まっており，米欧と中国の交渉は複雑を極めよう。

ところで，グローバル・ビジネスの主役は依然として先進国に拠点をおく巨大グローバル企業である。そのあとを，韓国，中国企業が急迫している。中国，インドが内需に重心を置く経済発展を行いつつある中で，巨大グローバル企業が新興国市場に参入する動きは，地場企業にとって，脅威と見られないであろうか。一方，中国などで力をつける地場企業は先進国企業の買収に強い関心を示している。こういう双方のニーズの実現はグローバル規模での win-win ゲームを持続させるだろうか。本論文では，こうした世界金融危機後の中国・インド経済動向とグローバル企業の動きを概観する。

1. 国際金融危機，世界経済危機へ転換とアジア経済
（1）米国経済メカニズムの変形と欧州経済の亀裂

世界金融危機の起点は，一般に，「リーマン・ショック」とされるが，その兆候は1年以上前に欧州・東欧で発生したバブルの破裂＝銀行危機にあった（Morris [2008]）。世界的な過剰流動性による欧州の銀行によるアイスランド，ギリシヤや東欧新興国への過剰融資とその結果としての不動産バブルの崩壊によるものだった（欧州はいまなおその問題から脱していない）。果たせるかな，それは，米国発のサブプライムローン・バブルの破綻の引き金となる。しかし，2007年段階では，米国エスタブリッシュメントの大部分は，米国政府・連銀などの巧みな舵取りに大きな期待をかけ，自国経済の先行きに楽観的であった。結局，米国政府は，サブプライムローン問題の処理に行き詰まり，リーマン・ブラザースを犠牲にして，事態を短期間に収拾しようとしたが，思惑ははずれ，株価は大暴落，強靭そのものに見えた米国の金融システムは，1929年以来最悪の破綻を見ることとなった。2009年，新たに政権の座についたオバマ大統領は，G20諸国に呼びかけ，巨額の財政資金注入と金融緩和策の共同実施での事態切り抜けを志向した。そのあおりを受けて，ロンドン金融市場も混乱し，英ポンドは大きな下落をし，英国および大陸欧州諸国も，多額の財政支援と金融緩和に踏み切った。

しかし，アジア通貨危機以後，金融システムを再構築し，慎重な経済運営をしていたアジア主要国では，金融システムに重大な打撃を受けた国はほとんどなかった。したがって，正確にいうと，今回の深刻な金融危機は，欧米の金融危機，すなわち，北大西洋金融危機と呼ぶべきであろう。

（2）世界経済危機の発生と国際波及

　世界金融危機が発生したとき，日本政府は楽観的で，日本には大きな影響は及ぶまいという見解を発表した。しかし，その予測は単純に楽観的希望の表明に過ぎなかった。それは，世界金融危機が，実体経済の大混乱と大収縮をもたらしたことに加え，本国で資金不足に陥った欧米の投資銀行やファンドが日本の株式市場や不動産投資から資金を引き揚げたためである（太田［2009］）。日本企業の中では，アジア太平洋なかんずく米国への直接・間接輸出が多く，米国内でも現地生産を大規模に行っていた自動車・同部品，電子・電機，機械産業などが大打撃を受けた。日本では2009年9月に，民主党を中核とする連合政権が誕生したが，新政権に明確な成長戦略や構造調整政策が無いことが，日本経済の落ち込みを助長した。2009年に，日本経済が先進国中，最悪の経済状況に陥ったのはそのためであった。とはいえ，日本のメガバンクなどは概ね自己資本に余裕があり，危機的状況に落ち込んだわけではない。

　アジア諸国経済の落ち込みも，日本と同じような経路をたどった（ただし，米国で日本企業が直接・間接に行っているような規模で，現地生産しているアジア企業はほとんどないし，日本円がドルに対して，円高基調で推移したのに対し，韓国などの為替レートは弱含みか，横ばいだったということも輸出産業や観光産業の収支の明暗を分けた）。

　中国は，2009年6月から，当局の管理のもとで行っていた小刻み為替レート調整（基本的に人民元高）を停止し，増税の還付率を上げることなどにより，労働集約産業への打撃の極小化を図った。とはいえ，対先進国輸出などの大きな落ち込みによって，沿海部の労働集約産業はかなりの影響を受け，一時は農民工1000万人以上が帰農する事態となった。

　こうした世界の情勢を図示すれば，図1のようになる（『通商白書09年版』から引用）。それまで，先進国と新興国という二つのエンジンをもっていた世界経済は，新興国のみが追加的に市場を作るという片肺飛行に移行した。問題は，先進国の不況が，近い将来，終息し，以前のような双発エンジンの状態にもどるかどうかである。筆者は，そういう見通しにかなり否定的である。その理由については後述する。

2．今後の先進国経済および新興国経済の展望
（1）世界ベースでの拡張的財政金融政策の実施

　今回の世界的な金融危機，経済危機の解決がどういう風に展開しつつあるかについて概説する前に，約10年前に発生したアジア通貨危機の時の状況につ

図1 国際金融危機の実体経済への波及

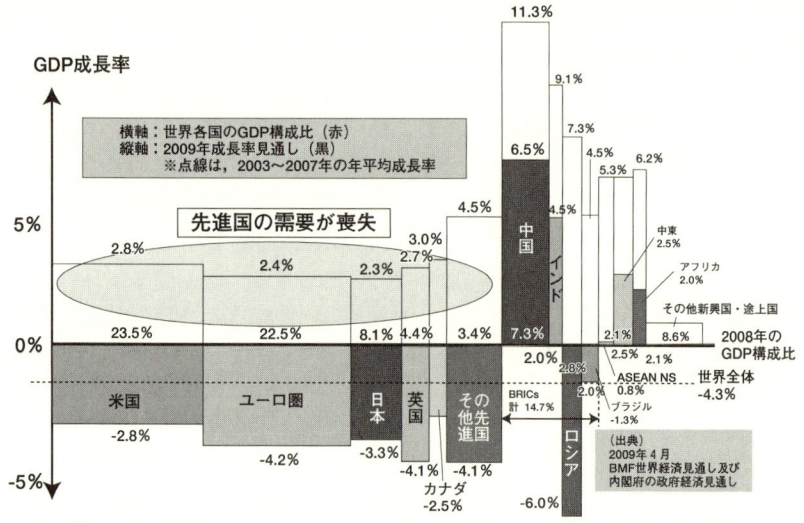

(出所：『通商白書09年版』)

いて触れておきたい。

アジア通貨危機が発生したとき，米欧とくに米国政府の対応は冷淡という以外の言葉を見出すのは困難である。ヘッジファンドなどによる短期外国資金の東アジア資本市場への大量流入と，急速な流出を主因とする「21世紀型」金融危機が発生したとき，米国政府・当局は，問題の根源は東アジアの腐敗・癒着・血縁主義であるとして，日本が1997年10月にIMF／世銀香港総会で提案した「アジア通貨基金」（AMF）構想に強く反対し，IMFの構造調整融資によって，危機に陥ったタイ，インドネシア，韓国に，金融システムの転換，国有企業の民営化などを短期間で行うよう要求し，その要求を貫徹した。それが，これらの国の後遺症を予想外に大きなものにした。

アジア通貨危機発生直前まで，東アジア諸国は，外国からのホットマネーの流入で，バブル現象が見られたが，IMFや世銀は，経常収支の赤字は直接投資の大量の流入でカバーされており，危険でないと判断し，特段の警告を行わなかった。犠牲になった諸国は，米国政府，OECD，IMFの強い要請によって資本市場を迅速に開放した国だったのである。その要求を時期尚早と拒否した中国は，米国政府の説得によりAMF設置には反対したものの，短期資金の流出にも見舞われず，人民元の対ドル為替レートを維持し，中国経済モデルの優越性を自讃した。日本政府は，AMF設置には失敗したが，「新宮沢構想」

によって,東アジアへの緊急資金供給を行うとともに,他の東アジア諸国と協調して,「チェンマイ・イニシアティブ」や「アジア債券イニシアティブ」を実現した（Kinoshita,, Yamazawa, & Kwan [2007a] 参照）。

　一方,戦後最大の金融危機に陥った米国政府・当局は,客観的な原因究明をほとんどすることもなく,今回の危機はグローバル・インバランスに起因して不可抗力的に発生したとして,解決に向けた主要国の共同アクションが行われなければ,世界は本物の恐慌に突入するとして,先進国と新興国の代表を交えたG20会合で,国際協調による大幅な財政政策実施と金融緩和措置をただちに行うとの了解をとりつけた[1]。新興国も,その合意に沿った対応をしたが,世界金融・経済危機を発生させた当事国が,自国の責任と事後対策に十分なコミットメントをしないまま,国際的「コンセンサス」を求めるやりかたに,強い不満を抱いたであろうことは誰の目にも明らかだった。こうした米国主導の既成レジームへの不満・亀裂が明白になったということは,戦後パックス・アメリカーナの申し子というべき米英中心のグローバル金融支配構造の終焉が始まったとみなしてよいであろう。米国流国際金融インフラは極度に不安定性を増し,新興国からその大改革が求められている（といっても,大改革案のコンテンツは,米ドルの1極支配体制を複数通貨体制に変えるといったもので,そう具体的ではない）。ただし,ヘッジファンドの運営の透明性確保,タックス・ヘイブン問題糾明などについては,新興国だけでなく,大陸欧州,日本政府も強く要求している[2]。しかし,事態の進捗は,遅れている。米国が世界金融・経済を主導する皇帝の地位を降りても,責任を持って舞台回しができる次の皇帝が現れたのではない。世界は,米国の総合力がなお国別で突出しているという不安定な皇位不在期に入ったのである。

（2） 米国の過大消費に依存する世界資金還流メカニズムの破綻

　米国政府・当局のいう「グローバル・インバランス」論は,「リーマン・ショック」発生までの自国の超低金利政策の続行,金融システム・金融証券化商品などへの適切な監督責任を回避するための国際訴訟時の弁護士的議論以外の何物でもないが[3],経済学的にいえば,米国の過剰消費（貯蓄以上の消費）

---

1) 結論として,それ以外の現実的な方法はなかったであろう。しかし,問題は公平で透明なプロセスの存否である。権威ある国際機関が,原因を究明したうえで,各国・地域がなすべき義務と検証方法や罰則を決める,また,再発防止措置も定めた条約を締結するという方法も論理的にはありえた。
2) ただし,中国は,香港をタックス・ヘイブン扱いすることに強く反対した。
3) その点については,P. クルーグマン,J. スティーグリッツなどの米国の一流の経済学者が認めている議論である。米国の産官学でも,そういう不安定な状態を是正すべきという提言がなんどもなされている。

を可能にする仕組みが長く存在していた，ということである。この点は，真実である。それは，米ドルという信用貨幣（ペーパーマネー）を使った国際資金還流によって可能となっていた。

米国の事業環境は世界で並外れて素晴らしいからという思い込み，ないし，手持ちのドル債権の毀損を恐れて，海外資金が巨額の経常収支赤字（米国の場合は，これは，貿易収支赤字に近い）をカバーしてきたのであった。

この仕組みは米国人にとっては，世界の蟻たちによって，自己の収入を超える生活を保障してもらえる極めて好都合なものであるが，経常黒字国にとっても，容易に輸出市場，資本運用市場を手にできるものであったため，アカデミック世界などで，この仕組みは持続的でないという結論が出ても，双方とも事実上それを黙過してきたのである。

しかし，一旦，この仕組みが持続的でないことが白日の下にさらされると，別の内外の政治力学が働きだし，これまでと違った新たな均衡を求めての運動が始まるのである。すなわち，米国では，企業は新規設備投資を控え，雇用を減らした。消費者は，自己防衛のため消費を減らし，財・サービスの流れは細った。銀行は不動産貸付の資産保全に動く。縮小均衡の動きである。一方，海外から現状の仕組み修正の要求の先頭に立ったのは中国で，米国債購入の条件として，米政府による健全なマクロ経済運営の実施を求めた。それは，中国が米国に対して，不良債権国に対しコンディショナリティの実現を迫るIMFの役割を果たしているようであった。それとは，別に，中国政府は，人民元をアジア諸国の中国品への支払い通貨とするのを認めたり，「走出去」政策を強めて，2兆ドルを超す手持ちの外貨準備（ペーパーマネー）を，国有企業に，海外の実物資産に変えさせるような措置を次々と採った。数年前まで，米国は中国にとって，銀行の不良債権をどうやって処理するかといったことの指導教官であったことが，信じられないような激変ぶりである。米国が中国に「G2」の提案をしたのは，こういう文脈のもとであった。中国政府は米国とは重要事項でできる限り協力するが，世界の重要事項を米中だけで決めることはできないし，不道徳だとして拒否したが，この話を聞いた中国国民が舞い上がったのも無理はなかろう[4]。しかし，中国にとって，現在から将来への展望はそんなに楽観を許すものではない。既成の国際金融プラットフォームは，好むと好まざるにかかわらず，国際公共財であり，中国は，冷戦終了とWTO加盟によって，それに自由にアクセスできることにより，貿易，対内・対外直接投資，人

---

4) 例えば，木下［2009c］や『朝鮮日報』（Web記事）「【コラム】ひた走る中国，薄れる韓国への関心」2010年1月4日付を参照。

の流れを拡大し，現在の「富強」を手にしたのである。

　欧米に台頭してきた保護主義が，既成国際公共財を中国などの強いコミットメントなしに安易に渡してしまったことの後悔を含んだものだとしたら，先進国，新興国にとって，危険極まりないものである。WTO ドーハラウンドは 10 年中に有効に成立するだろうか。政治家は，選挙に勝つために，グローバルな利益を捨てて，ポピュリストの法案に一票を投じる可能性がある。欧米ベースのグローバル企業の立場は微妙だが，基本的には，ビジネス機会を失いたくないという願望が強いので，破局を恐れ，粘り強く交渉する傾向がある。

　他方，新興国側も安閑としておられる状況にはない。世界各国・地域を緊密に結び付けてきた既成の国際公共財は，コストなしに維持され，自動更新されていくものではない。そういう事実に目をふさいで，次の受け皿ができるまえにそれを破壊してしまえば，世界は，戦前のようなブロック経済，ないし，事実上の鎖国に追い込まれざるを得ない。

　良心的で，事実究明に熱心な「国際派」は進むべき進路を知っているが，先進国であれ，新興国であり，ナショナリスティックな「国益」論の大きな声には対抗できない。

　先進国および新興国の指導者が，事柄の重要性を知悉していることを強く期待する。リスクは，国民がそれを十分理解せず，先進国や新興国の「横暴」に憤り，暴発してしまうことである[5]。新興国政府は，不人気を覚悟で，正しい国民教育をすべきである（木下［2009c］など参照）。また，こういう時期のメディアの役割は決定的に重要である。

3．世界市場の中の新興国市場の台頭とアジア
（1）中国など新興国経済の急速な回復

　国際経済危機に最初に果断な反応を示したのは中国であった。ひとつには，権威主義的政治体制がそれを可能にしたという事情がある。中国政府は，こういう緊急事態を想定して，4 兆元という巨額の財政支援を準備していたという向きもる。さらに，近年の財政状況がよいという状況も幸いした。資金のすべてが中央政府から出されたわけでなく，地方政府も応分の負担を行った。西

---

[5] 例えば，中国の場合，2008 年には，輸出の大幅減にもかかわらず，例えば，自動車の国内販売台数は 40% 増加し 1360 万台と，世界一の座を確保した。したがって，国民にすれば，世界中のビジネスマンは中国に来なければ，商売にならないだろうと考え始めるかもしれない。つまり，中国は世界の中心にある，と。しかし，自動車の原料や燃料の大半は海外からドル建てで輸入されているのであり，「油断」があれば，全ては無に帰するのである。WTO，BIS，国際原燃料市場，国際金融市場を含む国際公共財の維持は世界のすべてのメンバーに不可欠なのである。

北部などの鉄道網などインフラ建設や農民が家電製品を買う場合の補助金の供与や農道整備など農村重視、雇用創設の姿勢は明白である。もっとも、重複投資、無駄な投資も多く、環境配慮も十分されていない[6]ようである。

今回の世界経済危機で、中国で最大の打撃を受けたのは、沿海部とくに広東省の深圳や東莞、浙江省の工業団地などの労働集約産業だった。注目すべきは、この事態にどう対処すべきかについて、党幹部の間で路線闘争が見られたことである。温家宝首相は、地方の多数の零細企業の倒産による社会不安を最も恐れた。広東省の総書記・汪洋氏は、この危機は、むしろ、付加価値のほとんどない現在の産業構造を転換する良い機会だと述べた。今回危機前から、低廉な労働者確保の困難や停電の増加から広東地域などから撤退し始めていた台湾、香港などの小企業は、輸送や居住条件の劣化を嫌って、内陸（遠隔地）よりも、貿易のしやすいベトナム、カンボジア、インドなどへの転進を目指した。彼らは、しばらく模様眺めして、一部は、ベトナム北部、カンボジア、インドネシアなどに転進した。しかし、再度、中国南部の事業環境を見直して、中国回帰を決めた企業も少なくないようだ。当然のことながら、賃金コスト、許認可手続き、市場までの輸送時間、生産性、言語、それに税率などが、転地決定の重要な要素となっている。中国は広く、発展段階も地域ごとに違うので、一つの規格をすべてに適用するのは困難であろう。

2009年の中国全体のGDP成長率は8.7％を記録、現5カ年計画最終年次の10年にも8％以上の成長を遂げると見こまれている。外資の進出は多くなくとも、中国内陸部の成長率は、巨額の財政支援により沿海部のそれを上回っ

表1　アジア新興国のGDPの実質成長比率比較　（単位：％）

	04年	05年	06年	07年	08年	09年 e
中国	10.1	10.4	11.6	13.0	9.0	8.7 [7]
インド	7.5	9.5	9.7	9.0	6.7	7.0 [8]
タイ	6.3	4.6	5.2	4.9	2.9	n.a
インドネシア	5.0	5.7	5.5	6.3	6.1	n.a.
ベトナム	7.8	8.4	8.2	8.5	6.2	n.a.
マレーシア	6.8	5.3	5.8	6.2	4.6	n.a.
フィリピン	6.4	5.0	5.3	7.1	3.8	n.a.
シンガポール	9.3	7.3	8.4	7.8	1.1	n.a.

注：eは推計値。
出所：ADB（2009）, Key *Economic Indicators* および Press Release dated December 15,2009。

6) それは、COP 15 の交渉の際の中国の独得の路線にも表れた。
7) 政府発表の実績値。
8) 2009年12月時点での政府の見通しでは、7.75％。

表2　粗資本形成率と民間消費性向（いずれも対 GDP 比）（単位：%）

	粗資本形成率		民間消費性向	
	2000	2008	2000	2008
中国	35.1	44.4	46.2	36.1
インド	25.9	38.9 ('07)	63.7	54.7
タイ	20.5	28.6	56.0	54.8
ベトナム	27.6	41.1	68.6	67.3
日本	24.8	23.5	60.2	57.8

出所：ADB（2009），Key Economic Indicators.

表3　経常収支の対 GDP 比率と予測値（単位：%）

	08 年	09 年 e	10 年 e
中国	9.8	7.1	6.5
インド	▲2.6	▲1.5	▲2.0
タイ	▲0.1	6.0	1.0
ベトナム	▲11.8	▲7.0	▲9.0
インドネシア	0.1	2.0	2.1
フィリピン	2.5	2.8	2.5

注：e は推計値。
出所：ADB, Asian Development Outlook, 2009 Update.

た。ただし，それを永続的と見る専門家は多くない。

（2）アジアの新興国，「世界の成長センター」を持続

　インド，インドネシア，ベトナムなどのアジアの新興国，さらに OECD の DAC メンバー入りをした韓国も，金融財政政策や慎重な為替レート政策で，経済の落ち込みを最小限に抑え，経済回復途次にある（表1参照）。このように，欧米経済が低迷する中で，アジアの新興国は新規に大きな需要を新たに生み出す「世界の成長センター」の地位を固めつつある。

（3）グローバル・インバランス縮小の条件

　ここで注目したいのが，中国の民間消費性向の低さである（表2参照）。「グローバル・インバランス」の解決（リバランス）のためには，インド，タイ，ベトナムなどの新興国の中でとりわけ低いこの民間消費性向を引きあげるとともに，粗資本形成率を引き下げる必要があることは中国の多くの知識人が認めるとことである[9]。

　次に，表3を参照されたい。これは経常収支の対 GDP 比率を示したものだが，中国のそれは並外れて高い。これを，できれば，世界的な平均許容水準

9）例えば，呉敬璉［2009］参照。

といわれる3％程度に下げる必要がある。そのために，粗資本形成率を下げ，民間消費性向を上げる必要がある。

　呉敬璉氏のいう中国経済の「完全なモデルチェンジ」による民間消費性向の引き上げの実現こそ緊要であるが，そこへ至る道は厳しい。この問題の核心は，党・政府が「三農問題」の解決と，企業部門の巨大利潤の民間部門（民生）へのシフトをどこまで真剣に取り込むかにかかっている。

　中国が過去30年間，8％以上の経済発展[10]を続けてこれたのは，筆者の考えでは，第一に，1940−50年代に，農民などが保有していた土地を国家が無償で取得し，これを「改革開放」後に，地元のディベロッパーや外資などに時価で売ることによって，地方政府が比較的簡単に潤沢な財政資金を入手でき，それを原資に大きな開発事業が可能になったこと（田畑［1995］，第二に，同じやりかたで，低廉にインフラ，工場団地を確保でき，投資環境の改善を図り，大量の外資を呼び込めたこと，第3に，穀物価格の自由化と農民の移動制限により，労働対価と穀物価格を低廉に抑え，かつ，ハイブリッド品種利用と大量の施肥などによって最小限の資本投下で，穀物増産（自給）ができたこと，第4に，潜在失業者状態にある農民を多数工業団地などで農民工として使役し，労働集約産業分野や鉄鋼，石油化学品などで「世界の工場」となったこと，第5に，香港，台湾，東南アジアなどの華人・華僑など多国籍企業からの対中直接投資，委託生産，中国企業との戦略提携，技術提供，先進国からの直接投資や技術提供，日本などからの輸出信用や公的資金援助，中国社会への寄付，などを得たこと，第6に，都会に多額の教育投資を行ない，経済発展に必要な人材を確保したことの複合効果（**TFP**の上昇など）であった。その市場路線を強力に推し進めたのが，ほかならぬ鄧小平だった。

　中国で，超低廉かつ膨大な農民労働力の利用が長期間可能だったのは，今や世界で中国にしか存在しなくなった「農民戸籍」という親の身分に依拠する仕組みが維持されてきたためである。この制度より，1億人以上の農民は，農民工と年収の4割弱の追加収入を都市で得つつ，一方で，限界生産力に近い賃金で，農民工として，労働集約産業やインフラ建設に従事する，そして，その

---

10) 中国の発展メカニズム（モデル）は他のアジア諸国・地域と大きく異なる。韓国も台湾も1960−70年代には，出稼ぎ農民をうまく使って海外の労働集約産業を誘致したことがあった（国内経済の発展により，労働集約的輸出加工区は短期間で不要となり，技術志向の新竹の電子電機などの工業団地に変わった。韓国，台湾の場合は，不十分ながら農地解放が行われ，農民戸籍が作られる基盤はなかったし，数千キロ離れた離村からの「民工潮」が生じる余地もなかった。外資は，農村の脇に工場を建て，農民は自転車などで工場に通った。なお，ベトナムには，農民戸籍は存在したが，中国と比べて厳しいものでなく，長期にわたり農民工の超低賃金を維持する装置とはならなかった。同国政府は2003年，農民戸籍を廃止した。

送金に依存する故郷の家族による零細農業によって，13億人に必要な5.5億トン前後の農産物の大半を自給するという壮大な国家目的を達してきた。この政策は，大半の農民が，年金，医療保険などの社会保障や適切な医療サービスを受けられない生存賃金に近い賃金水準を21世紀初めまで維持してきた。胡・温政権は，三農問題の漸次的解決を目指す「和諧社会」建設を進めてきた。しかし，これまでのところ，所期の成果は上がっておらず，所得・教育・社会保障格差の拡大に不満を持つ農民は増えている。

この問題の根本的解決には，（イ）都市住民からの納税を大幅に増やして，農業補助金を増やす，（ロ）農村での組合活動強化による機械化導入を進める，などの複雑な措置を必要とする[11]。既得権化した都市住民が，そうした目的の増税に応じるかなど，大きな政治課題がからんでいる。

いまひとつの企業利潤の民間セクターへのシフトができるかどうかは，党・政府の政治意思にかかっている。この問題は，国有企業の成長をいつまでも許容するのかという問題と連関する。この点は後述する。

上記2点の著しい改善が当分無理ということになると，民間消費性向の上昇は期待薄となり，欧米などとの金融・通商摩擦が解消される見込みはない。このジレンマから脱出する一つの手段は，（イ）人民元の対ドルレートの大幅な上昇を容認して，産業構造を転換する（＝1970-80年代に日本が行った方式），（ロ）資源関連企業に，資源税を課して，その税収を地域振興基金などに回すといった方法である。

（イ）の人民元レートの上昇の容認が2010年1月になってもなされないのは，労働集約輸出産業での雇用確保を重視した，優れて政治的な問題である。中国政府は，ドルペッグをやめて変動為替レートに戻せば，経済発展の安定性が失われ，世界にとって打撃が大きいと述べている。しかし，その主張の妥当性は科学的になされるべきであり，当事国の意向で決められてしまうのはフェアといえない。Krugman［2009］は，『ニューヨーク・タイムズ』紙の中で，中国のドルペッグは「重商主義」だとまで述べて，非難している。

既述の，新華社による建国60周年記念の「今後10年の中国経済に関する

---

11) 2009年12月5-7日に開催された中央経済工作会議での10年の経済政策の基本方針に，それらの方向性がきめ細かく示されている。また，新華社が行った建国60周年記念の経済アナリストとの共同分析「特集　今後10年の中国経済に関する10の予測」（2009年10月発表）によれば，2020年には，「都市化率が約6割に，戸籍制度規定は徐々に緩和され，農村人口は主に中小都市に移動。都市部の人口は8億に達し，都市化率は約60％となるが，先進国の都市化率80％とはまだ大きな開きがある。特に中小都市で戸籍制度の規制が徐々に緩和され，農村人口は主に中小都市へ移動する。しかし，都市部に巨大なスラムが形成される可能性があるため，現行の戸籍制度を完全になくすわけにはいかない」との予測が発表されている。

表4 農業部門就業者比率推移と07年の農業部門付加価値比率（対全部門）

(単位：%)

	1995	2000	2007	農業部門付加価値率（07年）
中国	52.2	50.0	40.8	11.1 (27.2)
インド	n.a.	59.9	56.1('05)	18.1 (>32.2)
タイ	46.7	44.2	39.5	10.8 (27.3)
インドネシア	44.0	45.3	43.7	13.7 (31.4)
ベトナム	71.3	64.4	53.8	20.3 (37.7)
マレーシア	20.0	16.7	14.8	10.0 (67.6)
オーストラリア	4.9	3.7	3.3	2.4 (72.2)

注：( ) は農業部門付加価値率／農業従事者数で，全産業の中での農業部門の効率性を示す（ただし，農業部門付加価値には，農外所得や国家の補助金も含まれる）。
出所：ADB (2009), Key *Economic Indicators* より作成。

10の予測」によれば，「人民元の国際化は加速し，人民元の上昇傾向は強まる。10年以内に人民元が自由兌換通貨となることは難しいが，人民元は安定した上昇を続けるだろう。2020年までに対ドルレートは60％以上上昇し，年平均伸び率は4.5％」としている。

　これは，中国のこれまでのTFP（全生産要素生産性）の伸び率からも十分正当化されるものである[12]。もし，そのようなことが実現すれば，今後のGDPの伸びを年率7.2％と低く抑えて見ても，為替レート上昇により，GDPは10年後には，現在の3倍弱になり，内需規模は一段と拡大することになる。他方，為替レート上昇により，人民元建て資源価格は大幅に下がり，資源企業の利潤が激増しよう。食糧については，表4に見るように，中国は国際的な価格競争力が弱いと見られるが，人民元高によって，さらに価格競争力を失う。しかし，国策として，主要穀物の自給策を続けるとすれば，農業部門への補助金を増やさざるを得ない[13]。しかし，これは生産性上昇を伴う補助金ではないので，農民の実質購買力は上昇せず，民間消費性向の上昇にはつながらない。農業従事者の数や機械化の程度は違うが，国民経済における農業の立ち位置としては，現在の日本の農業に近い形になっている可能性が高い。

　（ロ）の資源関連企業への課税が今後行われるかどうかは，判然としない。現時点では，中国政府は，国有石油／天然ガス企業を国際メジャー化しようと考えており，納税期待企業と見ていないようである。しかし，将来，環境対策

[12) 2009年12月3日に内閣府で講演した中国改革基金会国民経済研究所長・樊鋼氏が上げた計数によれば，1979～88年，89～98年，99～05年におけるＴＦＰの年間上昇率はそれぞれ3.4%，4.4%，3.7%と経済成長率の30～40％を占めた。

13) その段階で，自給率を少し下げ，差は米国などから輸入してはどうかという意見が出てくるだろう。

表5 工業部門就業者比率推移と07年の工業部門付加価値比率（対全部門）

(単位：％)

	1995	2000	2007	工業部門付加価値率（07年）
中国	23.0	22.5	26.8（06）	48.6（181.3.）
インド	n.a.	16.3	17.2（05）	29.6（＜171.5）
タイ	15.1	15.0	15.7	45.1（284.7）
インドネシア	13.4	13.5	13.2	46.8（354.5）
ベトナム	6.6	10.1	14.5	41.5（273.8）
マレーシア	23.7	23.8	19.1	46.7（244.5）
フィリピン	10.6	10.4	9.5	31.6（332.6）

注：中国の工業部門（Industry）は第2次産業を読み変えた。
出所：ADB（2009），Key *Economic Indicators* より作成。中国は『中国統計年鑑』による。

や資源保全などに多額の資金が必要になれば，これら企業への課税が検討されることもありえよう。

　農業とは事情は違うが，工業部門の1人たりの比較生産性（GDP中の工業部門の付加価値シェアを，工業部門従事者総数で割った比率）では，中国は近隣国と比べて，決して高くなかった（表5）。それは，これまでは低賃金の農民工を多数使用する人海戦術で，工業部門の付加価値は支えてこられたということである。大手企業の利潤額は極めて大きいが，そこには十分な雇用吸収力はないのである。もし，国内事情から，今後も工業人口を大きく減らすことができないとすれば，工業部門の一人当たりの付加価値率（生産性）を上げるしかない。そのためには，イノベーションによる商品価格の引き上げと賃金上昇を吸収する生産性の向上（資本・技術装備率の上昇などによる）。

　ここでの核心的な問題は，今後の中国のイノベーションの主要な（国内の）担い手をどこに求めるかということである。中国社会科学院・工業経済研究所が，2009年12月12日に北京で開催された「2009年中国企業競争力年次総会」において発表した2009年度の「最も競争力ある海外上場企業上位10社」には，中国石油化工株式有限公司，中国石油天然気株式有限公司，中国海洋石油有限公司，中国移動（香港）有限公司などの大型国有系企業がずらりとランク入りしている。中国政府は，国有企業の合併などにより，国際競争力の強い企業群を作ろうとしている。樊鋼氏が提出した既述のデータによると，一定金額の工業企業の平均利潤率は，国有企業のそれの倍にも及んでいる。それなのになぜ，国有企業を中心に再編しようとするのか。国家目標達成には国有企業が適切という判断になるのかもしれないが，イノベーション能力と海外での摩擦[14]の観点からゼロから議論する必要性があるのではなかろうか。

表6 アジアでの多国籍企業の売上高

	多国籍企業数	売上高(10億ドル)	アジアでの売上げ比率	欧州での売上げ比率	北米での売上げ比率
多国籍企業500社	336社	30.7	23.0%	32.1%	52.4%
アジア系多国籍企業	51	33.3	73.0	7.8	16.9
日系多国籍企業	44	35.9	74.7	7.3	15.6
その他アジア系	7	17.2	62.2	10.2	25.2
欧州系と北米系	284	30.3	6.6	37.2	58.8
欧州系多国籍企業	99	33.0	7.9	63.6	22.8
北米系多国籍企業	185	28.8	5.6	13.9	78.1

出所:Rugman [2005], *The Regional Multinationals: MNEs and Global Strategic Management.*

4. グローバル企業の対中・対インド新戦略
(1) グローバル企業の従来の対アジア戦略

多国籍企業研究の一人者の一人 Rugman [2005] によれば,「多国籍企業」の中で,真に世界3極(アジア,欧州,北米)で活動している企業は少なく,大半の企業は,自社の本拠地を中心に,もうひとつの地域くらいで主要な活動をしている,という興味深い研究結果を発表している。とくに,日系やその他アジア系の多国籍企業は,世界での売上げ総額に占めるアジアでの売上げ比率は,6~7割に及んでいる。逆に欧米系多国籍企業はアジアでの売上げ比率は10%以下である。

(2) 今後の多国籍企業の行動方向

今後,多国籍企業の行動は変わるであろうか。それは確実に変わるだろう。3つの要因がその変化をもたらす。

第1に,今後の世界における成長センターは,アジア地域であろう。第2に,輸出志向から内需志向の傾向が強まるであろう。その中には,モノづくりや資源開発でない,サービス事業やインフラ構築も含まれよう。第3に,アジア通貨とくに人民元の対ドルレートは中長期的に上昇する可能性が強い。

このような展望のもとに,多国籍企業は,どういう形態による新展開をするだろうか。貿易によるのか,直接投資によるのだろうか。R.マンデルは,企業は「貿易に障害がなければ,貿易で行い,貿易では対応しにくい場合には,

---

14) 中国政府が進めている「走出去」政策では,潤沢な資金を使って海外の資源,ブランド・技術保有企業を買収する計画が中心になっているが,中国の購入,買収企業は概ね政府が強く支援している大手国有寡占企業である。海外の被買収企業および同じ対象を購入したいという先進国企業は民間企業であり,一時的に,資金流入があるので,歓迎されてもやがて,「イコール・フッティング」でないという議論が高まりやすく,すでに,オーストラリアで海外の国有企業による豪企業買収に関し規制法が成立したほか,欧米で摩擦が起こっている(木下 [2009c])。

直接投資で対応する」と述べた。この法則は絶対ではない。FTA や EPA が増えると，貿易が増える可能性が多いが，他の要因も働くので，簡明な展望はしにくい。タイに産業クラスターを持っている日系企業はタイからインド，インドネシア，ベトナムに部品などを移送するケースが増えるだろう。通常の貿易でも，直接投資でもない委託生産（OEM や ODM）という形がある。これは，コストを下げ，経営リスクを減らす効果が期待できる。ただし，高度の技術移転や複雑なファイナンスが絡む PPP（政府民間パートナーシップ）の場合には適合しない。パソコン，携帯電話やその部品組み立て，アパレルの縫製などが典型例で，台湾やシンガポールの EMS（電子生産サービス）企業やファウンドリーが有名である。彼らは生産工程を中国，ベトナム，カンボジアなどコストが安く，アクセスが容易なところで行うケースが多い。

そうした要因から，欧米系多国籍企業は，その資産や営業活動分野をポートフォリオ分散的に利益拡大最適化に沿って，アジアにシフトするだろう。日系企業も，中国，インド，ベトナムなどのアジアシフトをもっと増やすだろう（したがって，日本国内向けのシェアは，減るだろう）。円高が進めば，このシフトは加速されるが，円安であっても，中国などの内需向けの投資は，それら諸国の成長率やライバルの動向などに影響され，減少しないケースも多いだろう。欧米向け製品の海外生産も従来ほどでないにしても，継続するので，生産トータルコストの引き下げのために，中国，東南アジア向けの委託生産や直接投資も行われる。

結　辞

上記の分析から，今後の中国，インドへの多国籍企業のかかわりについて，概ね次のことがいえるのではなかろうか。

1. 消費過剰の米国が支えた従来の世界経済・資金フローのパターンが戻ることはなく，世界の消費・生産の重心は，欧米からアジアにシフトするだろう。
2. 先進国の経済成長率が低迷しても，先進国に拠点を置く優秀な多国籍企業の成長が鈍るとはいえない。それら企業は，種々の要因と自己の競争力や弱点，ライバル企業の動向，進出先のリスクを総合的に判断しつつ，最適化を図るだろう。シフトの形態は，貿易，委託加工，直接投資，技術提供，PPP など様々であろう。受け入れ国としては，経営資源の移転がなされやすく，フットルース出ない直接投資の導入に最も関心を示すだろう。
3. アジアへの欧米日韓などの多国籍企業のラッシュは，受け入れ国での市

場競争を激しくし，商品・サービス価格の上昇を押さえる働きをするだろう。そうした状況の中で，受け入れ国は選択的に外資を導入する傾向を強めるだろう。地元企業の利益とも連動しやすい経済ナショナリズムはその動きを強めるであろう。
4．外資に過度に厳しく当たる国は，生産技術や経営ノウハウの導入に遅れ，産業クラスターの育成に遅れをとるだろう。
5．巨大産業クラスターづくりで先行した中国，タイは，資源部門以外の外資誘致面で，インドネシア，ベトナム，フィリピンより優位に立つ可能性が高い。もちろん，要素価格の変化やそれ以外の国の事業環境の改善によって，事情が変化する可能性はある。

参考文献

木下俊彦［1978］,「中国の経済発展パフォーマンスと今後の産業・貿易政策—日中貿易拡大の論理を考える」『海外投資研究所報 中国特集』,3月増刊，第4巻第4号，1—48頁。

木下俊彦［1988］,「戦後における日本の技術導入と政府の役割」『NIRA Report』総合研究機構，2月，NRC-86-5（委託研究。（中文訳）「戦後日本引進技術発展経済的経験」『日本市場経済』中国社会科学院日本市場経済研究中心，北京，1996年第1—4期，1—11頁）。

田畑光永［1995］,『鄧小平の遺産—離心・流動の中国—』岩波新書。

木下俊彦［1996］,「東アジアにおける経済危機の発現形態としての資産価格大変動とマクロ経済運営論究のための研究メモ」（日本経済研究センター・日本経済新聞社との共同研究）『経済成長と金融』，第6章，78—94頁。

木下俊彦［1998］,「東アジア：対外資金依存型経済発展の脆弱性の克服に向けて」『国際問題』（財）国際問題研究所，4月号，No.457，26—44頁。

木下俊彦［2002］,「海外企業活動と経済活動—海外直接投資のマクロ的効果と日本経済に与える影響」『海外投融資［特集］日本の対外直接投資』〔設立10周年記念〕,（財）海外投融資情報財団，7月号，110—118頁。

杉田俊明［2002］,『国際ビジネス形態と中国の経済発展』，中央経済社。

木下俊彦［2003］,「ASEAN10と日韓中FTAの展望」（浦田秀次郎・日本経済研究センター編）『日本のFTA』日本経済新聞社，110—118頁。

原剛編著［2005］,『「中国」は持続可能な社会か—農業と環境問題から検証する』同友館。

Williamson, J. Peter [2006], *Winning in Asia Strategies for Competing in the New Millennium*, Harvard Business School Press.

Fernandez, Antonio et. Al, [2006], *China CEO, Voices of Experience from 20 International Business Leaders*, John Wiley & Sons（Asia）

Kinoshita, Toshihiko, Yamazawa, Ippei & Kwan C.K. [2007a], "Japan and Asia- How Do We Meet the Globalization Challenge Together?", (co-authored with Ippei Yamazawa & C. H. Kwan), A Publication of the Waseda University Program on Contemporary Asian Studies (COE-COS, NUS Press, Singapore, pp.68-99.

木下俊彦 [2007b],「日本企業のビジネスモデルと日中経済」(浦田秀次郎他編著『経済共同体への展望』(早稲田大学 COE プロジェクト), 岩波書店, 第2章.

Kinoshita, Toshihiko [2007c], "Japan and ASEAN—with reference to Vietnam," an article listed at Thanh Nien Daily, dated October 15. 下記 HP 参照:
http://www.thanhniennews.com/search/?q=Toshihiko+Kinoshita&image.x=10&image.y=11

Morris, Charles R [2008] *The Trillion Dollar Meltdown*, Public Affairs.

天野倫文, 大木博巳編著 [2006],『中国企業の国際化戦略 『走出去』政策と主要7社の新興市場開拓』, ジェトロ.

木下俊彦 [2008],「中国型経済発展の特質とリスク—日中は相互に何を学ぶべきか」, 内閣府経済総合研究所主催・第1回日中ワショップ (@北京, 3月28日) における発表資料) http://www.esri.go.jp/jp/archive/hou/hou040/hou037.html

Kinoshita, Toshihiko [2008] "Changes of Japanese Corporate Business Model Under Global Pressure: Evidence Justifying KPM" & "Examples of Changes of Japanese Corporate Business Model: Why is KPM Essentially Important Now?, (Shigenobu Ohara & Takayuki Asada ed.,) *Japanese Project Management*, KPM— Innovation, Development and Improvement, World Scientific, London & Singapore, pp83-110 & pp.403-424.

Ghosh, Joyata [2009], "Why we had to Reshape Economic Development", *Economic Sharing & Alternative*.

Fernandez, J.Antonio & Underwood, Laurie [2009], *China CEO*, John Wiley & Sons (Asia) Pte.

木下俊彦 [2009a],「世界の金融危機とP2Mへの新たなニーズ—機能重視型ハイブリッド経営で日本企業は生き残れるのか」『国際プロジェクト・プログラムマネジメント学会誌』, Vol.4, Number 1.

木下俊彦 [2009b], 世界「経済危機と中国の環境・農業問題—地球温暖化問題と『三農問題』を中心として—」, 内閣府経済社会総合研究所主催第2回日中経済ワークショップ用提出論文, 3月28日, @北京・The Peninsular Hotel.

木下俊彦 [2009c],「中国:期待される『責任ある世界のステークホルダー』としての役割」, 内閣府経済社会総合研究所主催第3回日中経済ワークショップ用提出論文, @北京・長富宮.

関志雄 [2009],『チャイナ・アズ・ナンバー・ワン』, 東洋経済新報社.

セン, アマルティア (加藤幹雄訳) [2009]『グローバリゼーションと人間の安全保障』, 日本経団連.

OECD編著(門田清訳)[2009],『科学技術人材の国際流動性　グローバル人材競争と知識の創造・普及』,明石出版。(原文:OECD, *The Global Competition for Talent: MOBILITY OF THE HIGHLY SKILLED*, 2008)

Tan, Sei Tin, et al., [2009], *Economics in Public Policies－ The Singapore Story*. Marshall Cavendish Education

Magee, David [2009], *Jeff Immelt And the New GE Way－Innovation, Transformation and Winning in the 21st Century,* McGraw-Hill Companies.

太田康夫[2009],『地価融解　不動産ファイナンスの光と影』,日本経済新聞社。

天児慧[2009],『日本再生の戦略』,講談社現代新書。

中嶋圭介[2009],「『巨大高齢国家中国』の誕生　食いつぶされる人口ボーナス—新たな成長モデルを模索」『金融財政ビジネス』,4月6日号。

三上喜貴[2009],『インドの科学者　頭脳大国への道』,岩波書店。

(Web記事)「【コラム】ひた走る中国,薄れる韓国への関心」『朝鮮日報』10年1月4日付。

呉敬璉[2009],「中国経済の完全なモデルチェンジをいかに実現するか」10月14日付web (http://japanese.dbw.cn) より。

Krugman, Paul [2009], "Chinese New Year," *New York Times*, December 31.

第2部　東アジアのエネルギー・安全保障と米新政権

第5章　東アジアのエネルギー安全保障とリスク
―海洋資源・輸送をめぐるリアリズムと相互複合依存―

澁谷　祐*

「石油はそれ自体が重要なだけでなく，リアリズムと複合的相互依存の双方の側面を含む問題である。原材料の中で石油は依然例外的である」
（ハーバード大学のジョセフ・ナイ・ジュニア教授，2009年4月）

1．はじめに

　IEA（国際エネルギー機関）の見通しによれば，2009年の世界の石油需要は，世界経済危機の影響を受け，（OECDにおける石油消費大幅減のため）8千485万バレル／日と前年比マイナス1.7%と大幅減少となる見込みであるが，一方，中国など途上国の石油需要は世界経済危機を乗り越え増加を続ける勢いである。同機関作成の「世界エネルギー見通し（2009年版）」によれば，2030年に世界のエネルギー需要は，現在の約1.4倍に増加する。増加分のうち中国とインドだけで約55％を占める（40％が中国，15％がインド）。東南アジア諸国なども増加分の12％を占め高い伸びを示す。この結果，中国は2025年直後に米国を抜いて世界最大の石油・ガス輸入国となり，インドは2020年直後に日本を抜いて世界第3位の石油・ガス輸入国となる見通しである。

　ところで中国，インドと東南アジア諸国の需要増加量の多くは中東湾岸産の石油・天然ガス供給に集中する見通しである。さらに東アジア向けの9割以上は陸路ではなくタンカーによってマラッカ・シンガポール海峡（本章ではあわせて「マラッカ海峡」という）を通って輸送される見通しである。

　マラッカ海峡以東の東南アジア海域において，タンカーの航行リスク，海賊・海上テロのリスクに加え，南シナ海における沿岸諸国の領有権と資源獲得リスク，米中のシーレーン（海上交通路）リスクなど潜在的要因が増えている。さらに東アジア海域において，尖閣諸島周辺の領有権問題，朝鮮半島の核ミサイル問題や台湾情勢がからんでいる。

　一方，北東アジア海域に目を転じれば，最近極東ロシア・サハリンは本格的

---

*　早稲田大学アジア太平洋研究センター特別研究員。

な石油・天然ガス輸出地域に成長しアジア太平洋市場における新たな供給源として台頭著しい。このため極東ロシアを出発点とする日本海の新輸送ルートが誕生したに伴い、東アジア諸国の中東石油依存リスクや「マラッカ海峡リスク」の軽減が期待されるに至っている。従って、本稿において東アジアにおけるエネルギー資源・輸送のリスクと相互複合要因の分析を試みることは有意義であると思われる。なお、東アジアのエネルギー安全保障協力体制の枠組については、著書『アジア経済発展のアキレス腱、第9章と第10章』（林・浜・澁谷［2008］）を参照。

2．マラッカ海峡の航行安全問題
（1）海峡のセーフティ論とセキュリティ論

マレー半島とスマトラ島などインドネシアの多島を隔てるマラッ海峡は、3つの海上交易ルートの要に位置する。即ち中東・欧州と東アジア諸国を東西に、大洋州と南アジア・欧州を南北に、更に東アジア域内諸国とそれぞれ放射状に結ぶ基点である。マラッカ海峡の総貨物通過量はスエズ運河の4倍、パナマ運河の10倍以上を示す半面、コンテナー船、バラ積み船の増加に加え、船舶の巨大化、原油・LNG（液化天然ガス）・LPG（液化石油ガス）や化学品など危険物質を含む輸送貨物の多様化のため航行安全・環境汚染リスク要因は倍加している。

他方、マラッカ海峡周辺は海賊・海上テロリズム問題を抱えている。従って、マラッカ海峡の船舶航行の安全確保問題について、航行安全（safety）と航行安全保障（security）の二つに分けて論究する必要がある。「9・11テロ」を契機に、一般に前者は伝統的脅威論に、後者はテロリズムなど非伝統的脅威論に分類される学説がある。もっとも海賊は歴史的に古く伝統的脅威であったが、現代武装海賊は変質し非伝統的脅威と化した（宮坂直史［2009］）。

（2）費用負担論と航行規制論の動き

マラッカ海峡の航行安全対策について、これまでインドネシア、マレーシアとシンガポールの沿岸3カ国と、特に日本民間のイニシアティブにより、航行援助施設の維持整備・交通管理等が行われた。しかし中国の台頭によって将来予想されるマラッカ海峡の船舶航行数とリスク増加のため、マラッカ海峡の航行安全確保に対して沿岸国・利用国・船舶会社等による衡平な費用負担が行われるべきとする機運が高まった。大多数の外国船舶は両国の港に寄港せず通航するだけで、両国はいかなる形での経済的恩恵をも受けていないとの批判があるため、「フリーライダー」（ただ乗り論）を是正し、受益者による応分の負

担論が提起されている。(林・浜・澁谷 [2008])。

2008年10月に，マレーシアのアブドル・ラザク副首相は，マラッカ海峡通峡船舶数の増大による安全・海洋汚染事故が懸念されるなか，(国連海洋法条約に留意しつつ) 通航船舶数の制限案を示唆した。ラザク副首相によれば，現在のマラッカ海峡通峡船舶数は年間7万隻以上を記録しこのまま航行未規制が続けば，2015年までに12万隻を超え，「マラッカ海峡は許容限界量を超える」と警告した。

マラッカ海峡は狭いところで幅が1.6kmしかなく，要所のフィリップ・チャンネルの深喫水航路帯は幅800mにすぎない。航路の渋滞は衝突事故の危険のみならず，海賊・海上テロ攻撃にチャンスを与え，11ノット程度で航行するタンカーはその3倍の速度を出せる小型艇の標的になる。また衝突事故によって原油・重油やLNG・ケミカルなど危険物質が海上に漏洩すれば汚染源となり，爆発すれば近隣住民に対する甚大な被害が予想される。最近では2009年9月にマラッカ海峡において石油製品・タンカーにバラ積み船が衝突しタンカーが爆発炎上，乗組員9名が死亡する事件が発生した。マレーシア海事研究所研究員は，マラッカ海峡の分離通航帯における強制パイロット制度の導入を検討する段階に達したと警告し，「もし任意の資金拠出がなければ，強制的なものにする必要がある」と語った (英国『ロイズ・リスト』紙電子版，[2009年9月2日])。

(3) 航行保険リスクのありかた論

英国のロイズ保険組合の合同戦争委員会 (JWC) は，2005年6月にマラッカ海峡を戦争とテロ攻撃が行なわれる可能性の高い「戦争危険地域」——戦争，ストライキ，テロ活動やその他脅威を与える事案——に指定した。危険シナリオによれば，アルカイダのテログループがマラッカ海峡でタンカーをハイジャックし，タンカーまるごと爆発物に仕立てて突っ込ませる可能性があるといわれた。ロイズ合同戦争委員会の戦争保険プレミアム決定に対してマレーシアのチャン・コンチョイ運輸相 (当時) は，「マレーシアの統計によれば，年間5万隻以上の商用船のマラッカ海峡航行の数と比べれば，海賊の襲撃事件は少なく，ロイズの判断は過剰反応で，同海峡が戦争の脅威にさらされた地域だとは思えない」と反論した (シンガポールのストレーツ・タイムズ紙)。「戦争危険地域」の指定により[1]，マラッカ海峡を航行する船舶に対する保険の掛け

---

[1] ロイズの戦争地域指定：パキスタン，タイ湾南部ソンクラとナラシワットの間，インドネシアのアンボン (セラム)，バリクパパン (ボルネオ)，ボルネオ北東部，ジャカルタ，マラッカ海峡と周辺港湾，ポソ (スラウエシ) ならびにフィリピンのミンダナオ島。

金が高くなることから，ASEAN 船主協会や国際商議所等は，ロイズの指定には問題があるとして，地域指定を再考するよう求めたところ，まもなくロイズは危険が去ったとして戦争地域指定を解除した。ロイズの提起した戦争保険プレミアム問題は，はからずも政府干与の「セキュリティ論」と民間保険会社の「リスク論」の対立関係を明示することとなった。

3．マラッカ海峡の代替ルート問題
（1）マラッカ海峡の迂回・代替ルート構想
　もしマラッカ海峡がなんらの理由から輸送途絶した場合，緊急避難的に，インドネシアのスンダ，ロンボク等の海峡を遠く迂回するルートが検討されているが，スンダ海峡は火山帯にあたる難所である上，両海峡はインドネシア領水に含まれるため航行について一定の手続きが必要であるといわれる。東アジアの輸入港までマラッカ海峡経由に比べ 2 - 3 日程度の日数を要し追加の輸送コストが発生する。
（2）マレー半島横断ルート構想
　マラッカ海峡の混雑危険リスクを回避・軽減するためマレー半島を短距離横断するパイプライン建設構想がタイ・クラ地峡計画など古くから数回検討され続け，そのたびに国内政治的理由で流産した。例えば，本格的なアイデアは 1960 年代の高度経済成長期における日本政財界の手によって考案された。マラッカ海峡の圧倒的利用者であった当時の日本企業は石油輸入ルートが一つの海峡だけに頼る危険を分散させる必要に迫られ，タイ南部のクラ運河計画やパイプライン建設計画を進めた。しかし 1970 年代に襲った 2 回のオイルショックによって日本経済が後退するとほとんどの計画は潮が引くように消えた（鶴見良行 [1994]）。2000 年代に入り中国・韓国の台頭によって状況は変化した。現在，タイは南部・クラ地峡に沿って延長 250km の大型の横断パイプライン建設構想（石油タンク群・石化コンビナート計画を含む）を日本や中国などに非公式に提案したといわれる。

　同時に，マレーシアにおいても複数の横断パイプライン構想が並走している。しかし，いずれのケースも中東産原油を一度積み替えれば追加コストの発生を免れず，このため経済性の予備審査の段階を超えていない。マレー半島横断パイプライン建設構想（タイ・クラ地峡構想をはじめ）は，マラッカ海峡依存度の軽減，東アジア経済発展の牽引力の観点から，（ミャンマーやパキスタンなどの陸上輸入ルートをみながら）タイ・マレーシア沿岸 2 ヶ国と中国・日本・韓国や産油国資本などが一緒にアジア協力プロジェクトとして取り組む

べき段階に来ているのではなかろうか。

（3）中緬パイプライン建設合意の意義

中国は，石油輸入国に転じた1990年代からマラッカ海峡やスンダ海峡等に依存しない「第3の石油輸入ルート」を探してきた。輸送ルート選定にあたって経済性のみならず，安全保障上の考慮があった。その最大理由はシーレーン（海上交通路）問題である。マラッカ海峡のシーレーンを米海軍ににぎられつつ石油輸送を続けるのは耐え難いという中国の「マラッカ・ディレンマ」がある（Robert R. Kaplan ［2009］）。

他方，中国・雲南省政府は，「マラッカ海峡リスク」のないミャンマーに接近し，インド洋・ベンガル湾揚げの地点を探した。両国政府は長年交渉を続け，ついに2009年中緬パイプライン協定合意に漕ぎ着けた。現地紙によれば[2]，中緬パイプラインはベンガル湾のランブリー島から陸路北上し，いわゆる「援蒋ルート」に沿って越境して中国雲南省・昆明までのびる延長1千500kmの距離である。中東・アフリカ産の原油が輸送される。このパイプラインが完成すれば（2013年目標），中国はマラッカ海峡依存度（現在80％）の削減，3－5千kmの輸送距離の短縮化と最大30％コスト削減がそれぞれ可能と試算された（雲南大学国際関係学院・畢世鴻教授）。さらに，中国はインド洋のパキスタンのグワダル港開発計画に参加し，中国新疆省・カシュガルと結ぶパイプライン建設計画を進めているといわれる。

（4）マラッカ海峡戦略をめぐる中印対立

マラッカ海峡周辺海域において発生した海賊・テロ多発（2006年ころ）はインド洋側においてインド海軍の「ルック・イースト」戦略を招き入れる原因となった。インド海軍は，アンダマン海・ニコバル諸島の要塞化を決定した。ミャンマー領のココ島の軍事基地をけん制するためだったが，ココ島の租借権を中国海軍は要求した。ところが中国海軍は2008年12月に，ソマリア沖海賊対策を契機にマラッカ海峡を超えてインド洋に現代史上初の艦船派遣を行ったが，この中国海軍の動向はインド海軍のマラッカ海峡戦略にとって衝撃だった（Robert Kaplan ［2009］）。

中国の胡錦濤主席は，2009年11月11日，マラッカ海峡を視察した。北京人民大学・時殷弘教授は，胡錦濤主席のマラッカ海峡視察は，中国がエネル

2）中国共産党政治局常務委員・李長春は09年3月26日，ミャンマーの首都ネピドーにおいて，ミャンマー国家平和発展評議会のタン・シェ議長及びミン・ウー第一書記と会談した。李長春とミン・ウー第一書記は，中緬両国間の原油／天然ガス・パイプライン建設協定と水力発電共同開発協定等に調印した。

ギー安全保障上，マラッカ海峡に注意をはらっていることを国際社会に向けて示したものとの見解を示した（香港系・『明報』ネット，［2009年11月12日］）。

4．東南アジアの海賊と海上テロ
（1）海賊襲撃事件の発生抑止論
クアラランプール（マレーシア）の国際海事局（IMB）によれば，マラッカ海峡と周辺海域において2003年には未遂も含め210件の海賊攻撃事案が確認されたが，2008年には100件と大幅減少した。その理由は，インドネシア，マレーシアとシンガポール沿岸3カ国の海軍・警察等取締機関による合同パトロールが実施に移され，武器所持取締の一般的な強化，主要港湾施設内への部外者立ち入り制限の措置等によると考えられる。一方，航行船舶側において，危険水域での船上見張り員の増員，警報設備の整備や高圧放水銃の設置など自主的な（ハード分野の）努力とともに，「アジア海賊対策地域協力協定」（ReCAAP，2004年採択）の情報共有制度（ソフト分野）などが海賊発生の抑止に寄与した。ただしマレーシアとインドネシアはReCAAPに加盟していない。なお，2004年末に発生した北部スマトラ沖地震・津波も海賊事件発生の抑止に大きな効果を発揮したと推定される。

（2）越境追跡権の限界
マラッカ海峡は狭く沿岸3カ国の領水にほぼ占められ公海部分は少ない。従って，（国連海洋法条約で規定された）海賊取締りに関する公海の制度を適用する余地はきわめて小さい。いずれかの沿岸国の領水において海賊襲撃事件が発生しても，実行した海賊船が他の沿岸国の領海に逃げ込めば，（相互に同意がない限り）「越境追跡」（hot pursuit）は認められない。このため海賊が減らない理由の一つとされた。

（3）ソマリア沖海賊対策と異なる性格
マラッカ海峡と比べソマリア沖海賊の場合[3]，海賊発生の背景・性格，規模や海賊対策等について全く異なる。ソマリア沖の海域は日本の国土面積の6倍と広く通航する年間2万4千隻の船舶をすべて監視保護できない。また，海賊行為の潜在的利益が極めて大きく，捕らえられる見込みが小さいため，致

---

[3] ソマリアとイエーメンにはさまれたアデン湾は，紅海・スエズ運河とペルシャ湾（アラビア湾）を結ぶ海上輸送路に当り，世界の石油貿易量の15％相当量が通過する。2008年1年間に同湾で世界比3割相当の92件の海賊襲撃事件が発生し，世界で最も危険な海域になった（国際海事局＝IMB発表）。

死能力を持つ軍隊を派遣しても海賊襲撃を完全に抑止できるかどうか疑問である。

（4）海上テロリズムの発生抑止

「9・11テロ」（2001年）を契機に，マラッカ海峡を含む東アジア地域の海洋安全保障環境は劇的に変化した。2004年に米太平洋軍司令官は「地域海洋安全保障構想」（RMSI）を提唱し，海兵隊派遣を含む共同パトロール計画を提案した。しかし，インドネシアとマレーシア両国は米軍駐留に繋がると反対した。マレーシアのアブドル・ラザク首相は「主権の原則に基き，沿岸国の承認を得ず外国軍が海上パトロールを行うことに反対する」と強調し，米第7艦隊など外国勢力のプレゼンスを批判した。

インドネシアとマレーシアの2カ国は「マラッカ海峡は沿岸国の領海，国際海峡，排他的経済水域であり，他国の介入は看過できない」と繰り返し声明した。2004年7月に沿岸3カ国海軍による調整された共同パトロール「MALSINDO」計画が始まった。半面，二国間ベースではインドネシアは柔軟姿勢に転じ米国のレーダー設置案を，また日本の巡視艇の貸与案などを受諾した。これらの措置によって海上テロ事件の抑止に対して一定の効果をもたらしたとインドネシア側は評価している。

（5）群島国家・インドネシアの地位

マラッカ海峡の一部とロンボクおよびスンダ両海峡を擁し，世界最大の群島水域を有するインドネシアの沿岸線は延長8万1千キロにも達する。そのため遠隔地を全てパトロールすることは不可能であるので国際協力を必要としつつ，その一方で，インドネシアの主権を脅かされたくないという意識がインドネシア政府には根強い（第3回「日本とインドネシアとの海洋安全保障ダイアローグ」〔バタム・ダイアローグ2007〕報告書，2008年3月，海洋政策研究財団）。

インドネシアは，ジャワ島，ボルネオ島とセレベス島等により囲まれた地域のうち，国際海峡として自国が承認する以外の海域は，自国の群島水域であると宣言し，外国船舶が航行するときにはインドネシア政府に航海許可を求める大統領令を公布した。スンダ海峡，ロンボク及びマカッサル海峡，モルッカ海峡を経由する線は，インドネシアが設置を決めたシーレーンである。一方，米国は国際海峡であるマラッカ海峡につらなる，ジャワ島北部のジャワ海を経由して，東にチモール海に至る東西方向の無害通航を要請した。（なお，国際海洋法条約はインドネシアの群島国家論を支持した。他方，米国は同条約にまだ批准していない。）

インドネシアは日中米などの主張する「マラッカ海峡生命線論」に冷静に対

応し，マラッカ海峡における軍艦による商船護衛は認めない方針である。過去20年，南シナ海が安定していたのは，米第7艦隊のプレゼンスによるのではなく，インドネシアを含む関係国が二国間，多国間およびASEANにおける交渉を通じて南シナ海の非軍事化を進めたための成果であるとインドネシア高官は評価した。

(6) シンガポールの海上危機管理モデル

海運貿易立国・シンガポールの海上危機管理は際立っている。同国は，コンテナターミナルについて世界一の取扱量を誇り，スエズ以東における最大級のオイル・センターで危機管理に対するセンシティビティはきわめて高い。

(7) 海上テロ対策とインドネシア・フィリピン

マラッカ海峡と周辺海域におけるテロ発生の類型は，運航支配型，船舶攻撃型，港湾施設破壊型及びテロ関連の密輸の四つがある。運航支配型について2003年3月にスマトラ沖においてインドネシアのケミカル・タンカーが武装集団に乗っ取られ，1時間ほど操舵された事件。船舶攻撃型について，未遂事件であったが，2000年と2001年にはマレーシアにおいて米船舶を狙ったイスラム過激派による計画が，また2001年にはシンガポールにおける米船舶を攻撃するジェマ・イスラミア（JI）の計画があったと報告されている（村井・真山［2007］）。

アチェ紛争と海賊・テロリズムについて，インドネシアからの分離独立を求める「自由アチェ運動（GAM）」は2005年に武装解除し，翌年アチェの地方自治を認めるアチェ統治法が施行されたため，マラッカ海峡における航行安全リスクは大幅に改善された。

2002年8月にインドネシア・バリ島において大規模テロ事件が発生し，イスラム過激派組織「ジュマ・イスラミーヤ（JI）」が摘発された。フィリピン（JI系のアブ・サヤフ）やタイ南部では国内治安上の脅威となっている。東南アジアはアフガニスタンに続く対テロ戦争の「第二戦線」ではないかとの指摘について，「9・11テロ」のずっと前から地元武装勢力の行動であると批判された。東南アジアにおけるイスラム原理主義との関連で，非戦闘員に対する暴力を肯定するテロ組織は，聖戦イスラム主義を唱える急進的組織の一部にすぎず，東南アジアを中東に次ぐ「第二のテロ危険地域」とみなす実態は存在しない（村井・真山［2007］）。

(8)「アンバラット海域」領有権問題

外電（2009年6月17日電子版）によれば，インドネシア国防省の代表団が去る6月9日，マレーシアで，両国が領土権を主張している「アンバラッ

ト海域」について協議を行った。同海域は，両国が国境を接しているボルネオ（カリマンタン）島の東の沖合に位置しており，豊富な石油・天然ガス資源が存在するとみられている。1979年にマレーシアが海図の作成を実施して以来，両国が主権を主張し，緊張状態が続いている。国際司法裁判所が2002年に，シパダン島とリギタン島の領有権をマレーシアに認めて譲歩したので，それ以来アンバラット海域はインドネシアにとって，自国のプライドを回復させるための重要な問題となった。同海域問題は2国間マターであるが，南シナ海領有権問題を抱えるASEAN（東南アジア諸国連合）内に不協和が生じる可能性も出てくる。

2009年7月に再選をはたしたユドヨノ大統領（インドネシア）は「アンバラットはインドネシアのもの」と述べたうえで，「外交的手段で解決する」と従来通りの立場を示した。

なお，ASEAN地域フォーラム（ARF）閣僚会議（2009年7月23日）は，「南シナ海の（南沙諸島領有権）問題を2002年のASEAN行動宣言に沿って平和的に解決する意思を歓迎する」旨議長声明し，再確認した。

5．南シナ海の大陸棚資源とシーレーン問題
（1）「海の大慶油田」計画の意義

中国側の南シナ海は，石油・天然ガスの生産量，確認埋蔵量について全国比それぞれ4.5%，6.7%を占め（2004年），まだ低い地位である。しかし中国政府は2020年までにそれぞれ20%の比率に高める計画である。しかしそこは主に南シナ海の深海フロンティアである。

中国側の南シナ海の深海部（水深3百－3千m）には220億バレルの原油埋蔵量の存在が確認されている（2008年の南シナ海の原油生産量は合計47万バレル／日）。中国は2020年までに中国最大油田である大慶油田に匹敵する95万バレル／日の原油生産量を見込んでいる。総額約2千億元（2兆8千億円）を投資する南シナ海の深海開発計画は「海の大慶油田計画」と呼ばれる。南シナ海の鉱区は外資開放鉱区が中心で，崖城・香港間の天然ガス・パイプラインは既に輸送利用中である。南シナ海の深海開発計画は中国大陸棚戦略の機軸となっている。

（2）中国の資源確保戦略

中国は1989年に「海洋権益の擁護」論を開始し，1992年には東シナ海，南シナ海全域を中国の領海とする「領海および接続水域法」を公布した。また，江沢民総書記は同年，「領海の主権と海洋権益の防衛」に言及した。（1993

年に中国は石油の純輸入国に転じた。)

2001年に中国国務院による「21世紀石油戦略」発表と同時に,「海洋石油の増産計画」(第10次5ヵ年計画)が決まり,南シナ海の大陸棚資源の「積極獲得方針」が固まった。

中国が南シナ海と東シナ海の領有の主張を強めたのは,1968年に国連アジア極東委員会(ECAFE)の資源調査委員会が,そこに有望な海底石油資源が埋蔵されている可能性のあることが指摘されて以来のことである。しかし南沙諸島についてまだ実効支配に至っていない時期であった。中国の指導者・鄧小平の回顧録(『鄧小平文選 1982-1992』)によれば,「中国は武力占領か,あるいは主権問題を棚上げして共同開発するかについて,いずれ解決しなければならない」と語り(1984年当時),南沙諸島の資源支配に意欲を示した(小島朋之ら[1995],270頁)。

(3)資源ナショナリズムと大陸棚延伸論

資源ナショナリズムはフィリピン政府の目を南シナ海の大陸棚の海底資源に向かわせた。しかしそこは中国の主張する南沙諸島の一角を含み,中国の大陸棚延伸論と交叉する海域である。フィリピンのアロヨ政権は議会の親中派の反対を押さえ,3月に「領海基線法」を成立させ,国連委員会に対しルソン島東側の海盆について大陸棚延伸の申請を行った。これに対して中国側は,大陸棚延伸上の南巌島(スカーボロ礁)と南沙諸島は常に中国領土の一部であると抗議した[4]。

(4)南シナ海の海底資源の共同開発論

中国海洋石油(CNOOC)と台湾の中国石油(CPC)は両社折半によって,南シナ海の潮台鉱区(Chao-Tai)における探鉱開発を進めているが,2008年の中台交渉によって現在契約の探鉱期間は2年間延長された(2010年末まで)ように,交渉舞台の背景には機微な中台関係がある。

2005年に中国は,フィリピン,ベトナム相手に首脳レベルの個別交渉した結果,南シナ海における領土問題の棚上げを条件に,それぞれ共同資源探査を行うことで合意が成立した(2005年3月,北京)。当時,南シナ海は「対立から協力の海に」進化したといわれたが,結局現在に至る4年間の成果発表もなく3カ国合意は事実上休眠化した模様だ。

2009年5月6日にマレーシアとベトナムは国連委員会に対して共同で南シ

---

4) 中国側からみて,南シナ海における領海線・資源紛争の相手国は,①南沙(スプラトリー)諸島をめぐる5カ国(ベトナム,フィリピン,マレーシア,台湾とブルネイ),②西沙(パラセル)諸島をめぐるベトナム③トンキン湾をめぐるベトナムなどがある。

ナ海における200海里に基づく大陸棚延伸計画を申請した。これに対して，中国の国連代表部は翌日同委員会に向かって「中国の主権，主権的権利と管轄権を侵害している」と審議に反対した。ベトナムらの周辺5ヶ国はいずれも南シナ海の大陸棚に対して一定の主権を主張しているが，中国はいずれも認めない方針を貫いている。

ベトナム戦争後の歴代の米政権は，中国を牽制するためベトナムの地政学的位置を重視し，南沙諸島領有やシーレーン問題についてベトナム支持政策に転換した（久保文明・赤木莞爾ら［2004］）。

（5）南沙諸島の部分的実効支配

南シナ海における中国の覇権にもかかわらず，現在ブルネイを除く関係5ヶ国（マレーシアを含む）は何らかの形で，南沙諸島の一部分を実効支配している。ベトナムも一部の島に部隊を駐屯させており，他の国も滑走路・軍事基地などの建造物を造って人を送り込んで既成事実化に努めている。西沙諸島（中越二国間関係）と比べ南沙諸島の場合，5カ国の主張が複雑にからみ中国の優位が確立していない現実がある。中国本土から南沙諸島は1千300km^{2}と遠く離れ，領有の既成事実化に大きく出遅れた。

（6）米国の東アジア海洋安全保障戦略と日米協力

米国のリチャード・アーミテージ（元米国務副長官）とジョセフ・ナイ（ハーバード大教授）ら米国の超党派研究グループは2007年2月に，「日米同盟：2020年のアジアを正しく構築するために」(The U.S.-Japan Alliance: Getting Asia Right through 2020)と題する報告書を発表した（いわゆる「アーミテージ・レポート第2版」）。同報告書は，マラッカ海峡を「アジアの生命線」と位置づけ，日米両国にとって海賊対策など海洋安全保障に関する日米両国主導による地域協力を提言し，米国のイニシアティブに対するインドネシアの不信感を指摘し，中国が外洋海軍力を増強していることに対して懸念を示した（美根慶樹，第6章「東アジアの安全保障と米新政権」参照）。

半面インドネシア・北部スマトラ津波（2004年）の災禍に際して，米海軍は空母を派遣し被災者の大規模援助活動を行ったが，これによりインドネシア国内における対米好感度は大幅アップし，米国のソフトパワー戦略（人道支援）の成果の一端として評価された。

（7）南シナ海のシーレーン防衛論

（イ）中国海軍の防衛論

2006年から始まった中国の「第11次5ヵ年計画」においてシーレーン防衛を含む海洋権益・海洋資源の重要性が再認識された。中国の海洋戦略は，沿

岸防衛から南シナ海，さらにマラッカ海峡，インド洋をにらんだシーレーン防衛論に発展している。

中国の軍事機関誌「中国戦区軍事地理」は次のように概説している。即ち，南シナ海はアジアと太平洋の十字路に接続しているので，わが海洋力を発展させ，戦略的海路を抑え，海洋権益を保護するのに重要な意義をもっている。特に日本，米国，ロシアと韓国の多くはここを経由しなければならない。日本はこの海域を「海上生命線」と呼び，米国は，東南アジアから輸入するゴム等の戦略物資と米西海岸向けの中東原油の輸送はここを通らなければならない。なお，台湾は，南北交通路の中間に位置し，中国はバシー海峡，東シナ海南部，南シナ海北部，南西諸島西武付近を押さえることが可能で，「台湾は中国海域から太平洋に進出するとき唯一コントロールできる地域である」。

台湾海峡とマラッカ海峡の間を結ぶ延長2千800kmの南シナ海のシーレーン（中国専門家は「油路安全」と呼ぶ場合がある）をめぐって中米両国は対峙している。米国は伝統的に「公海の自由」のもと，シーレーンを「国際公共財」として認め，米海軍艦船が海域パトロールを行っている。他方，南シナ海沿岸諸国は中国の外交的フリーハンドを制限するため「南シナ海行動に関する（1992年）特別声明」に合意した（田中恭子［2000］）。

（ロ）米国によるシーレーン防衛の「独占」

米海軍艦船はアジアとペルシャ湾をつなぐシーレーンを防衛している。南シナ海ももちろん含まれる。日米関係の専門家のケント・カルダー氏は，シーレーン防衛の意義について，中国，韓国やインドなど日本以外のアジア諸国によって使用されていること，次に唯一の本格的な外洋航行機能をもつ米海軍の艦隊によって（独占的に）守られていることを強調した[5]。

6．日本海；核ミサイル，領有権とエネルギー資源
（1）日本海の地勢

日本海はユーラシア大陸と日本列島の間にある内海であるが，西太平洋の縁海に位置し，日本列島とサハリン，北朝鮮，韓国とロシアに囲まれている。英語ではSea of JapanやJapan Seaと表記されている（現在，国連及び国際的な地図の大半はこれを使用している）。これに対して韓国は「東海」と呼称し

---

[5] 米国がシーレーンを独占することで中国への政治的，軍事的優位性を保てる。しかしシーレーン防衛は米国にとって重要性は派生的なもので，米国に直接利益をもたらすわけではない。シーレーン防衛は，日米関係の文脈のなかにおいて米国にとって大切な「同盟の自己資本」である。（ケント・カルダー著，2008年，「日米同盟の静かなる危機」，167-168頁）。

非難している。ユーラシア大陸とサハリンの間の間宮海峡（タタール海峡），サハリンと北海道の間の宗谷海峡でオホーツク海と繋がっており，北海道と本州の間の津軽海峡では太平洋と，九州と韓国の間の対馬海峡で東シナ海と繋がっている。北方と南西海域は豊富な水産資源が得られ，鉱物資源や天然ガス，新潟沖ではわずかながら石油の存在など経済的にも重要な海域とされる。

（2）日本海のエネルギー地政学

東シナ海ガス田紛争や北朝鮮の核実験など日本海周辺は冷戦構造がまだ続く危険地域である。東アジアのエネルギー地政学を展望すれば，朝鮮半島の核（ネガティブ要因）と東シベリア・サハリンの資源エネルギー（ポジティブ要因）の相反する事態が混在しているといえる。

日本列島とアジア大陸の南北を逆さにした地図をつくってながめて見れば，地図の上に向かって突き出ている朝鮮半島は，右側の東シナ海と左側の日本海を扼しているが，南北分断国家のままである。中国は歴史的に南シナ海・東シナ海・黄海・渤海に対する覇権国家だが，日本海への出口（豆満江＝図們江河口）は事実上閉ざされ，中国は「日本海国家」とは言えない。他方，最近極東ロシアは東シベリア・サハリン資源開発の成功の波に乗ってアジア太平洋市場に登場し新たなプレイヤーとなった。

（3）朝鮮半島の核問題と日本海の海上輸送

北朝鮮は，長距離ミサイルの発射（2009年4月）と地下核実験（同5月）を行い，日本海を再び「冷戦の海」に陥れた。これを受け国連安保理は北朝鮮追加制裁のため北朝鮮関係船舶の臨検を決議した。朝鮮半島の核，台湾海峡，東シナ海ガス田や竹島（独島）などの要因を抱え，エネルギー資源の海上輸送上に位置する対馬海峡は世界のホットゾーン（チョークポイント＝輸送隘路）になった[6]（北朝鮮の核をめぐる安全保障問題については，美根慶樹，第6章「東アジアの安全保障と米新政権」参照）。

（4）東シナ海の岩礁をめぐる韓中対立

東シナ海の離於島（＝リビド＝韓国名称）または蘇岩礁（中国名称）の帰属をめぐって韓国と中国の対立が激化している。この岩礁は干潮時にもその岩頂は海面下 4.6m の海中にあり，岩が海面上に姿を現すことはないが，韓国はこの岩礁（暗礁）を自国の島であると主張し海洋調査施設を建設した。これに対

---

[6] 2008年10月「中国海軍の戦艦4隻が（情報艦以外では）はじめて津軽海峡を通過した」（NHK報道）。対馬海峡は中国・韓国のコンテナー船や貨物船の北米航路上にあたる。日本海から津軽海峡を抜け太平洋に出て大圏コース（1万400km）をたどり米国ロサンジェルス（ロングビーチ港）に至る。

して，2006年9月中国外務省は「蘇岩礁は（国際法上の島ではなく）東中国海北部の水面下にある暗礁であること」，また「韓国との間で領土紛争は存在しない」と主張，韓国側の一方的な行動は全く法律的効力がないと抗議した。両国政府はこの海域に暫定経済水域を設定し交渉を続けているが難航している。2009年5月に韓国政府は大陸棚延伸計画を国連大陸棚限界委員会に提出した（『産経新聞』『日経新聞』［2009年5月12日］）。なお，日中間における東シナ海ガス田の領有権をめぐる交渉については林・浜・澁谷編著『アジア経済発展のアキレス腱』（220頁）を参照。

（5）韓国とロシアのエネルギー協力問題

2009年8月7日に韓国知識経済部の李允鎬（イ・ユンホ）長官とロシアのシマトコ・エネルギー相がモスクワにおいて会談し，「韓ロエネルギー協力行動計画」に合意した。この行動計画は2008年9月に李明博（イ・ミョンバク）大統領がモスクワを訪れメドベージェフ大統領と会談した際の合意を再確認したものである[7]。

この合意の主要内容は，（イ）ロシア産天然ガス供給計画のＦＳ調査，（ロ）東シベリアの油田・ガス田の共同探査と東シベリア原油パイプライン（フェース2）に対する韓国の建設協力，（ハ）朝鮮半島における発送電ネットワークの構築，（ニ）南ヤクーチヤ炭鉱やウラン共同探査・開発，（ホ）西カムチャッカ沖鉱区の共同開発，（ヘ）北朝鮮を経由するシベリア産ガスのパイプライン輸送計画（後出参照）か，あるいは東海（日本海）の海底パイプライン建設・LNG液化計画などのメニューである。

7. 極東ロシアのエネルギー地政学の課題と展望
（1）「アジア太平洋国家論」

ロシアのデメトリー・メドベージェフ大統領は自著の論文「アジア太平洋地域における動的かつ平等なパートナーシップの強化に向けて」（2008年11月）において，金融危機をはじめとする世界的な問題の解決のためにアジア太平洋地域が担う役割の重要性を強調し，アジア・太平洋諸国との地域間協力（APECなど）は，ロシア極東及びシベリアにとって特に重要な意味があると強調した[8]。

---

7) 李明博（イ・ミョンバク）大統領とロシアのメドベージェフ大統領は2008年9月，モスクワで首脳会談を開き，両国関係を「相互包括的協力パートナー関係」から「戦略的協力パートナー関係」に一段格上げすることで意見は一致した。
8) ロシア紙「週刊ダーリニ・ボストーク通信」，2008年11月14日。

しかし2004年12月，ロシア地方知事の大統領任命制に関する法律が施行され，大統領の地方政治権限が強化されたため極東ロシアとの間で溝が深まっているともいわれる。(世界不況の影響を受けロシア経済は疲弊しているところ)資源の多い極東地域は「資源も関税もすべて取り上げられ，われわれには還元されない」と不満を言う地元民の間には「極東地域独立論」という過激な声さえ出ている。「極東の安全保障」で重要なのは「軍事」よりも「エネルギー・環境・交流」であるとの地元市民の指摘があるという[9]。

　これらの論調の背景に，ロシア連邦の中央政府と地方政府間の「経済・財政戦争」の縮図が浮かびあがる。極東ロシア・沿海地方住民の多くは，極東ロシアのエネルギー資源の利益をモスクワからの物取りゲームとしてではなく，長期的かつ国際的パースセプティブにたって，国際協力による豆満江（図們江）開発計画のように「極東経済協力基金」活動をアジア太平洋諸国と行えば「地方自立の趨勢」につながるのではないかと期待しているといわれる[10]。

　さらに，クレムリン側と極東ロシア側との間において，東シベリア・太平洋（ESPO）パイプライン建設計画について，モスクワが太平洋ルートを選んだのは，国際的戦略にもとづく判断の帰結というより，極東ロシアの政治家たちの意思表示を受け容れた結果であるとの見解がある[11]（横手慎二，第5章「ロシアと東アジアの地域秩序」，160頁）。

（2） 極東ロシアの発展とガス・パイプライン拡充計画

　極東ロシアにおける幹線ガス輸送システム「サハリン―ハバロフスク―ウラジオストック」が2009年7月着工された。あわせて「ヤクーツク―ハバロフスク―ウラジオストック」輸送計画，カムチャッカ地方とイルクーツク地方の輸送計画がそれぞれ進められている。これらのガス生産輸送計画は，2007年9月に策定されたロシア産業エネルギー省「東方ガス計画」にいずれも合致している。極東ロシアのガス需要に充足されるだけでなく近隣諸国向けにも供給輸出する計画を視野にガスプロムとロスネフチ連繋を軸にパイプライン計画が進んでいる。沿海地方へのガス供給開始は2012年開催のAPEC首脳会談（ウ

---

9) 富山国際大学現代社会学部教授・鈴木康雄，2009年10月21日，読売新聞。
10)「ロシア連邦極東地域研究報告書」，日本国際問題研究所，2008年3月。
11) 極東研究所副所長のミヘーエフ（2003年当時）によれば，「極東ロシアの経済的向上は展望できる将来，北東アジアへの統合なしには実現不可能」であった。そこで，ロシアは抜本的な輸送整備とエネルギー開発のために大規模な外国資本を導入すべきであり，そのためには「この地域を北東アジアの統合プロセスに効果的に適合させるため，特別な経済運営条件の形成」が必要であった。ミヘーエフは2004年にかってヨーロッパ諸国を結びつける原動力になった「石炭と鉄鋼」の役割は，アジア太平洋地域ではロシアのエネルギー資源が果たすことになるという見通しを示した。（横手，173頁）。

ラジオストック）に間に合わなければならない優先プロジェクトである。
　前掲・ウラジオストックに至るこのガス・パイプライン建設が完成のあかつきに，次に北朝鮮を通って韓国まで延伸する構想を韓国はロシア側に（前掲参照）提案した。

（3）ESPO パイプライン（第1段階）完成と大慶ルートの意義

　「東シベリア・太平洋石油パイプライン」（ESPO）第1段階が完成し，2009年12月25日に操業を開始する予定（原油出荷量は2009年末；約30万トン，2010年末；1千500万トン計画）である。2009年4月にはESPOパイプラインの大慶ルート（支線）の建設が始まった。この支線はスコヴォロジノ（アムール州）から中ロ国境までが67km，そこから中国・大慶までが960kmの距離である。大慶ルート建設のため，中国側は250億ドルの長期融資の見返りに20年間にわたって毎年1千500万トンのロシア産原油を引き取る提案をロシア側に行い，2009年3月に最終合意をみた。大慶ルートは2005年7月に合意された中ロ首脳会談における「エネルギー協力項目」の中の優先課題であったので，両国間の戦略パートナーシップを強める最大の成果物として記録されるに至った。

（4）オホーツク海・ベーリング海問題と対米関係

　タス通信によれば，ロシア天然資源省のドンスコイ次官は2009年10月1日，オホーツク海の大陸棚延伸の申請を準備している（北方領土周辺は申請に含まれず）と声明した。もし国際的に認められれば，ロシアの排他的経済水域（EEZ）の外側にある5万6千km^{2}の海域面積（四国のほぼ3倍に相当する）が新たにロシアの大陸棚になる[12]。ロシアは2001年にオホーツク海の大陸棚領有を国連大陸棚限界委員会に申請したが，北部については調査データの不備を理由に却下され，南部については日本と調整するよう勧告されたという。（なお，2008年7月18日，メドベージェフ大統領は連邦法「ロシア連邦大陸棚」修正に署名した。）

　ロシアの石油ガス専門家ミハイル・スボチン氏によれば，現在ロシアでは，大陸棚から取れる天然資源は採掘量全体の約1％に過ぎず，サハリンプロジェクトなどの大規模開発プロジェクトがようやく始まったばかりであると強調した。

　北太平洋のエネルギー地政学は冷戦崩壊後，大きな変化はなかった。9・11テロ（2001年）後に，米ロ関係は一時好転し，両国間のエネルギー商業協力

---

12) 共同通信，2009年10月2日。

関係は進展したが，イラク戦争後のブッシュの政権後期（2006年ころから）にはクールになった。オバマ政権の極東ロシアのエネルギー外交重視論はまだ明確ではないが，ロシア側においては長期化する世界経済不況の前に，プーチン首相は，これまでの資源ナショナリズム論を緩め，欧米資本を含む外国資本導入に対してエネルギー開発誘致政策に対して柔軟姿勢に転じているのは興味深い。

北太平洋エネルギー情勢の将来を占う古くて新しいカードはベーリング海の米ロ国境画定問題である。1990年に旧ソ連のエドアルド・シュワルナーゼ外相と米国のジェームズ・ベーカー国務長官（いずれ当時）の間で協定が成立した。しかし，その後ロシア議会は，国境線はソ連と米国海岸から等距離でなく，そのためソ連は5万km2の本来の海域面積を失ったと反対したため，協定は未批准におわった（米国側は1991年批准した）。しかし，北極開発をめぐる沿岸諸国の覇権あらそいは激化し，ベーリング海問題と必然的に連動せざるを得ない。日付変更線をはさんで米海域にのびる極東ロシアの大陸棚延伸論はベーリング海における新たなエネルギー資源問題に発展する可能性がある。

（5） 北太平洋海域のエネルギー安全保障問題

ロシア軍は広大なロシア領土において東，西，南の各正面を持つという軍事地政学的制約のためロシア極東部隊（ロシア極東軍管区，太平洋艦隊）への資源配分は従とならざるをえないとされる。その結果，ロシア極東正面は軍事的に弱い部分となるので，モスクワの政治・軍事指導部は，軍事的に緊張が生じないように，またもめごとや係争が生じないよう平和・静寂な戦略環境作りに努力している。即ちロシア極東部隊（通常戦力）はしだいに周辺諸国との戦闘を考慮した防衛能力の充実強化よりも経済活動をサポートするなどの機能の充実化を図るようになってきた。具体的には，エネルギー産業など経済活動を阻害するテロや海賊に対する対テロ機能及び経済活動の警備機能の充実強化である（三井光夫 [2003]）。

日本の「防衛白書平成20年度版」（防衛省）も，極東ロシア軍とロシア太平洋艦隊は，シベリア・サハリンの地下資源開発や地域の経済社会基盤活性化のためにもわが国や中国などアジア太平洋諸国との経済関係を重視していると評価した。2007年には日中米韓加口の6カ国による北太平洋海上保安サミットが開催され，海上テロ活動に関するガイドラインが策定された。

地球温暖化の影響で近い将来に北極開発が進めば北極海航路が開く可能性が強い。もしそうなればサンクトペテルブルグからバルト海・北極海・ベーリング海・太平洋・日本海を経てウラジオストクに至るロシアの沿岸航路はアジア

とヨーロッパを結ぶ海の大動脈になる可能性がある。北極海航路は，欧州までユーラシア大陸を鉄道輸送する「シベリアランドブリッジ構想」と競合・補完し輸送ルートの再編成を迫る可能性がある。

(6) サハリン沖のタンカー航行の危険度

サハリン周辺海域のタンカー航路は，日本の各港から，(イ)宗谷海峡（ラペルーズ海峡）を通りサハリン島のアニワ湾内の港に行くルート，(ロ)ロシア本土東岸沿いに航行しデカストリに行くルートと(ハ)サハリン島北東部オホーツク海側のサハリン1鉱区の原油生産現場に行くルート，の3本がある[13]。タンカーの海域航行はロシア標準の極地氷海・耐氷船階級をクリアしなければならないので難易度は高いといわれる。

新しい3本の日本海輸送ルートの展開に備え，タンカーによる油濁対策の教訓は活かされるべきである。1997年11月，ロシア船籍タンカー「ナホトカ」号（1万3千総トン）は9千トンの重油を積載し，上海からペトロハバロフスクに向け航行中に島根県沖で船体破断し，重油が流出（6千200トン）した。島根県から秋田県にかけての海岸に甚大な油濁被害が発生した。事故は老朽化による船体の強度の低下等が原因と考えられる。流出油による漁業などの被害補償額は合計約261億円に達した。中国，ロシアを含み国際油濁補償条約の枠内においても解決されるべき問題である。

(7) 「環日本海経済圏構想」の障害

「日本・韓国の資本・技術力」，「ロシア極東の豊富なエネルギー資源」と「中国・北朝鮮の安価な労働力」を結集すれば，「環日本海経済圏の形成」は進展するのではないかと1990年代～2000年代前半は期待されたが，世界不況の影響を受け現実的には停滞感が漂っている。その最大理由の一つは人口分布上，日本海沿岸には人口100万人以上の大都市・大消費地が存在しない。日本の大都市の多くは太平洋側にあり，韓国と北朝鮮も同様に東シナ海側に大都市が集中している。ロシアにとって極東地域は辺境の地であり人口減少地域である。中国は日本海に直接面する領土はない。現在ロシア極東で存在感を高めているのが中国と韓国である。

図們江（豆満江）河口地域開発計画も遅れている。北朝鮮問題がネックになっている上，ロシアは「大ウラジオストク自由経済地域」構想を優先しお互いバッテングしているといわれる[14]。

---

13)「ロシア海域航行のためのガイドライン」，日本海事協会，2009年6月。

(8) 日ロエネルギー協力の進展の可能性

　日本政府のロシア極東・東シベリアとの関係強化は，「極東・東シベリア地域における日ロ間協力強化に関するイニシアティブ」として，2007年6月ハイリンゲンダムサミットの際に当時の安倍首相からプーチン大統領に提案され，エネルギー，輸送，通信等8つの分野での協力関係が進んでいる。しかし，北方領土返還問題もあり，前掲・ESPOパイプライン建設計画（2003年当時）の「小泉行動計画」の熱気は中国・韓国に比べやや冷めている。

　日ロ原子力協力協定（2009年5月）によって，日本の使用済み核燃料が再処理される際，抽出された回収ウランをロシア・アンガルスクにある「国際ウラン濃縮センター」において再濃縮される計画の実現性が高まった。回収ウランは，ユネスコ世界遺産のバイカル湖の近くにあるアンガルスク・ウラン濃縮工場へ約1万kmかけて輸送されるためロシアの環境NGOが反対している。

　極東ロシアにおける石油・ガス探鉱プロジェクトについて，ロシア民間企業のイルクーツク石油と日本の石油天然ガス・金属鉱物資源機構（JOGMEC）は，イルクーツク州北部のセベロモグディンスキー石油天然ガス鉱区（資源量：石油1千500万トン，天然ガス500億m^3推定）の探鉱を行う合弁企業を設立（2008年5月）したにとどまっている。

(9) 対ロ期待論の検証を——むすびにかえて

　2006年から3年間，極東ロシアにおいて新たに原油（サハリンと沿海地方）・LNG（サハリン）の3つの輸出ターミナルが相次ぎ出現した結果，東シベリア・サハリン産石油・ガスの輸出量はロシア全国比3％（2009年）だったが，2020年に30％に増えると推定される。プーチン首相の主導する「東方エネルギー」戦略はヨーロッパ向けの石油・ガス供給を減らし，アジア太平洋地域において増やす方針を優先している。

　東シベリア・サハリン産のエネルギー資源は，その供給能力の大きさ，輸送距離の近さや新規ソースとして期待されるに至った。日本の場合，ロシアからの原油輸入はいままで実績はほとんどなかったが，全国輸入比3.7％（平成20年度）に増え，将来10％程度まで上昇する可能性がある。この結果，日本の原油輸入の中東依存度（いままで90％を超す水準）は，85％（同年度）まで低下した。アジア・太平洋域内市場におけるロシア石油供給に対する依存割合

---

14) ロシアの朝鮮半島問題専門家・アンドレイ・ランコフ氏によれば，朝鮮半島の統一はロシアの競争相手の地政学的な影響力を拡大し，ロシアにとって特に脆弱な国境地帯に著しい不安定をもたらすとの考えから，ロシアは概ね現状維持，すなわち安定かつ分断された朝鮮半島を望んでいると指摘した。

は現在まだ低いが2020年に6－7％台に増えるという見通しがある。もしそのようになれば，域内市場の中東石油依存度（現在80％）は70％台まで大幅に低下する見通しである（IEA　ワールドエネルギーアウトルック　2009年版）。

　半面，ロシアに対するエネルギー依存度の急激な高まりに対して，（ウクライナ・ガス供給問題に示されたように）対ロ警戒論が強いのは事実である。

　従って，ロシアの東シベリア・サハリン産エネルギー供給の台頭を期待しつつも，生産力のある中東ものと比べどこまで拮抗できるのか，供給の安定性・経済性は確保されるのか地政学的リスクは大丈夫かなどについて検証する必要がある。

参考文献

林華生・浜勝彦・澁谷祐編著『アジア経済発展のアキレス腱』文眞堂，2008年。

藤井秀昭「アジアのエネルギー安全保障」『アジア経済発展のアキレス腱』文眞堂，2008年，175－204頁。

吉田和男著『安全保障の経済分析』日本経済新聞社，1996年，73－78頁（国際公共財），284頁（シーレーン）。

村井友秀・真山全編著『現代の国際安全保障』明石書店，2007年，84頁（第5章　海上テロリズム）。

ジョセフ・ナイ・ジュニア『国際紛争；理論と歴史』（原書第七版，田中明彦・村田晃嗣訳，有斐閣，2009年4月）。（80頁と272頁の第七章の中の第3項「石油をめぐる政治」参照）。

玄大松著『領土ナショナリズムの誕生』ミネルヴァ書房，2008年2月。

田中恭子著『現代中国の構造変動第八巻（アジア太平洋の地域紛争)』東京大学出版会，2001年。

茅原郁生編著『中国の軍事力；2020年の将来予測』(株)蒼蒼社，2008年。

村井友秀・安倍純一・浅野亮・安田淳編著『中国をめぐる安全保障』ミネルヴァ書房，2007年7月。

長谷川啓之監修『現代アジア辞典』文眞堂，2009年7月。

うみのバイブル2000（下）通巻第7巻　事業名　公海の自由航行に関する普及啓蒙　団体名　国際経済政策調査会，第21章　シーレーン原論　山本誠（元海上自衛艦隊司令官）。

鶴見良行著『マラッカ物語』時事通信社，1994年。

(財)海洋政策研究財団編「『海洋安全保障情報月報』電子版，2007年9月号」。

小島朋之・高井清司・高原明生・阿部純一編著『中国の時代』三田出版会，1995年。

ケント・E・カルダー著『アジア危機の構図―エネルギー・安全保障問題の死角』日本経済

新聞社，1996 年。
ケント・E・カルダー著『日米同盟の静かなる危機』ウエッジ，2008 年 11 月。
小此木政夫・文正仁編『東アジア地域秩序と共同体構想』，横手慎二著「第 5 章；ロシアと東アジアの地域秩序」と「北東アジア安全保障共同体の現在と将来」，慶應義塾大学出版会日韓共同研究叢書）。
田辺靖雄『アジア・エネルギーパートナーシップ』エネルギーフォーラム社，2004 年。
藤井秀昭『東アジアのエネルギーセキュリティ戦略　持続可能な発展に向けて』NTT 出版，2005 年。
三井光夫「極東地域に所在するロシア軍の将来像」『防衛研究所紀要』第 6 巻第 2 号（2003 年 12 月）。
ジャン＝マリー・シュヴァリエ（増田達夫訳）『世界エネルギー市場』作品社，2007 年。
David Howell and Carole Nakhle, Out of the Energy Labyrinth, I.B.Tauris, 2007。
IEA（International Energy Agency）, World Energy Outlook 2009。

第6章　東アジアの安全保障と米新政権

美根慶樹*

1．オバマ政権の新風

（1）オバマ新政権は発足してからまだ一年未満であるが，すでにいくつかの分野で特色のある方針を打ち出し，世界の注目を浴びている。

　ブッシュ政権はよきにつけあしきにつけ，冷戦後の国際政治における米国の単独優位を象徴する政権であり，強い軍事力と自信を背景に世界を善玉と悪玉に二分して「悪玉とは交渉しない」と言明するなど話し合いで解決を探るより信念にしたがって行動し，米国に同調する国とは coalition of the willing を組みながら目標達成のために必要とあらば preemptive action や regime change も厭わず突き進む傾向があった。ブッシュ政権のこのような性格は unilateralism として批判された。

　オバマ政権は前政権とは異なり，これまで対立していた国々とも対話する方針を打ち出し，世界にさわやかな風を送り込んだ。とくにイランとは従来対話がなく相互非難を繰り返していただけに米国の新しい方針は新鮮な響きとなってこだました。イランとの初歩的対話はすでに 2009 年 3 月のアフガニスタン安定化会議（ハーグ）での政府高官の接触となって実現している。

　単純な善悪二分論でなくどの国とも対話しようとする姿勢は multilateralism を重視することにもなり，前政権の unilateralism とは対照的な外交が展開されるものと期待される。このような新政権の姿勢にはオバマ大統領の人柄が強くにじみ出ているが，それはオバマ大統領がその生い立ちから異なる文化，伝統に触れ親しむ機会が多かったという経歴とも関係があると指摘されている。

　一方，オバマ政権が前政権から受け継いだ環境は内外ともに厳しいものであり，近年まれにみる金融・経済危機の中での政権発足は容易でなかったであろう。さらに，内政面では医療体制の立て直しという歴代の政権が実現できなかったことに取り組もうとしているし，対外面ではアフガニスタン問題という難題があり，これらはそれぞれ別のことであるが，オバマ政権にとってはいずれも大変な重圧となっている。したがって，同政権の政策を見ていく場合に，ただ新風を吹き込んだということでは偏った見方になってしまうことを念頭に

＊　一般財団法人　キヤノングローバル戦略研究所特別研究員。

置いておく必要があるのはもちろんである。

（2）米新政権の外交方針は東アジアの安全保障にどのような影響をもたらすであろうか。オバマ大統領がこれまで行った表明の中にそれを窺う手がかりとなることがいくつかありそうだ。

まず，核政策の面では，オバマ大統領の就任から2か月後（2009年4月）に二つの大きな進展があった。一つはオバマ大統領がロンドンでメドベージェフ・ロシア大統領と現在のSTART I 戦略兵器削減条約が失効する本年末までに新たな戦略兵器の削減を目指して交渉を始めることに合意したことと，もう一つはオバマ大統領がその3日後のプラハにおける演説で軍縮全般に関する米新政権の方針を打ち出したことである。前政権時代，軍縮は「冬の時代」であったと言われていただけに，この二つは久しぶりに聞く前向きの出来事であった。

オバマ大統領は「核兵器を使用した唯一の国として行動する道義的責任がある」，「核兵器のない世界の平和と安全を追求する米国のコミットメントを明確に，かつ，確信を持って表明する」と素晴らしく積極的な決意表明を行った上，（イ）米国は核兵器のない世界に向けて具体的な措置を取る，（ロ）冷戦時の思考を終わらせるために国家安全保障戦略における核兵器の役割を縮小する，（ハ）他国も同様の行動を取るよう促す，などを強調した。これらの言葉は世界に向けて語られたのであったが，日本においては心の琴線に触れられたと思った人は少なくないであろう。

もっとも，オバマ大統領の核に関する演説はすべての点で積極的であったのではない。積極的でないと言い切るのは困難としても，少なくとも積極的か消極的かよく分からないところがあり，そのうちの一つが，核兵器を使用するか，しないかということである。これはNPT（核兵器不拡散条約）において長年議論されてきた大問題であるが，東アジアにおいても，とくに北朝鮮との関係で厄介な問題になっている。

2．北朝鮮の安全保障と米国の核政策

（1）北朝鮮の核兵器やミサイルは周辺の諸国に対し脅威を及ぼしているが，実は，北朝鮮も種々の不安を抱えており，脅威も覚えている。その根本的な原因は北朝鮮の国際的地位が不安定だということにある。

朝鮮戦争以来半島を二分してきた北朝鮮と韓国との関係は決着がついておらず，とくに韓国を支えている米国との法的関係は1953年7月の軍事停戦協定で休戦状態となったままであり，米国は韓国内に軍隊を駐留させ一朝有事には直ちに北朝鮮に対し攻撃あるいは反撃できる体勢を維持している。

朝鮮戦争が終わってからすでに半世紀あまりが経過した今日，米国が北朝鮮を攻撃することなど非現実的であるという印象が強いであろうが，北朝鮮から見た場合の国際関係は外部から見るのとかなり違っており，北朝鮮にとって米国は，米国のみであろうが，脅威なのである。

　朝鮮半島の法的不安定状態を解消するには複数の選択肢があり，もっとも普通の方法は朝鮮戦争停戦協定の当事者間で平和協定を結ぶことである。ただし，韓国は当時戦争の継続を主張して休戦協定に署名しなかったのでこの方法では韓国が含まれなくなる可能性があり，何らかの調整を加える必要がある。このほか，2005年9月の六者協議，2007年10月の南北首脳会談などでも一定の方式が提案され，暫定的に合意されたこともあるが，いずれも長短がありこの問題を最終的に解決するには至っていない[1]。

（2）一方，北朝鮮の安全保障を支えてきたロシアおよび中国は冷戦の終了と前後して韓国と国交を樹立し，北朝鮮をめぐる安全保障環境は激変した。

　肝心の同盟関係については，新生ロシアは旧ソ連時代の1961年に北朝鮮と結んだ「友好協力相互援助条約」を維持しなかっただけでなく，一時は北朝鮮と険悪な関係に陥ったこともあった。その後両国は友好関係を取り戻し，2000年になってようやくソ連時代の同盟条約に代わる友好親善条約を締結したが，ロシアは旧条約の軍事同盟条項を維持することを拒否し，一方の国が第三国から侵略された場合には口朝両国はただ「協議する」ことしか同意しなかった。これでは北朝鮮として，いざという場合にロシアからの軍事援助を期待することなどとてもできないであろう。

　中国と北朝鮮との友好協力相互援助条約は現在も有効であるが，北朝鮮とロシアとの新しい条約が締結されると，中国としても軍事同盟条項は廃棄したいと考えていると噂されるようになった。これが確かな根拠に基づいたことか知る由もないが，北朝鮮を攻撃する可能性があるのは米国であり，米国との関係を重視する現在の中国の姿勢にかんがみれば，中国がそのように考えていてもなんら不思議ではない[2]。

---

1) 米朝両国は「国交を正常化するための措置を取ることを約束した」（2005年9月19日共同声明第2項）ほか，「直接の当事者は，適当な話し合いの場で，朝鮮半島における恒久的な平和体制について協議する」こととした（第4項）。ノムヒョン大統領と金正日国防委員長の南北共同宣言では，「南と北は（中略）直接関連した3ヶ国または4ヶ国の首脳らが朝鮮半島地域で会い，終戦を宣言する問題を推進するため協力していくことにした」（聯合ニュース2007年10月4日）。

2) 欧陽善（富坂聰編）『対北朝鮮・中国機密ファイル』文藝春秋社（2007年）は，条約を改正すべきであるという意見があることを認めつつ，「いまは時期尚早である」と述べている。著者の欧陽善は仮名で，実際には中国共産党中央対外連絡部亜洲局の職員を中心に，中国社会科学院の朝鮮研究者が共同で執筆したとされている。真偽の程を確かめられない記述も少なくないが，中国共産党員でなければ知りえないようなこともいくつか含まれており，信憑性はかなり高いものと思われる。

冷戦の終了後，韓国，中国およびロシアなどは新しい国際環境に応じて対外関係を大いに改善したが，北朝鮮だけはあいかわらず米国との関係で問題を抱え，しかも中口両国に頼れる度合いが低下した分だけ安全保障環境が悪化したと見るべきであろう。そのような状況において北朝鮮が自らの力で安全保障を確保するほかないと軍事力の増強に突き進んでいったのは，北朝鮮なりに自然なことだったのであろう。核兵器および戦略ミサイルの開発・保有は決して認められることではないが，北朝鮮の軍事力増強路線の象徴であった。

（3）北朝鮮が米国から核攻撃を受けることを恐れていたのはたんに心理的な恐れだけでなかった。1990年代の初め，IAEA（国際原子力機関）による査察に北朝鮮が協力しなくなったとき，米国は北朝鮮に対する攻撃の可否を実際に検討していた。軍事機密に関することであるが周知のことであったとみなしてよいであろう[3]。

　米国は，そのような攻撃をすれば米軍がこうむる損害があまりに大きくなりそうなので対北朝鮮攻撃を断念したそうであるが，その後も米国は必要になれば核を含めあらゆる兵器で攻撃するという基本方針は変えなかった。ペリー国防長官は1996年に，もしいずれかの国が化学兵器で米国を攻撃する場合，「米国は持っているあらゆる兵器（any weapons in our inventory）から」反撃するという趣旨のことを述べている。同様の考えはブッシュ政権でも「戦略文書」や国務省の報道官によって繰り返されている[4]。したがって，北朝鮮からすれば状況次第で米国の核攻撃を受ける可能性があり，それが同国の安全保障上最大の脅威となっているのである。

（4）北朝鮮にとってこのような米国の核攻撃を封じ込めることが最大の課題であり，1994年の枠組み合意交渉において北朝鮮を核攻撃しないという約束を米国に求めたが，米国はこれに完全には応じず，「米国は北朝鮮に対して，核兵器で攻撃または脅威を与えないという正式の確約を与える（will provide formal assurance to the DPRK, against the threat or use of nuclear weapons by the United States）」とだけ表明した。これは米国が繰り返してきた核兵器の使用に関する基本方針と比べれば核攻撃をしないという趣旨がかなり強く出ている態度表明であったが，これで北朝鮮の安全保障問題が解決されたのではなかった。

3）ドン・オーバードーファー（菱木一美訳）『二つのコリア　国際政治の中の朝鮮半島』共同通信社 2002年。
4）ブッシュ政権の戦略文書については2003年1月31日付ワシントン・タイムズ紙にリークされたNational Security Presidential Directive 17（NSPD 17），国務省高官の発言としてはバウチャー報道官の2002年2月22日の記者ブリーフなど。

まず，この枠組み合意は北朝鮮の安全保障および朝鮮半島の非核化について米国と北朝鮮がそれぞれ行うべきことを記したものであり，言いかえれば，それは青写真のような計画書であった。したがって，そこで表明されたことは実際に履行されて初めて現実のものとなる。米国は核攻撃しないことについて「確約を与える」ことを未来形で述べており，その時点で確約はまだ完了していなかった。

　一方，北朝鮮が表明したのは，朝鮮半島非核化宣言を実行することと南北間で話し合いを行うことであった。これも予定の表明であり，実際には実行されなかった。要するに，枠組み合意において米国と北朝鮮はお互いに自国がなすべきことを述べあっていたのであり，その後一部が実行されたにとどまった。このことにかんがみても，北朝鮮の安全保障上の問題が枠組み合意によって確定的に解決したのでないことは明らかであろう。

　（5）北朝鮮は六者協議でも安全が保障されていないことを訴え，参加国の理解を得ていた。第1回目の協議終了に際し中国代表の王毅外務次官が行った議長声明は，「六者協議の参加者は，朝鮮半島の非核化を目標とし，北朝鮮側の安全に対する合理的な関心を考慮して問題を解決していく必要があることに合意した」と述べている。「北朝鮮側の安全に対する合理的な関心を考慮して」という表現を注目すべきである。それは，北朝鮮が協議の中で安全の保障を要求し，それに対し他の参加国はその要求を合理的と認め，さらにそのことを考慮して問題を解決していくこととしたという意味であろう。議長声明は議長限りのもので，その内容すべてに参加国が拘束されるわけではないが，北朝鮮の安全保障の必要性を六者協議の参加国は多かれ少なかれ認めたわけである。

　北朝鮮の安全保障問題に対する米国の態度は2005年9月の六者協議共同声明でもあらためて示され，米国は北朝鮮に対して「核兵器または通常兵器による攻撃または侵略を行う意図を有しない（has no intention to attack or invade the DPRK with nuclear or conventional weapons)」と言明した。

　しかし，これでも北朝鮮の安全保障上の問題は解決されなかった。米国が北朝鮮を攻撃する「意図を有しない」のは北朝鮮にとってもそれなりに評価できることであろうが，それはその時点では攻撃する意図がないと言っているだけのことであり，将来事情が変わればどうなるか分らないわけである。そもそも，この表現は枠組み合意の際の表明と比べても弱い。枠組み合意の中で述べたことは核攻撃しないという「正式の確約」を与えることであり，六者協議では「意図を有しない」という表明に過ぎなかったからである。

　（6）核兵器の開発は北朝鮮の安全保障にとって重要な問題であるが，政治的

な意味合いも濃厚である．すなわち，北朝鮮の核兵器はまだ初歩的な段階にあり，その数はせいぜい数個なので米ロなどの核戦力とは比較にならない．将来多少増えるかもしれないが，北朝鮮としては，国力からしても，米ロはもちろん，中国などに匹敵する規模の核戦力を持とうとしているとは考えられない．

　しかし，北朝鮮にとって重要なのは純軍事的な力よりもむしろ政治的効果であり，北朝鮮の核戦力は小規模であっても国際社会にとってすでに放置しておけない問題になっており，米国との関係においても北朝鮮は本来の力よりはるかに強い立場で交渉を行っている．もし北朝鮮が核兵器もミサイルも持っていなければ，米国も国際社会も北朝鮮を相手にしないのではないだろうか．かつて米国は北朝鮮とは直接交渉しないという方針を堅持していたが，今や状況はまるで違ってきており，米国は北朝鮮と頻繁に交渉するようになっている．オバマ新政権になっても北朝鮮と話し合いをしようとする基本的姿勢は変わっていない[5]．

　要するに，北朝鮮は数個の核兵器という軍事的には比較的小さい力で，米国という巨大な相手を交渉に引き寄せた．つまり，核を梃子に大きな政治的効果を上げたのである．

　この戦術が米国を相手によく利いたことを悟った北朝鮮は，歯に衣着せぬどころか，口汚く米国批判を行い，それでも米国は北朝鮮との関係をしきりに改善しようとしてきていると国内に宣伝している．この梃子を国内的にも活用しているのである．北朝鮮の国民は表面的には金正日体制礼賛一色に見えるが実情はもっと複雑であり，そのような宣伝に満足し切っているか疑問の余地はあるが，少なくとも，そのような居丈高な態度は国民のナショナリズムをくすぐり，国民生活面の不満をそらす力があるのであろう．

（7）もっとも，金正日はただ強面で振舞うだけでなく，核兵器および戦略ミサイルの開発と米国との交渉を巧みに操っており，正面衝突にならないよう抑制もしているようである．外部では好戦的だという印象が強いかもしれないが，戦争は仕掛けないのではないか．かりに北朝鮮が他国に対して軍事力を行使すれば，フセイン大統領のイラクを破壊したように米国は北朝鮮を攻撃する可能性が現実に出てくる．少なくとも攻撃の口実を与えることになる．そこまでするのは愚かなことであり，すべきでないことを金正日はよく知っているようである．かつて遊撃隊方式を盛んに用いていたとき北朝鮮は危険な冒険に走る恐れがあったが，現在，それに代わる戦術は，金正日の巧みなさじ加減によ

5）オバマ政権の姿勢を伝えるニュースは多数ある．たとえば，『朝日新聞』2009年8月25日．

る対外関係の操作である。

さらに，ややうがち過ぎの感もあるが，金正日にはしたたかな読みがあるのかもしれない。すなわち，「米国は北朝鮮に対して核兵器を使用しないという約束を完全な形で行うことはできないだろうから北朝鮮が核兵器の廃棄を徹底的に迫られることはない。そうであれば北朝鮮として，安全保障の問題が解決すれば核兵器を廃棄すると逆に物分りのよい態度を取っておけばよい。第三国との関係でもそのほうが有利である」という読みである。

これはきわどい芸当である。金正日は実質的国家元首である国防委員長として権力を一身に集中し，独裁者的な地位にあるからこそそのようなことができるのであろうが，他の国ではまず無理である。民主主義国家では大統領であれ，大臣であれ，官僚であれ数年もしないうちに次の人に交代する。また，政策の透明性が高い。彼らは自分が担当している間に実績を上げようと懸命になるので，困難な問題は後回しになりがちである。金正日からすれば民主主義国家にはこのような特性があるので付け入りやすいのではないか。

（8）一方，北朝鮮に対して非核化を求める側として重要なことは，核兵器やミサイルを開発する口実を北朝鮮に与えないこと，その保有が利益にならないようにすることであり，そのためには米国は核兵器を持たない国に対して核攻撃しないという原則を立てる必要がある。このことは，北朝鮮との関係だけにあてはまることでなく，どの非核兵器国に対しても該当することである。つまり，米国は非核兵器国に対しては核攻撃しないという原則を立てる，すなわち「消極的安全保障」を与えるべきである。現実には，北朝鮮は核兵器をすでに保有しているので，米国としては「核を持つ北朝鮮には消極的安全保障を与えないが，放棄すれば完全な保障を与える」という方針で臨むべきである。

（9）また，イランの場合はまだ核兵器を保有していないが，保有していない現在も，また，将来保有することになっても核攻撃を受ける危険があるということであれば，核兵器を持たないという方針を選択することにならなくても不思議でない。結局北朝鮮の場合と同じ問題がある。

イランとの関係でも核政策を転換し，「核兵器を開発しない限り核攻撃しないことを保証するが，核兵器を開発すれば核攻撃をする可能性がある」という態度で臨むべきである。つまり，国際約束に「違反すれば危険，違反しなくても危険」になっているのを「違反をしなければ安全，違反をすれば危険」という形に転換することが肝要である。

なお，北朝鮮に対しても，また，イランに対しても核兵器を使用しなければならない必要性は，彼我の軍事力の圧倒的な差にかんがみればもはやなくなっ

ており，核兵器を使用しないこととすることによって米国が失うものはほとんどないであろう。広島と長崎に原爆が投下された直後，米国においては米軍人の損失を防ぐために核兵器は必要であったということが，戦争を早く終わらせるためという理由とともに使われたことがあったが，このような発想は現在の世界ではどの国からも支持されないであろう。

（10）米国がオバマ新政権になり核軍縮について積極的な姿勢を見せている現在，消極的安全保障は核不拡散体制を強化する最良の手段であると確信する。非核兵器国に対して米国が消極的安全保障を与えることができれば，米国として核軍縮に臨む真摯な姿勢をアピールできるし，ブッシュ政権時代に損なわれた核不拡散体制の信頼性を回復するのにも大いに役立つであろう。

核兵器の廃絶も不使用も NPT 成立以前からの二大難問であるが，核兵器を完全に廃絶することより，軍事的には弱小の非核兵器国に対して核兵器を使用しないことのほうがはるかに容易なはずである。廃絶が横綱とすれば，不使用は大関である。

オバマ大統領は横綱を倒すと宣言して喝采を浴びたが，大関と取り組むことなく，北朝鮮の核問題を解決することはできない。

3．中国と東アジアの安全保障

（1）どの国の安全保障も他国にとっては安全を脅かす原因となりうる。北朝鮮の場合も自国の安全保障のために核武装したことが周辺諸国にとって脅威となっている。日本の場合も「専守防衛」が大原則であるが，周辺の諸国からそれを素直に認められているわけではなく，日本の軍国主義が復活しているなどと警戒されることがままある。自国の安全保障と他国に対する脅威はコインの両面である。

また，どの国も相手の国の軍備を過大に，自国の軍備は過小に評価する傾向がある。このために国家間の関係が緊張し，紛争に立ち至った例は歴史上無数にあると言って過言でないであろう。

このように軍事力は安全保障のために必要であるという側面と他国に対する脅威となりうるという側面の双方から見ていく必要があるが，中国の場合はどのような状況にあるだろうか。

（2）中国は数十年前までは外国から脅威を受けていたが，半世紀も経たない内に脆弱な立場から完全に脱却し，今や中国に対して軍事的な脅威となる国はどこにもないのではないか。中国はそれでもこのような情勢の好転は表面的な現象であり，潜在的脅威はなくなっておらず万一の事態に備えることを怠ることはで

きないという考えを維持しているようであるが，そのような見方が妥当であろうか。

　日本が脅威でなくなってから久しい。中国は日本に軍国主義が復活する危険があるという見解を完全に放棄したわけではないようであるが，それは将来の危険として，あるいは一部に存在する傾向として言っているのであり，現実に日本が中国にとって脅威であると断定しているのではないであろう。この問題は日中間のイシューではなくなっている。

　建国以来中国にとって最大の脅威は米国であったが，ニクソン大統領の訪中以降両国関係はいちじるしく改善され，今や世界中が米中両国の協力関係を注目するようになっている。

　ソ連とは一時期対立していたが，冷戦の末頃から関係が改善し，また，ソ連がロシアとなってからも友好関係を維持・発展させており，国連においては共同で西側諸国にブレーキをかける役割を果たし[6]，また，上海協力機構のような地域的協力を強化するなど国際社会で共通の立場に立つことが多くなっている。

　（3）しかしながら，中国は軍事予算を毎年かなりの率で増加させている。しかも，中国の予算については各国と異なる扱い方があり，兵器の研究・開発・製造費用は軍事予算でなく「経済建設費」などに含まれているので，これを斟酌すれば軍事予算はさらに大きくなる[7]。また兵器の入手価格は統制され本来の価格より安くなっているので，予算の実質的購買力は表面的な数字より大きい。また，軍人への優遇措置はカウントされていないという問題も指摘されている。

　中国の海・空軍力の増強はとくに顕著である。1980年，中国はICBMの実験を行い，その効果を確かめるためにニュージーランド近海へ18隻の各種船舶から成る船団を派遣し，途中どこへも寄港せずに実験結果を確かめて帰国した。これは中国海軍として初めての遠洋航海であり，注目された。

　1990年代に入ると中国近海での軍事演習が目立つようになり，95年の台湾の李登輝総統の訪米，翌年の総統選挙での李登輝の再任などに際して中国は台

6）たとえば，2006年9月頃から米欧諸国はミャンマー問題を安保理で取り上げようと試みたが，ロシア及び中国の反対でなかなか進まなかったので，拒否権を発動できない手続き問題として議題にするか否かを決定しようとした。しかし，2007年1月中旬にその決議も両国の反対で否決された。
7）米国国防省は中国の軍事力に関する年次報告書を発表している。2008年版では国防費について，中国の公表（2007年）では約459.9億ドルであるが，米国国防省の推定では970～1390億ドルであり，その差は第二砲兵の予算，武器輸入，研究調査費などが含まれていないことにあるとしている。また，2009年1月，中国政府は08年版の国防白書発表（2年ぶり）。これによると，国防費は1988年から20年連続で二桁の伸び率を記録している。

湾近海でミサイル発射を含む軍事演習を行い，不快感を示した。

　装備の面ではミサイル駆逐艦，原子力潜水艦などを含め各種艦船の近代化を進めている。1988年には原子力潜水艦からのミサイル水中発射実験に成功した。航空母艦は現在建造中で，2015年頃には就航させる予定だと言われている。

　2001年には海南島沖合い上空で米の偵察機EP3と中国海軍の戦闘機が衝突事件を起こした。これは中国に近い場所なので米側の行動に問題があった可能性があるが，それにしてもこれと接触事故を起こすくらい接近していった中国機はかなり大胆であった。

　中国の軍事力が周辺諸国にとって脅威を及ぼしているという意味では，このような通常兵器面での増強もさることながら，数十年も前から開発され，実戦配備されている核兵器と運搬手段であるミサイルははるかに大きな問題である。しかも，中国はNPT（核兵器不拡散条約）によって，核兵器を保有することが他の四ヶ国とともに世界で例外的に認められており，核戦力の点では周辺の諸国との関係で一方的に有利な立場に立っている。

　中国は軍事力整備を非常に計画的に進めてきた。中華人民共和国が誕生して以来きびしい国際環境の中におかれていた中国にとって有効な国防体制を建設することは国家として喫緊の課題であったが，きわめて限られた国力では全面的に軍を近代化することは不可能であり，政府が明確な計画に基づきその課題を段階的に達成しようとしたのは当然であった。

　毛沢東が核兵器と戦略ミサイルの開発を急ぐ決定を行ったのは1955年から56年のことであり[8]，最初から水爆の開発まで進むことを目指していたと見られている。なぜならば，原爆実験を行った頃にはすでにかなりの量のプルトニウムが生産されており，最初の原爆としてはプルトニウム型のほうが容易に製造できるにもかかわらず，最初から水爆に発展させるのに適しているウラン型原爆を作っていたからである。また，ウラン型はプルトニウム型より小型化できるので原子力潜水艦にも向いていた。中国の核開発はこのような二重の理由で最初から水爆の開発を目指し，開発は順調に進展して原爆実験からわずか3年後に水爆実験を成功させた。

　(4) 問題は以上のような軍備増強がどのような考えで行われ，また，今後についてはどのように発展していくのかであり，その内容いかんによって周辺諸国に与えている脅威は強くもなりうるし，また，逆に緩和されることもありうる。これは複雑な問題であり，一枚の答案用紙で答えられることではないが，

---

8) 平松茂雄『中国の安全保障戦略』勁草書房（2005年）133頁。

少なくともつぎのような諸点を勘案して見ていく必要があるだろう。

第1に，中国の最近の対外的積極姿勢がどのような考えに基づいているかである。とくに中国海軍の外洋への進出はかなり明確な方針に基づいて行われていると見られるが，それは世界各地における資源確保の試みと密接に関連しているのではないだろうか（第5章参照）。中国の海洋調査船は西太平洋や南シナ海で活動を活発化させており，1988年にはベトナム，台湾との間で争いになっていた南沙諸島の一部に海軍陸戦隊を強行上陸させ，中国領土であることを示す標識を立てるなどかなり強引な行動も行っている。日本の周辺海域でも種々の「調査活動」を行って日本人を刺激している。

1989年の全人代政府活動報告は「海洋権益の擁護」論を展開し，1992年には東シナ海，南シナ海全域を中国の領海とする「中華人民共和国領海および接続水域法」を公布した。また，江沢民総書記は同年，共産党一四全で「領海の主権と海洋権益の防衛」に言及しつつ国民に対し国家の発展と繁栄に寄与すべきであると呼びかけている。

これに先立って伝統的な国家領域とは別に，「国家の軍事力がコントロールしうる，国益と関係する地理的空間的範囲の限界」があるとし，これを「戦略国境」と名づけるとともに，これが国家と民族の生存空間を決定づけるとする理論が主張されたことがあり[9]，これは軍事力で勢力範囲を決定するというのに等しい露骨な拡張的主張であるが，これはやはり海洋権益の擁護の文脈で考えられていたようである。

第2に，中国の軍事力がまだ米ロ両国の域には達していないことである。中国としては自己の軍事力をさらに強化させ両国に近づけようとする力が軍事的には働くであろう。中国にはこれを支持する強いナショナリズムもある。中国が軍縮に熱意を示さないのも米ロの軍事力との差が原因の一つであろう。中国軍は，湾岸戦争でハイテク兵器を駆使する米軍の力にショックを受けたと言われており，それがきっかけとなって装備の近代化に一段と力を入れるようになった可能性もある。

しかし，米ロと同等の軍事力を持つことにどのような意義があるのか。中国がすでに強大になっている軍事力をさらに増強すると，周辺諸国のみならず米ロなどに対しても一定の脅威を及ぼすことが避けられないのではないか。また，軍事以外の国政に対し不利な影響が出ないか。このような諸問題について，中国として明確な認識を持っているのであろうか。

---

9) 1987年4月3日の『解放軍報』徐光裕「追求合理的三維戦略辺境」。

第3は，中国としての国威発揚である。これには，かつて列強の帝国主義的侵略の犠牲になったという歴史と中国人としての誇りの両側面が背景にあるが，これも近年の国家建設成功の結果中国としての国威は大いに発揚され，状況は大いに変化してきている。北京オリンピックと言い，また宇宙事業の成功と言い，今や中国が世界に誇れるものがつぎつぎに誕生している。このように大きな成功を収め，偉大な国家に回復した中国として，その声望を落とすようなことはできないという力も働くであろう。

　この問題も軍事力のさらなる増強を促進する面と抑制する面を持ちうると思われる。軍事的に強大であることが偉大な中国としての国威発揚に資するのは言うまでもないが，対外的に脅威を及ぼす恐れがあるという意味ではそれは逆に働く可能性があるからである。

　また，中国の国威を発揚させるのは強大な軍事力とは限らない。中国経済のめざましい発展によって中国の国際的地位はいちじるしく上昇した。主要国首脳会議G8が開催される際，今や主要な開発途上国の参加を求めることが当たり前のようになりつつあり，また，G20という言葉に象徴されるように世界経済をリードするのはG8と言うよりむしろG20であるという傾向が強くなっている。中国はその中でももっとも注目されている国であろう。

　第4に，中国軍の近代化・増強を支えている経済は開放政策以来順調に成長し，今年は世界的な金融経済混乱のためかなり影響をこうむったが，それでも景気刺激策が効果を上げていることもあり8％の成長も不可能でなくなっている。中国経済の急激な成長は世界各国にとってよい刺激となり，世界経済の牽引車となっているとも言われている。GDPはすでにドイツを越え，2009年中に日本をも凌駕して世界第2位に躍り出る可能性もある。外貨準備はすでに世界1となっている。

　もちろん，中国経済は決してばら色一色ではない。そもそも出発点があまりにも低すぎたので経済の発展段階は先進諸国に追いついていないし，新たに生まれた種々の格差が大きな問題となっている。7億人を越える農民はいまでも非常に低い生活水準にある。都市においても豊かさを享受できるのはごく一部の人であり，大多数の人の生活はそれほど向上していない。Krugmanの言うように，中国の急激な成長は資本と労働力の大量投下によるものであり，生産性の向上はまだ低い段階にあるのであろう。しかも無限にあると思われてきた労働力でさえもはや簡単に確保でなくなってきていることは中国自身認めている。また，年に数百億ドルのオーダーで流入していた外国からの投資が今後も同じ程度に継続されるか保証はない。このように中国経済は高度の成長過程に

あるものの課題もつぎつぎに作り出されており，いつまでもこれまでのように優先的に軍事力の増強を支え続けることは困難になる可能性がある。

　中国はかつて，経済発展よりも政治・軍事的強国になることを重視する傾向があったが，そのような考えはしだいに後退しつつあるのではないか。改革・開放政策を始めてまもなく（85 年），鄧小平は「かなり長期間にわたって大規模な戦争が起こらずにすむ可能性が生まれている」と言いはじめた[10]。以前は，米ソ二超大国による戦争は不可避であるという見解であったのは周知のとおりである。もっとも，その数年後に発生した天安門事件に際し各国から人民の抑圧を批判され，中国はかつての居丈高な態度に戻った。現在でも表向きは政治優先の建前を崩さないかもしれないが，傾向として中国はさらなる経済発展のためにも平和な国際環境を欲しており，そのことが中国の軍備にも微妙な影響を及ぼす可能性があり，将来は，軍備増強に専念するだけではかえって中国にとって不利益が生じてくるという認識につながっていく可能性もあろう。

　第 5 に，これもかなり遠い将来のことかもしれないが，平和が長期間継続すれば，中国がこれまで懸命に喧伝してきた外国の脅威が実はほとんど存在しないこと，少なくともこれまで想定されていた姿とはかなり異なっていることに気づくことはありうる。中国の対日不信についても同様の側面があるかもしれない。すなわち，中国が対日不信を抱くのは過去の不幸な歴史にかんがみれば無理からぬことであろうが，実態はすでに変わっており日本はすでに過去とは決別し，根本的に違った生き方をしていると言えるのではないか。

　中国はあいかわらず古い日本が残存しているということにこだわっているとしても，そのような心理的問題は日本側の継続的努力と時間の経過により和らいでくるであろう。日本と中国の間の信頼関係回復は複雑で忍耐と時間を必要とすることであり，このような信頼関係の強化を妨げるナショナリズムが日本にも中国にも存在するが，両国ともそのような要因を乗り越えて信頼関係を回復・構築していくことは可能であろう。

（5）米中両国は 2009 年 7 月，ワシントンにおいて戦略・経済対話を行った。このような対話は透明性の低い中国の軍事力をよりよく理解する上で積極的な意義を持ちうるものである。どの国でも国防に関わることは秘密にしておきたがる傾向があり，かつてのソ連はもちろん，現在のロシアでも，また米国でも国防に関することはすべて公開されているわけではない。核兵器の正確な保有数を公表している国は皆無である。そういう意味では中国だけが透明性がな

[10) 中央軍事委員会拡大会議での鄧小平の発言。平松茂雄『軍事大国化する中国の脅威』時事通信社（1995 年）35 頁。

く，他の国には透明性があるということではない。しかし，現状では，核兵器やミサイルはもちろん，通常兵器に関しても中国の透明性は抜群に低いし，国際社会はそのことに不満を抱いている。

日本には米中間の戦略・経済対話は「Ｇ２」の始まりだと言って騒ぐ傾向がなきにしもあらずだが，米国は中国の軍事と経済をよりよく理解し，また中国が国際社会の同じルールに従うことを期待して対話を行っているのであり，基本的には日本にとっても裨益するものと考えられる。

4．人間の安全保障の重視

（１）東アジアの自由主義諸国，台湾，韓国および日本には安全保障の面で共通点がある。これらの国は，中国およびロシア，それに限定的ながらも北朝鮮，とくにその核兵器とミサイルの顕在的あるいは潜在的な脅威にさらされており，米国との同盟関係に頼って安全保障を図らなければならないという大きな枠組みがある。そのような状況の中で，各国とも自己防衛力を最大限に強め，また，米国との同盟関係の信頼性を高めなければならず，そのためになすべきことは多々あろう。その意味で各国にはさまざまな難問があり，その解決は重要な国家的課題であるが，それを論じる余裕はない。最後に，すべての国に共通する新しい安全保障のあり方を論じておきたい。

それは人間の安全保障の重視である。国家にとって安全の確保は主権国家としてもっとも基本的で，重要なことであり，自己努力による他，特定の国との同盟関係や，また近年は国際連盟や国際連合など多国間で平和と安全の維持も行われるようになっている。このような従来からの安全保障は国家を対象とするものであり，それを確保することによって個人の安全が図られると考えられてきたが，最近は，人間個人の安全を直接的に確保することも重視されるようになってきた。

具体的には大きく分けて二つの潮流があり，その一つは人道的観点から人間を紛争や武器の被害から守らなければならないということであり，もう一つが，戦争以外の原因，武器以外の原因による場合も人間の安全を確保しなければならないということである。

（２）北朝鮮が極端な軍事優先主義であり，また，そのような方針を取っているのは北朝鮮としての安全を確保しなければならないという考えからであろうことはすでに説明した。北朝鮮はなけなしの資源を軍事に重点的に配分しており，その比率は国家予算の20～40％くらいに上っている可能性がある。これに大水害が加わったこともあるが，一時期は多数の餓死者が出たと噂され

たこともあった。これは誇張されているかもしれないが，WFP（世界食糧計画）は最近まで現地で活動しており，一般人は食料が欠乏していることを実際に目撃している。「国民が餓死しても国家はなくならないが，軍事を疎かにすると滅亡する」ということも言われているそうである。これも誇張かもしれないが，北朝鮮は，冷戦が終了していく過程の中で東欧諸国があっけなく崩壊したのは軍事をおろそかにしたからだと公に批評していること，また，いわゆる「先軍思想」が北朝鮮の指導原理であることなどは周知の事実である。

　軍事力が国家の存続を支えるということは原則としては北朝鮮に限らないことであり，そのこと自体については北朝鮮は特異な状況にあるわけではないが，国民の犠牲がそのために極端に大きくなっているのは問題であり，いつまでもそのような考えを維持することはできないはずである。しかも国家体制の維持のために軍事力が必要というのは，国外からの脅威や攻撃に備えるためだけでなく，国民自身の反体制行動に備えるためであることを意味しているのではないか。それも歴史的には多くの国で繰り返されてきたことであるが，そのようなことがあるからこそ人間の安全保障を重視していかなければならないと最近は考えられるようになっているのである。おそらく北朝鮮の考えは現在世界でもっとも国家中心になっているのではないかと思われる。

　（3）中国は北朝鮮とは同じでないが，どれほど人間の安全保障を重視しているか疑問の余地が多々ある。かつて，「中国はどんなことがあっても核兵器を生産する。（中略）たとえズボンははかなくても完成された兵器を製造するであろう」と陳毅外交部長が発言したことがあった[11]（1963年10月，日本のジャーナリストとの会見）。1989年6月の天安門事件でも，中国は人権を軽視しているとして国際的批判を浴びた。これに対し，中国は欧米のそのような批判の意図は共産党政権の打倒を狙った「和平演変」であると反発した。

　このような中国の反応は，一面では「白髪三千丈」や「張子の虎」のような中国人の豊かな言語表現によって誇張されているであろうが，発展段階の低い中国としては個人の利益よりも国家全体の利益を優先せざるをえないという考えがかなり強かったことは間違いないであろう。最近の開発目的のための強引な区画整理などを見ていると中国における個人の安全確保はいまだ遠い道であるという気持ちを禁じえない。

　しかし，人間を犠牲にする軍事力の重視政策は長続きしないのが歴史の法則

---

11) 1963年10月28日の日本人記者団との会見における陳毅外交部長の発言。ただし，この発言は，フルシチョフ首相が「中国が無理して原爆を作ればズボンがはけなくなる」と挑発的なことを言ったのに対して反発したものであった。『朝日新聞』1963年10月29日。

であろう。北朝鮮も，たとえば金正日亡き後，いろんなことが起こりそうだが，極端な政策は長く維持できないであろう。中国は巨大な象であり，また生き物であって変化もするので固定的に見続けるべきでない。中国の変化は国家の安全保障についても，また，人間の安全保障についても生じてくるのではないか。

（4）中国経済の世界経済へのかかわりが深まるにともない，中国と世界の国々では摩擦が増加する一方，相互に依存する関係も深まっている。

摩擦は，たとえば，中国の周辺地域における資源に対する要求とそれを確保するための一方的行動やアフリカにおける経済面での協力の進展とそれにともなう労働者の送り込みなどに関係して発生しており，現段階では中国の行動は国際的なルールや慣習に調和していない面も少なくない。

他方，相互依存関係の深化は，たとえば，中国による米国債の保有増大にともない起こっている。中国は近年米国債の購入を急増させ，2008年に日本を抜いて世界第1位となった後もさらに買い増し，本年の3月末には7千679億ドルとなった。そうなると，米国経済の不景気が深刻化して米国債の市場価値が下落するのが心配になり，最近中国は首脳レベルでも米国債の価値が下がらないよう十分注意して欲しいと要望している。これは注文をつけているのと同じことであろう。これに対し，Geithner財務長官はその点は十分配慮しており，米国債の保有に心配は要らないと説明している。米国としても，中国が心配になって米国債を売りに出すとそれこそ市場価値が下落し，混乱が惹起されるので心配なのである。これと類似の問題が日本でも十年前に起こっており，現在でも日本がそれを手放すことになると中国ほどではないかもしれないが，やはり混乱が起こるであろう。ただ，日本の場合は同じ先進国でG8の仲間であるからどのような行動を取るか米国としてもある程度予測可能であり安心感があろうが，中国の場合はもっと心配であろう。昨今の金融・経済危機はこのような相互依存関係が深化していることを如実にさらけ出したわけである。

中国と世界の相互依存の例は多々あり，中国製の工業製品についても起こっている。最近中国は世界の工場と言われることもあるように，大量の工業製品を世界各国に輸出し，その結果，各国は中国製品に依存するようになってきている。中国製品に安全性の問題が起こったのをきっかけに，米国でChina freeで生活できるか研究した人があり，その結論は，そうすると生活は非常に困難になるという結果だったそうである。このような相互依存関係の深化はグローバリゼーションによってますます顕著になっている。

（5）このようなグローバリゼーションと相互依存の深化は様々な影響を及ぼし，中国自身にも跳ね返ってきているのではないか。中国の改革・開放が西側の文化・価値観を中国へ流入させる効果をともなっているのは明らかである。国民生活を強いコントロールの下に置いておきたい中国にとってこれは何とか排除したいことであり，「精神汚染反対」，「ブルジョワ自由化反対」などのキャンペーンで，あるいはインターネットに対するコントロールを強化することなどにより対応に努めているようだが，これが一筋縄ではうまくいかない。長期的に見れば成功する可能性がきわめて低いのではないかと思われる。

　また，中国の急速な経済発展の陰でその利益を享受できない人たちが多数発生し，その不満が増大している。少数民族の不満にも共通の問題があり，さらに，最近は食の安全に関し大問題が続発し，死者も発生している。中国当局はこれらの問題について神経過敏に反応し情報の制限に躍起となっているが，それでもある程度の情報流出は止まらなくなっている。中国の経済発展は沿海発展戦略を核として実現してきたが，いずれは内陸も，またこれまで経済発展を享受できなかった人たちも恩恵を受けられるようになるという保証はない。このような問題を通じて，中国においても人間の安全保障の重要性についての認識が高まっていく可能性がある。

　一方，経済成長により国民の生活水準が上昇していけば政治や軍事よりも国民生活に大きな関心を持つようになる可能性もある。つまり，中国の経済発展はうまくいっても，あるいは問題が起こっても人間の生活に対する関心を強化させる結果となるのではないかと思われる。

（6）安全保障は主権国家にとっての基本問題であり，国が安全であって初めて人間も安心して生活できるというのが昔からの考えであり，人間の安全保障はごく最近議論されるようになったのは事実である。また，国家安全保障と人間の安全保障を比較すると，前者は直接的，後者は間接的であると思われているであろう。

　しかしながら，国家の安全保障は原則として国家ごとの問題であり，ある国の完全が確保されると他の国の安全は損なわれることも多いのではないか。つまり，国家の安全保障は他国の犠牲において成立する場合が多いということである。典型的なのが戦争であり，勝った国の安全は確保されるが，負けた国の安全は打ち砕かれる。

　これと異なり，人間の安全保障はそもそも国家の違いを前提にしていない。台湾でも，韓国でも，日本でも中国でも同時に目標として掲げることができるものであり，しかも互いに矛盾は生じない。人間の安全保障は世界のすべての

人間について同時に成立しうる。人間の安全保障は，原則としてプラスサムである。

これを推進するために国家安全保障は必ずしも必要でないし，国家安全保障は人間の安全保障にとってかえって不利に働く場合もある。紛争の中で人間を守らなければならないという人間の安全保障が強調されるようになった一つの流れは，まさに国家安全保障だけでは確保できない問題があることに注意が向けられるようになって起こってきたことである。

さらに，従来は，国家の安全を確保することが先決問題であると考えられてきたが，国民一人一人の安全確保を重視するようになると，国家の安全保障はそのための手段であるという考えがしだいに前面に出てくるようになり，しかも，絶対必要な手段でもないし，十分でもないという認識が強くなってくるのではないか。そのような考えがさらに進み，国民の安全が他の方法で確保されるのであれば，国家として恐ろしい兵器を持ち出す必要は少なくなっていく可能性がある。このように考えれば東アジアの諸国にとっては，人間の安全保障を推進することによってこの地域全体の安全を高められる可能性があるのではないかと思われる。

（7）米国は国家安全保障のチャンピオンであり，また，どの国よりも深く世界的規模で平和と安全の維持にかかわっており，そのために国家安全保障をおろそかにできない状況にある。とくに中東地域においては米国が高い優先度を置く問題の解決が糸口さえまだ見えてこない状況にある。

しかし，米国内には人間の安全保障を重視する強い世論も存在する。とくに，人権の擁護という面では米国内のNGOは強い影響力を持っている。オバマ政権は対話を重視し，また，軍縮に積極的な姿勢を見せており，問答無用的なところがあった前政権と異なり人間の安全保障にも力を入れていく可能性がある。この意味でも，オバマ政権の誕生は東アジア地域の安全保障にとって好ましい環境を作り出しつつあると見てよいと思われる。世界が金融・経済危機の影響から脱却していない現在は，新しい感覚で物事を見ていくのに適しているのかもしれない。

第3部　中印経済発展の課題と展望

第7章　中国改革開放30年の政策展開過程
——その成果と課題

浜　勝彦*

1. はじめに

中国は2008年12月に，改革開放政策への転換から30年を迎えた。

この30年間に，中国は改革開放政策を展開した成果として，高い経済成長，市場経済への転換，経済のグローバル化を実現し，中国国民の生活水準を高め，中国の国際的地位を高め，中華の復興という前世紀の中国人の悲願の達成に向けて大きな一歩を進めた，と評価できる。

しかし，こうした成果をさらに固めて中国の発展を真に確固としたものとするには，こうした成果に内在する負の側面と政策的制約を克服して，持続的な発展を確かなものとすることと，その基礎となる社会・政治の安定を実現することが課題となっている。2009年には世界金融危機の中で，これらの課題克服が試されているのである。

本章では，まず，最近の中国当局が，世界金融危機の中で，どのようにこれに応戦し，高成長を維持しているのかを，改革開放30年の成果と結びつけて分析する。

そして，本論として，改革開放30年の政策展開過程を三つの時期に分けて，その政策展開における主な特徴を取り上げる。これらを踏まえて，中国の改革開放と本格的な発展が現在直面しているいくつかの課題を指摘する。

30年の時期区分としては，第一段階として，1980年—92年の改革開放政策の模索を，第二段階として，1992年—2002年の中国市場経済の形成を，第三段階として，2002年以来の胡錦濤体制になってから，急拡大して厚みと広さを実現してきた経済に対してマクロ・コントロールの枠組みをどう構築しているかを，見ていきたい。

2. 2008年からの国際金融危機への応戦
(1) 国際金融危機への応対

まず中国が市場経済に転換した1992年からの各経済指標の伸び率を示す表

---

*　創価大学名誉教授，社団法人中国研究所理事長。

表1　市場経済下中国の経済指標

(伸び率〔%〕)

年次	GDP	固定資産投資	消費財小売額	消費価格指数	都市住民可処分所得	農民純収入	財政収入	実際外商直接投資	輸出	輸入	外貨準備
1992	14.2	44.4	16.8	6.4	9.7	5.9	10.6	152.1	18.2	26.3	·10.5
1993	14.0	61.8	13.4	14.7	9.5	3.2	24.8	150.0	8.0	29.0	9.0
1994	13.1	30.4	30.5	24.1	8.5	5.0	20.0	22.7	31.9	11.2	143.5
1995	10.9	17.5	26.8	17.1	4.9	5.3	19.6	11.1	22.9	14.2	42.6
1996	10.0	14.8	20.1	8.3	3.9	9.0	18.7	11.2	1.5	5.1	42.7
1997	9.3	8.8	10.2	2.8	3.4	4.6	16.8	8.5	21.0	2.5	33.2
1998	7.8	13.9	6.8	·0.8	5.8	4.3	14.2	0.5	0.5	·1.5	3.6
1999	7.6	5.1	6.8	·1.4	9.3	3.8	15.9	·11.3	6.1	18.2	6.7
2000	8.4	10.3	9.7	0.4	6.4	2.1	17.0	1.0	27.8	35.8	7.0
2001	8.3	13.0	10.1	0.7	8.5	4.2	22.3	15.1	6.8	8.2	28.1
2002	9.1	16.9	11.8	·0.8	13.4	4.8	15.4	12.5	22.4	21.2	35.0
2003	10.0	27.7	9.1	1.2	9.0	4.3	14.9	1.4	34.6	39.8	40.8
2004	10.1	26.6	13.3	3.9	7.7	6.8	21.6	13.3	35.4	36.0	51.3
2005	10.4	26.0	12.9	1.8	9.6	6.2	19.9	·0.5	28.4	17.6	34.3
2006	11.1	23.9	13.7	1.5	10.4	7.4	22.5	4.5	27.2	19.9	30.2
2007	13.0	24.8	16.8	4.8	14.2	9.5	32.4	18.6	25.7	20.8	43.3
2008	9.0	25.7	21.6	5.9	8.4	8.0	19.5	23.6	17.5	18.5	27.3
2009 1-9月	7.7	33.4	15.1	·1.1	9.3	8.5	--	--	·21.3	·20.4	

出所：『中国統計年鑑』各年版、『新中国五十五年統計資料彙編』中国統計出版社、2005年、国家統計局2009年10月22日より作成。

1によって近年の中国経済のパフォーマンスを振り返ってみたい。

1992年以来，市場経済への転換に伴う経済過熱に対してマクロ・コントロールが強化された。1998年からはアジア金融危機の影響による成長の鈍化が見られ，内需拡大への努力が行われ，その一環として西部大開発戦略が実施された。2002年に胡錦濤体制に転換して，1人当たりGDP 4倍増計画が打ち出されてから，急速な成長に転じている。近年は，高成長に低インフレということで，外貨準備も貯まり，経済発展のパフォーマンスとしては非常に好ましい状況を実現してきたといえる。その背後にはもちろんエネルギー・環境問題の深刻化と各種の構造問題が覆い隠されているものと考えられる。

こうした中，2008年には消費者物価指数が5.9%となり，大きな問題となった。前年後半から急速にインフレ状況が出現したためで，インフレ抑制の財政・金融政策が行われて，どんどん抑え込んだ。しかし，その抑え込みからの転換は遅きに失し，2008年9月の世界金融危機に遭遇して初めて転換が本格

化した，という見方が多い[1]。政府は4兆元の巨額投資による経済成長促進へと急転換した。2009年は8％を超える高成長を実現すべく努力が行われ，結果として8.7％に到達した。

　巨額の政府投融資の投入による景気刺激策は，建設投資と内需を刺激し，中国だけの突出した高成長を実現したわけであるが，その政策後遺症として，いくつかの弊害が指摘されている。

　一つは，エネルギー・環境問題に対処するための構造調整政策を実行するために，これまで地方政府の投資を抑制する努力が行われてきたわけだが，今回の経済刺激策で，政府の環境・エネルギー水準枠に達しない投資が進行して，構造調整政策の効果が不利な影響を受けることになった。

　二つは，今回の政府投融資が，主として国有部門に向けられて，民間企業の投資空間が狭められており，これは改革の方向に逆行するものだとの批判が強い。

　三つ目は，政府の投融資が，対象プロジェクトから，株式市場や不動産市場に流失して，インフレ傾向を助長しているとの見方が強い。

　さらに，経済政策に関する中央政府と地方政府の力関係が，地方政府に有利になっている事がうかがわれる事例がある。2009年9月の統計公報が発表された段階で，統計局筋が明らかにしたところでは，9月のGDPの全国集計と地方のGDPの集計を比較してみると，地方のGDP集計が2.5兆元ほど（11.5％）全国GDPを上回るという[2]。すなわち地方における経済成長追求の政権運営が統計数値にまで反映されて，それを中央当局が統合・消化できない。こういうところにも中国の現在の経済運営の問題点が表れていると考えられるのである。

3. 改革開放政策の探索── 1980〜1992
（1）改革開放の出発点──旧ソ連との比較

　まず第1段階である改革開放の初期段階について検討する。その第1の特色は，旧ソ連との際立った対照である。中国が改革開放政策に転換した1980年ごろは，まだ建国から30年しか経ていなかった。農業生産責任制を導入し，規制を緩和して，経済を自由化するから自分で稼げといわれた場合に，農民そ

---

[1] 袁鋼明「マクロ経済政策の激変と世界金融危機のなかの中国経済」『中国年鑑2009年』中国研究所2009年5月所収。
[2] 「人民時評：2.5兆はどこから来るか，GDP"水増し"問題を解決すべきである」『人民網』2009年11月6日。

表2　改革・開放初期の4段階

	第1段階	第2段階	第3段階	第4段階
改革・開放の高潮	1980	1984	1988	1992
改革・開放理論	・党の工作の重点を近代化建設に置く ・実践による真理の検証	・新技術革命論 ・(1984.10) 社会主義商品経済論	・(1987.11) 社会主義初級段階論 ・(同) 国家が市場を調節し、市場が企業を誘導	・科学技術は第1の生産力 ・(1992.10) 社会主義市場経済論の確立
改革政策	・農家経営請負制の展開 ・工業企業党で利潤留保の実験	・都市・工業部門で改革開始 ・工場長責任制の実施 ・利潤上納から納税制へ ・二重価格体系の導入	・私営企業の公認 ・企業経営請負制の実施 ・副食品価格の自由化 ・価格体制改革案の策定	・企業の経営メカニズムの転換 ・「税利分流」実施と統一法人税の導入 ・「分税制」実施
対外開放戦略	・(1978.12) 対外開放への転換	・一つの世界市場の承認 ・東側にも市場開放 ・一国二制度論 ・「貿―工―農」体制	・(1988.1) 沿海地区経済発展戦略 ・「両頭在外」「大進大出」	・全方位対外開放 ・上海に重点を置く
対外開放政策 地域的拡大 政策・優遇 その他	・(1980.8) 深圳、珠海、厦門、仙頭に経済特区設置 ・(1979.7) 広東省と福建省に特殊政策 ・(1979.12) 円借款受入れ開始 ・(1979.6) 合弁法	・(1984.4) 14沿海都市を対外開放 ・(1985.1) 長江デルタ、珠江デルタ、閩南三角区を対外開放 ・(1984.5) 全国で100％外資企業設立許可	・(1988.3) 沿海ベルト地帯対外開放 ・(1988.4) 海南省成立、全体が特区 ・(1988.7) 「台湾同胞投資奨励規定」 ・(1987.9) 深圳で土地使用権外商に販売 ・(1988.1) 貿易企業で経営請負責任制の全面実施	・(1990.4) 上海浦東新区開発決定 ・(1991.末) 深圳、上海で外国向株発行 ・(1991) 外資による団地開発管理弁法 ・(1992.3) 海南島洋浦経済開発区の外資による開発決定 ・(1991.1) 貿易企業の独立採算制導入、貿易補助金廃止

(出所) 浜勝彦著『中国　鄧小平の近代化戦略』アジア経済研究所1995年　14頁

れから企業者がどこに行って何を売ればどのくらい儲かるか, ということがただちに計算できる旧市場体制の認識というものが, まだ保持されていた。その

ために，改革開放で自由化が進められたときに，草の根の経済が急速に伸びてきた。もう1つは華僑が存在するということ。この二つの点が革命70年の旧ソ連では見られなかった中国の比較優位性であったと言うことができる。

（2）安定団結，足で石を探って川を渡る

私が強調したいのは特色の第2点で，中国の改革開放政策においては，まず安定，団結が大前提で，政治の安定が経済発展を促し，経済発展が安定を促すという好循環を目指した。足でもって石を探りながら川を渡る（摸着石頭過河）ということで，手探りで改革開放を進めて，安定，団結を乱すとなると，しばらくこれを止めて他の道を探るというかたちで慎重に改革開放を進めた。

（3）4年ごとの波型発展

その具体的内容の大きな特徴として私が整理した結果は，表2に示されている改革開放初期の4段階ということになる。

主な柱だけ取り上げてみると，その第1段階として，80年には農家生産請負制が爆発的に拡大し，また経済特区ができた。第2段階の84年には，改革を都市・工業でやりたいということで社会主義商品経済論が出てきた。第3段階の88年には社会主義初級段階論が公認理論となり，沿海地区経済発展戦略が実行されるに至った。第4段階は92年の鄧小平の南巡談話で社会主義市場経済の確立を目指すということになった。どうして改革開放で4年ごとに高まりが起こったのかということの理由は歴史研究の課題であるが，全体の特徴としては波型の経済発展がみられた。自由化する（放）とインフレになり混乱して（乱），これを調整する（収）と沈滞して（死），また自由化を図る（放），ということになるので，1つの政策の波が全国展開するのに1年くらいはかかり，「放乱収死」の一種の4年ごとの経済循環ということが結果として現れてくるものとみられる（図1参照）。

波動の第2の特徴は政策の継続性である。調整の過程で政策の手直しは図られたけれども，基本は維持されて，さらに次の段階で新しいものが展開していくという形で段階的に拡大深化できた，ということが言える。波動のもう1つの特徴は，いずれにせよ新しい段階の開始においては鄧小平自身のイニシアティブが決定的な影響を与えている，ということである[3]。

中国の改革開放期30年の経済成長率の変動は，図1に示されているように，第二段階に入った1992年の市場経済への転換以降，大きな変化を見せている。それ以前の波形は指令性計画経済の下に，乱高下を繰り返したが，92年から

---

3) 浜勝彦『中国—鄧小平の近代化戦略』アジア経済研究所1995年　序章参照。

図1　1978―2009年の中国のGDP伸び率

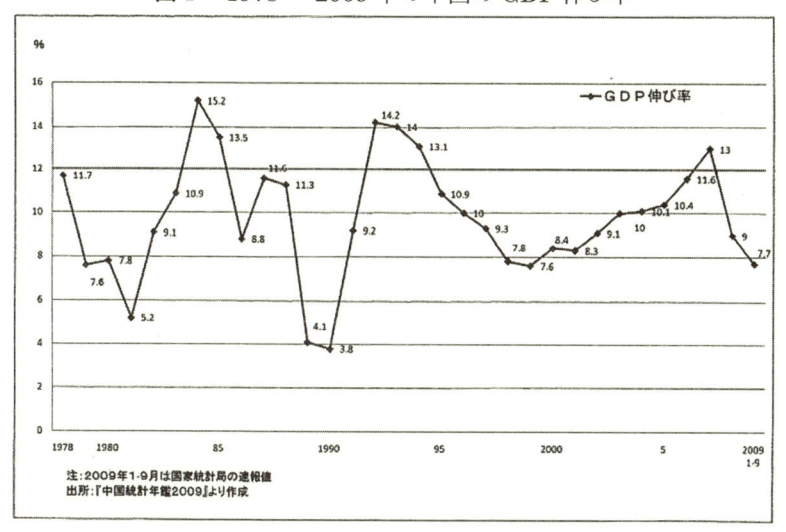

は政府のマクロ・コントロールは金利，貸付等の間接的手段に転じ，その効果は即効性に欠け，波型はなだらかなものとなった。

（4）社会主義初級段階論と趙紫陽

　社会主義初級段階論の登場は極めて重要である。この理論により，私営企業が憲法で合法化された。鄧小平のイニシアティブに沿って趙紫陽がこれを強引に進めたものであると見られる。2009年，趙紫陽が口述した『改革歴程』という本が香港新世紀出版社から出版された。それによると，胡耀邦が80年代初めから政治面の改革を先頭に立って進めていたために，元老・保守勢力の反発は胡耀邦に向けられていた。趙紫陽は経済改革の実務で，むしろ保守的なスタンスと見られていた。趙紫陽が87年，88年政権を担当した期間に鄧小平の意を体して胡耀邦が意図してもできなかった改革の突破，理論的な突破を実現した。すなわちそれが政治体制改革と社会主義初級段階論になるわけである。そういうわけで趙紫陽は鄧小平の指示によって改革開放政策をさらに一段と強烈に前に進めたのだが，前に進め過ぎたために孤立し，結局，鄧小平からも見放されたかたちになって，天安門事件で失脚した。また，趙紫陽の沿海地区の経済発展戦略は，90年代，2000年代に実際に大きく花開くわけだが，趙紫陽と結びついた「沿海地区経済発展戦略」という名前では言われなくなってしまったのである。

(5) 体制外改革, 増量改革論

中国では改革開放の第1段階と第2段階の違いを説明するのに, 第1段階は増量改革, 体制外先行の改革であって, 第2段階の90年代から全体的な改革を推進したという言い方をしている[4]。

第1段階は体制外先行の改革である。すなわち農村の生産責任制とか, 郷鎮企業, 経済特区などは旧来の体制の外で増えた分の増量改革である。増分改革と言っている人もいる。そういうかたちで国有企業の改革など抵抗の大きなところを迂回して, 抵抗が少ないところから改革が進んだ。最近の政治体制改革議論においても増量改革が良いのではないかと言う議論が登場することになる。

これはむしろ90年代後半になってから, 経済がほとんど民営化されてしまった段階で整理された言い方であって, 80年代にはこのような言い方は聞かれなかった。80年代の初期の段階は前述のように, 安定, 団結, 足で石を探って川を渡るというかたちで, 試行錯誤で慎重に進めていった。その結果が体制外改革, 増量改革となったということである。

4. 中国的市場経済の形成―― 1992 ～ 2002
(1) 中国的市場経済と中国的資本主義

第2段階は中国的市場経済の形成の段階である。私はここでは中国的資本主義の形成という用語を使わない。その理由は以下のとおりである。実際の中国的資本主義は, 官僚的資本主義あるいは国家主導資本主義で, しかもそれが初発的で荒々しい資本主義のすそ野の上に成り立っているものと見られるが, それに対する国家や党の関与は他の国とは違ってきわめて大きな存在である。用語として「資本主義」と言う言葉を使う場合, これを主導する国家や党の作用を示す適切な形容詞が見つけにくい[5]。中国が資本主義だと定義すると性格規定と用語問題に研究を要するということもあり, 本論ではさしあたり「中国的市場経済」という言葉を使用する。

(2) 国有企業改革の進展と民営経済化

1992年の南巡談話の後, 93年に中国的市場経済の枠組みを示す党中央委員会の決議が行われて, その青写真として, 分税制, 中央税, 地方税, 社会福祉

---

4) 呉敬璉著, 青木昌彦監訳, 日野正子訳『現代中国の経済改革』NTT出版 2007年。
5) 中国に関する具体的用語例としては,「官僚金融産業資本主義」(小島麗逸『現代中国の経済』岩波書店 1997年参照),「官製資本主義」(呉軍華『中国静かなる革命』日本経済新聞出版社 2008年) がある。

図2　1978 — 2009年の中国の貿易総額

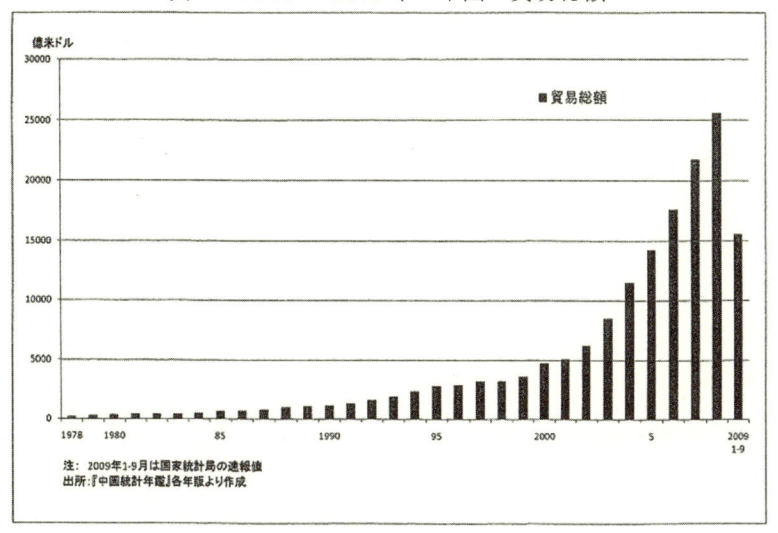

注：2009年1-9月は国家統計局の速報値
出所：『中国統計年鑑』各年版より作成

制度，市場向け金融制度といったほとんど日本と変わらないような市場経済のチャートが描かれた。その中にはすでに遺産相続税とか贈与税も含まれていたが，中国においてはこの方面の改革は今も実施されていない。90年代には「大をつかみ，小を自由化する」ということで国有企業も中小企業は自由化・民営化する，大企業では株式化を進め，全体としてリストラを行ってきた。97年には15回党大会で国有経済の戦略的調整を決定した。大型国有経済も株式化，民営化する。同時に民営企業は経済の重要な構成要素であるとして，民営企業を体制内のものとして認めた。97年以降毎年2万社の国有企業が減って，これらが民営化したものと見られている。同時に，今までの郷鎮企業，民営企業，温州の企業などで多くが共同企業のかたちをとっていたが，これら企業の完全民営化が97年以降に進んだ[6]。こうして，90年代後半に中国的資本主義の構造が急速に確立されていったと見ることができるのである。

（3）経済国際化をめぐる論争
（ア）経済国際化の進展
　中国のドル建て貿易総額の棒グラフである図2からも見られるように，1980年代の貿易は現在の段階からすると非常に初歩的な段階にあったことが

6）大橋英夫，丸川知雄『中国企業のルネサンス』岩波書店2009年。

図3　1979－2009年の中国の外国直接投資実行額

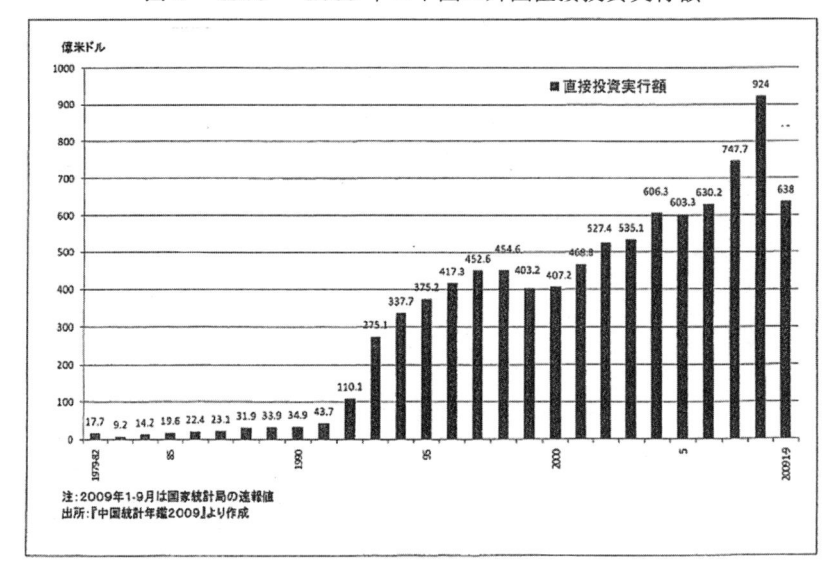

分かる。90年代になってかなりの伸びを示した。そして2000年代に入ってからの伸びは3年で倍増の驚異的ともいえる勢いであることがわかる。こうした中で，世界金融危機の影響は，2009年の貿易総額で前年比13.9％減という大きな落ち込みをもたらした。これまで貿易総額は，アジア金融危機の1998年に微減となったほかは，ずっと伸び続けてきたもので，初めて大きく落ち込んだということが見て取れるのである。

図3の中国への外国直接投資でも同じような傾向がみられる。すなわち1990年代に外国直接投資が中国に流れ込んできて，毎年大体400億ドル水準で推移した。1980年代のアセアン全体に対する域外からの直接投資が年間最大400億ドルくらいだったので，その分が毎年中国1国になだれ込んできて，この外国直接投資が中国の経済の変化に大きな役割を果たしたのである。さらに2000年代に入っても急伸していて，最近の中国経済のグローバル化の勢いを示している。

中国への外国直接投資の実行額は2008年に924億ドルだったが，09年には年間900.3億ドルとなり，前年比2.6％減で，中国に対する直接投資が落ち込んでいるということが確実になっている。アジア金融危機のとき以来の減少である。

（イ）経済国際化論争

90年代の中国経済のもう1つの重要な問題点として，新しい国際関係の進展の中で，エネルギーと食糧は基本的に自給すべきではないか，ということで，輸入では対外依存度を何％にするのが適当かということが議論された。大体10％が安全の基準ではないか，という方向で自給論争が進められた。エネルギーでは自給の石炭が多いので，対外依存するとすれば石油が中心となる。石油消費の半分以上を輸入してもエネルギー全体では10％に収まるかもしれないという計算ができる[7]。食糧についても同じような論争が行われた。レスター・ブラウンが「中国をどう養うか」という論文を書いてくれたので，中国でも問題関心が高まり，中国農業部自身，非常に助かったとブラウン氏に表明したと伝えられている[8]。

結果として二つの市場――すなわち外国市場と国内市場，二つの資金，二つの資源を積極的に利用するという政策が次第に固まってきて，2000年代に入って全面的に実行に移されることになる。例えばカザフスタンから石油を輸入するパイプラインを建設することが97年に合意された。当時は結局失敗して，5年から10年後に実行されることになった。しかし，97年合意だけでも，カザフスタンに根拠を置くウイグル独立派組織がカザフスタンで活動しにくくなり，独立運動が不利になったというような政治的，外交的効果が観察されたのである。

（4）コントロールへの政府の苦闘

荒々しく発展する経済と過熱をどうコントロールするか，政府は苦闘を迫られた。行革では石油産業を再編して3つのメジャーを作って対外的にも乗り出す能力を持たせた。2003年の国有資産監督管理委員会の成立によって，国有企業への投資者としての政府の機能をこれ1本に集中して，他は，価格・金利，産業構造政策，法制などのマクロ・コントロール政策によることにした。90年代には民営化の猛烈な推進と外国投資が巨額に存在するために，アモイ事件を象徴とするような密輸事件が各所に見られて，密輸取締り警察が99年1月に設置された。すなわち軍と警察，地方政府が信頼できない。それを取締るために大砲を備えた軍艦を持つ密輸取締り警察を設置した。朱鎔基首相は密輸事件などに見られる地方の暴走を治めるためには「100の棺桶を準備してくれ，最後の1つは俺のだ」という決心でもってあたり，コントロールのために苦闘したのである。

---

[7] 浜勝彦「改革開放期における中国石油産業政策の展開過程」『創大中国論集』創刊号 1998年3月。
[8] 浜勝彦「中国の食糧・農業危機と農業保護政策への転換」『国際問題』1996年6月号。

（5）西部大開発と生態系建設

　河川問題が深刻化した1998年に丁度アジア金融危機が発生して，内需を拡大し，内陸部を振興するために西部大開発戦略を推進した。河川の源流を植林するための対策として「退耕還林」政策が実施された。当時朱鎔基首相が，食糧買付価格を引き上げたために，食糧は1年分くらいの在庫が貯まってしまい，食糧が腐ってきていて保管をどうしたら良いのか悩んでいた。そこに，この「退耕還林」という方策があることが分かり，食糧を補助のためにそちらにまわすというアイデアを実行することを決めた[9]。「退耕還林」政策では，経済樹林には5年間，自然生態林には8年間食糧給付を実施した。しかし，食糧事情が厳しくなったため，それが一巡したところで拡大をストップして，今までやった重点部分だけを保持するという政策に変更されている。

5．経済の急伸とコントロール枠組みの構築——2002～
（1）経済コントロールの枠組みの構築

　改革開放の第3段階は胡錦濤体制になって以降である。2002年に成立した胡錦濤体制はSARSをコントロールすることに成功して，初期において経済発展戦略の構築に非常に意欲的に取り組んだ。それは経済のマクロ・コントロールにおける政策的枠組みを構築すること，科学的発展観の成立，調和社会論の形成等の内容をもっていた。

　経済のマクロ・コントロールにおける政策的枠組みを構築することの主な内容は，シンクタンクの大兵団作戦と閣僚級の指導グループの設置であった。2005年5月に国家エネルギー指導グループが発足した[10]。これまでエネルギー政策を集中的にコントロールする部門が実は中国では形成されておらず，特に石油産業の位置づけが明確でなかった。石油派が冷遇されていたという問題点があった。石油派は華国鋒体制の主流を構成していたために，これに替わった鄧小平時代に冷遇された。江沢民時代には石油産業を3つの国際級石油大企業に再編するという改革を進め，石油派が力を取り戻した。いくつかの閣僚級の指導グループを作って経済を集中的にコントロールする枠組みが作られた。その政策を探るために各種シンクタンクを大幅に動員して，経済の実情を探らせた。特にエネルギーと農業については，2002年から2005年に各種

9）浜勝彦「四川省における『退耕還林』事業」『中国西部大開発基礎調査報告』社団法人中国研究所2002年3月所収。
10）浜勝彦「中国のエネルギー『危機』と省エネ発展戦略の展開」林華生，浜勝彦，渋谷祐編著『アジア経済発展のアキレス腱』文真堂2008年所収。

シンクタンクの大規模な調査活動が行われて，それらをとりまとめた。これは温家宝首相が指揮して自分の構想に基づいてやったということで，温家宝の政治指揮力の冴えがここに表れていると言える。

（2）科学的発展観と産業構造調整

胡錦濤体制が強調する科学的発展観は，人間を中心とする協調的持続的発展を図るというものである。それは同時に調和社会の建設と反腐敗の政策というものとセットになっている。それらをもとにして 2005 年以降は産業構造調整政策が進められてきた。この産業構造調整政策の内実は，中国がこのまま成長していくとエネルギーと環境問題がどんどん悪化してくる。国際標準にキャッチアップするためにも第 11 次 5 カ年計画（2006 年から 2010 年）において，GDP 当たりのエネルギー消費量を 20％，主要汚染物質排出量を 10％削減するという目標を設定した。年間にすると 4％と 2％で，ともかく年間の省エネのノルマを決めてそれを実行することになった。しかしそうすると地方政府の発展方針とは対立してくることになり，そこで地方諸侯との利害調整が難しくなってきた。それでも断固やりぬかねばならないということで，相当無理をして実施しているところに世界金融危機が発生した。そのため，コントロールを一気に緩めることになり，地方政府がかなり自由にその発展を図りうるようになった。2009 年度に入ってからこの構造調整政策が非常に大きな困難に遭遇していると見てよい。

（3）調和社会論と危機管理体制

胡錦濤体制は 2000 年代前半，親民政策を強調して，党の政治支配力を強化してきた。調和社会建設の裏には危機管理体制が存在する。すなわち突発事件管理予備案，突発事件対応法が制定されており，それにより調和社会建設の裏側を危機管理体制が支える構造になっている。GDP が 1 人当たり 1000〜3000 ドル，あるいは 5000 ドルくらいになるテイクオフの過程においては権威主義的支配が必要であるという理論を背景にして，こういった危機管理体制を 5 年なり 10 年なり維持してゆくうちに社会が脱皮して経済社会が近代化する，という見込みに立っている。すなわち韓国，台湾のケースがモデルになっており，危機管理体制プラス調和社会論が党を支える理論的背景なのである。

2007 年からの胡錦濤体制後期になると，地方で起こる各種の事件に対して，警察的，治安的対応を迫られ，積極的な要素としての親民政策，調和社会論が色褪せてきているというイメージがもたれるようになっている。こうした中で，党の一部リーダーや知識人の中では地方諸侯と特権階層の抵抗を突破して政治改革により民主化を進めなければならない，という危機意識が高まってき

ているのである。

6．改革開放 30 年の成果と課題
（1）30 年の成果と課題

改革開放 30 年の成果についてみると，2010 年には中国の GDP は日本を超えて世界 2 位になる見込みであり，多くなる外貨の蓄積および財政収入の拡大で政府の支配力が格段に強化されている。もちろんこれらは改革開放の大きな成果なのだが，しかし改革開放政策で残された問題が多い。特に 93 年の市場経済のフローチャート表によると，遺産相続税，贈与税なども予定にあるが，現在も実現していない。経済における再分配である社会保障体制が都市ではバランスのとれたものとなっておらず，農村ではまだ普遍的に形成されていないという状況にある。政治制度改革については，まだ 80 年の鄧小平の演説，87 年の政治制度改革決議の課題がほとんど実現されていないという問題点があると思われる。以上のような改革開放政策の展開の現状を踏まえて，今後の展望に関連して，改革開放の残された課題として，4 点を取り上げておきたい。

（2）政治改革を考える

2007 年の中国共産党 17 回大会では，「社会主義民主政治を発展させる」という目標の下に，「政治制度改革を深化する」とした。問題は政治改革をどう進めるかと言う点である。改革開放 30 周年を迎えた 08 年の暮れから 09 年にかけて『人民日報』に登場した論調として，3 つの具体案がある。2008 年 12 月 3 日に中共中央編訳局副局長の兪可平が，中国民主の「増量発展論」を主張した。それは主として党内の民主と，基層民主すなわち底辺の民主とを結合して，ここから取り組んで行き，もしできるところがあれば他の部分でも突破を行う，とした。兪可平の主張は，2006 年 10 月に『民主主義は素晴らしいものだ』という本を出版したということで有名である。もう 1 つは国務院研究室副主任の江小涓が経済社会制度の「存量改革推進」を提唱する論文を 2009 年 4 月 1 日の『人民日報』に発表した。政治における「存量改革推進論」の所在がはっきりわからなかったところ，09 年 10 月の日本現代中国学会で季衛東上海交通大学教授の「政治改革"軟着陸"のための制度設計と中国憲政の前景」という講演があり，この内容がそれにあたるものであった。すなわち人民代表大会と政治協商会議は今までは実権の乏しい機関といわれていたわけだが，だんだんと実権を持つようにして質的に力のある機関にしていくということ，すなわち議会権力の質の強化を図るものである。あと 1 人，国務院発展研究センター研究員の呉敬璉は市場経済を積極的に推進してきた経済学者

だが，彼は「法制化した市場論」を08年12月3日の『人民日報』に発表した。市場における法律による支配と憲法の強化を切望したものである。呉敬璉は『現代中国の経済改革』という本を出しているが，その中で政治改革についても詳しく論じている[11]。

(3) 中国市場経済と腐敗

呉敬璉が前掲『人民日報』で言うには，既得権益層が導き悪い市場経済の泥沼にはまり込む可能性がある。それを防ぐには法律と憲法を経済の中で貫徹しなければいけないので，「今までは市場経済の呉敬璉と言われたのですが，これからは法制の呉敬璉と言ってくれ」と言っている。問題点は，今の中国は良い市場経済に向かうのか，権力資本主義の悪い市場経済に向かうのか，であると。良い市場経済に向けて進めるということが課題になる。腐敗との関係では一般の企業において会計準則の充実，実施が大きな課題となっているのはもちろんのこと，利子取得税，相続税，贈与税などが未だに実施されておらず，果たしてこれらが実施できるのかということが問題になっている。

(4) 格差と経済圏域，中央権力と地方権力

中国には沿海地区のメガロポリスを含む沿海地域，中部地域，西部地域がある。それからタテの権力機構では省クラスの政府があって，県クラスの体制，郷鎮の体制がある。2000年代初期から農民に税金と負担金を課すのを止めて，逆に国家から地方政府に財政資金を交付することになった。これはこれまで2000年間存在しなかった新体制であり，一体地方の県と郷鎮という体制は，中央の単なる出先ではなく民を代表する存在として，いかにあるべきか，ということが問われているのである。これがどういうところに軟着陸するのかはまだ明らかでなく，2012年か2020年ころまでに体制を整えるというスケジュールになっている。これは2010年代の中国の国家体制の足元を固める重大な問題の所在を示しているものである。

しかも，中国には沿海，中部，西部，3つの世界が一国内に存在している。そもそも中国は国が大き過ぎる，そのため地方の体制においても，構造調整の課題においても，地方の独自性なり，合理性を持つ地方のバージョンというものがありうるわけである。その意味で，一種の連邦制的な方向に行くのが合理的であると言える。

しかし，連邦制を実現することが非常に難しい。もともと大きくて統一した国土という歴史的伝統がある。毛沢東が文化大革命までの政治建設において地

---

11) 呉敬璉著，青木昌彦監訳，日野正子訳『現代中国の経済改革』NTT出版2007年。

方文化というものを徹底的に払拭してしまった。例えば広東省の嶺南派や安徽省の桐城派というような儒教の文化センターも消滅させてしまった。これから広東のリーダーに，あなたのところは連邦制で自主的にやって良いですよといわれても，連邦制とはなんでしょうか，と聞き返されるような感じであり，結局中央が巨大な力でコントロールするところに戻っていかざるを得ない。地方権力と中央権力の兼ね合いがこれからの非常に大きな課題になると考えられる。

（5）民族問題と国家の統合

　国家の統合にかかわるもう一つの重要問題は民族問題である。民族問題ではチベット問題，ウイグル問題が大きな問題になっている。私が注目しているのはチベット族，ウイグル族の周辺に居住する回族である。中国人の顔をしているけれども回教を信じている民族グループで，08年のチベット騒動のときも回族の商店が襲撃された。09年の新疆における騒乱事件においても漢民族のデモの中に回族の人たちが加わっていて，記者のインタビューに答えているというようなことがあった。回族の人々が現在どういう状態にあるかは明らかではない。

　清朝の歴史から見ると，回族が反乱を起こしたために，新疆にウイグル族のヤクブ・ベク国というものがでてきて，その後の東トルキスタン民族運動のもとになっている。天才的軍事戦略家の左宗棠がまず回族反乱を平定して，それから新疆のヤクブ・ベク国を平定した。もしこの回族の反乱を鎮定できなかったら，東トルキスタンはアフガニスタンとかパキスタンのような国になっていたという可能性が存在したといえる。このような意味で，今後大陸本土の混乱，回族などの中間地帯での混乱，それから少数民族の運動が同時に発生した場合には政治的に大きな選択を迫られることになり，自治力アップにつながる機会が生じてくるかもしれない。現在は内政不干渉を含む平和共存5原則が国際的に承認されており，さらにアメリカは今回の経済危機の中で中国の内政にあまり関与することを避けており，当面外からチベット問題，ウイグル問題に対して圧力を行使する力はあまり強くないという状況が続くと思われる。

第8章　インド型経済発展モデルとグローバル不況

清水　学[*]

1．はじめに

　インド経済は1991年の経済自由化政策への転換以降,「停滞」から「成長」への転換が注目されてきたが，2003年度（2003年4月－04年3月）にさらに第2の投資ブーム期に入った。対GDP比投資額は1990年代では25%であったが，03－04年度以降は34%程度に上がってきている。高貯蓄・高投資の典型的な高成長パターンで2007年度まで5年間，連続して年率8%を超える実質成長率を記録し，2007年度は10%に達した。2005年10月末の1400億ドルであった外貨準備高は急増し，2年半後の2008年5月には3146億ドルのピークに達した。しかし第2の投資ブーム期の過程で，インドも世界信用経済危機に揺さぶられた。米国発の信用金融危機を起点として拡大した世界的な経済危機は，その規模の大きさと危機の拡散スピードの速さを特徴とし，特に金融面でグローバル化の波に巻き込まれている地域，国ほど大きな影響を受けた。1929年の世界恐慌が想起され，そこからの脱却のためには，先進資本主義国の多くがゼロ金利に近い通貨金融政策を採用し，金融政策の不十分さを巨額な財政出動によって補うなど，とり得る政策手段をフル動員した危機対応策をとらざるを得なかった。2008年9月中旬のリーマン・ブラザーズ破綻から1年を経過した本稿執筆時において，世界的な信用危機は一定の沈静化を見せており，主要国，中国，インド，ベトナムなど新興経済圏の株価も基本的に回復基調にある。

　しかし今後世界経済がこのままV字型の景気回復につながるかに関しては不確定要因が大きい。何よりも米国など各国が大規模な財政出動に依存した一時的な救済などのある意味ではなりふり構わない危機対策の遺産がのしかかっており，「ノーマル」な状態に何時，どのようなプロセスで戻るかという問題を残しているからである。どのような条件が熟した時に，その政策の結果からの「出口」，つまり「ノーマル」な状況に回帰する調整プロセスを深刻な経済危機を再度引き起こすことなくスムーズに通過し得るかという複雑な課題である。金利引上げ等の政策のタイミングは特に難しい。米国では景気回復の兆しが見えながらも高失業率が相変わらず消費回復のテンポを抑制している。日

---

[*]　帝京大学経済学部教授。

本ではデフレ問題が浮上しているが，他方では超金融緩和政策がキャリー・トレード，商品投機などを通じ，構造的な過剰流動性インフレを準備しつつあるのではないかという懸念もあり，いつまでも金融の超緩和政策を維持することに対する不安もくすぶっている。キャリー・トレードによる中国，インド，ベトナムなどでの資産インフレも真剣に懸念されている。世界経済が「ノーマル」な状況に復帰するまでには，もう一度大規模な調整期を経るかもしれないという，いわゆる「二番底」の懸念は消えていない。

　現今の経済不況をとりまく状況は1929年の恐慌期と比較されながらも，他方では異なる側面も多い。金融面では米国への一極集中を示す一方で，物的生産つまり実物経済分野では中国・インドなどの新興経済圏の比重が高まるという現象が併存している。後者は世界経済の構造的な多極化現象の進展である。そのなかで，いわゆる「デカップリング論」が唱えられた。中国，インドなど新興経済圏が，米国向け輸出市場の収縮や国際的な信用収縮という点で大きな影響を受けたことを前提にしつつも，他方ではそれだけでは説明できない独自の発展メカニズムが一定程度機能することに注目したものである。BRICsに代表される新興経済国が米国経済とは必ずしも歩を一にせずに，世界経済の収縮するなかでこれら地域が一定の独自の発展の軸となることを期待する議論である。「デカップリング論」の当否の判断基準はあくまで相対的であるが，一定の有効性を見せたことも事実である。

　インド政府が2009年11月30日に発表した同年7－9月期の実質GDPの前年同期比は7.9%増で，4－6月期の6.1%増を大幅に上回った[1]。当初の成長率見通しを前年比6.5%から上方修正する可能性が強まり，2008年度の対前年度比成長率の6.7%をうわまわる見通しさえ出てきている。インドの貿易額の対GDP比は40％程度であり，内需の動向は特に重要である。また農家消費が個人消費の約半分を占めている点も重要で，これが比較的堅調であったことが「デカップリング論」を支えていると見られる。ただし肝心の農業生産が2009年度に干ばつの影響をどれ位受けるかは懸念材料である。他方，IT関連，自動車，薬品などの輸出の伸長は比較的順調であった。本稿は「デカップリング論」などを考える上で必要なインド経済の構造的特性を考察することを課題にする。しかし紙数の制約もあり，しばしばインド論などで誤解されている点，不十分にしか理解されていない経済社会的の課題に考察の範囲を絞ることにする。

---

1)『日本経済新聞』2009年12月1日。

2. 経済危機と総選挙

　インド経済も 2008 年秋以降急速に深化した世界金融経済危機の直撃を受け, 米欧向け輸出が停滞・急落し, 株価の急落, 外資の流出, ルピーの低落を引き起こした。しかしインドへの危機の波及は, サブプライム・ローンに関連した証券化金融商品の購入を通じる直接的打撃を受けることはほとんどなかった。中国は条件を異にしており, 中国の金融機関, 国家ファンドは米国のデリバティブ関連金融商品あるいは海外の株式投資で直接的打撃もうけている。インドの場合は, 世界的な信用危機に伴う経済活動の収縮のインドへの波及という形で大きな打撃を受けた。成長の牽引力であった IT サービス, 特にアウトソーシング・サービス業は 600 億ドル規模の産業に肥大化していたが, 主たる輸出先である米国の需要鈍化が急速にマイナスの影響を及ぼした。商業銀行はサブプライム関連米国証券を購入していなかったため直接の打撃は受けなかったが, 流動性が急速にひっ迫したため貸し渋りに走り, またルピーの低落によりインド企業のルピー建て外貨建て債務返済負担が急増し経営を圧迫した。インド政府は 2008 年 10 月には経済政策の優先度をインフレ対策から景気刺激政策に急遽転換させた。2009 年 5 月には総選挙を控えていたため, インド政府は片方ではインフレ問題をも無視できなかったが, 景気対策も緊急の課題になったのである。卸売物価指数は急落したが, 消費者物価指数は必ずしもそれに対応して低下せず, インド政府と準備銀行 (中銀) は複雑なかじ取りを強いられた。連邦政府は石油関連を除く中央消費税を 4 ％引下げ, ガソリン, ディーゼル価格をそれぞれ 6 ％, 10% 引下げた。

　2008 年 10 月 20 日にインド準備銀行 (RBI) はレポ (中銀による商業銀行向け短期資金の貸付金利) を 9 ％から 8 ％に切り下げたが, その後 2009 年 4 月にかけて金利を 6 回にわたって引き下げ, 再買い入れ金利を 4.75% とした。インド・ルピーは対米ドルで約 10% 低落し, 2009 年 3 月には心理的な節目である 50 ルピー＝1 米ドルの水準を割っている。ムンバイ証券取引所の主要 30 社株価指数 SENSEX は 09 年初頭までに一時期半分まで低落した。

　2009 年 4 月 16 日から 5 月 13 日の間にかけて第 15 次連邦下院選挙が経済危機の渦中に行われた。周知のように議会制民主主義が定着しているインドにおいて, 選挙特に連邦下院選挙は経済政策の方向性を判断するうえで極めて重要な意味を持っている。連邦下院選挙では, 与党の国民会議派を核とする統一進歩連合 (UPA) と, ヒンドゥー民族主義を掲げるインド人民党 (BJP) を核とする国民民主連合 (NDA) との 2 大勢力の一騎打ちであった。他方, 選挙直前にインド共産党 (マルクス主義派) (CPI=M) を中心に一部の地域政党

を巻き込んだ 8 党連合による第 3 戦線も結成されていた。インド共産党（マルクス主義派）は 2004 年以降，少数与党連合の UPA を閣外で支持してきており，重要な政策決定を左右しうる立場にあった。しかし同党は 2008 年 8 月に締結された米印原子力協定への反対の立場を鮮明にし，UPA と袂を分かった。エネルギー部門を通じる米国の影響力拡大を懸念したものである。選挙では不況，悪化する失業，農業農民問題，テロ対策が重要な争点となった。

　この選挙で与党国民会議派は大方の予想に反して 1991 年以来の大きな勝利をかざった。総議席 543 のうち，会議派を核とする UPA は 262 議席を獲得し前回の 218 議席を大幅に上乗せした。これに対して BJP を中核とする NDA は 159 議席にとどまり前回より 27 議席減らした。第 3 戦線は CPI-M が大幅に議席を失ったことにより 59 議席にとどまった。5 月 16 日に選挙結果が発表されたが，これに対する証券市場の反応は極めて好意的なものであった。株価指数 SENSEX は急騰し，ムンバイ証券取引所は急騰に対処できず，1875 年に創設されて以来，史上初めてという取引停止措置をとらざるを得なかった。バーラト重電機社の株式は 33％上昇した。ルピーも対ドルで 3.3％も跳ね上がり，47.78 ルピーとなった[2]。これは 1986 年 3 月以来最大の上昇幅である。インド経済界および外資の好意的な反応は，国民会議派政府が経済政策をより規制緩和の方向に進めるであろうと期待したためである。

　それまで UPA 第 1 次マンモハン・シング内閣は，インド共産党（マルクス主義派）やインド共産党などの左翼政党の閣外支持を政権存立の条件としており，経済政策でも規制緩和・自由化には一定の枠がはめられていた。会議派の勝利と左派政党の後退のため，第 2 次シング内閣が保険業，年金基金運営，小売業への外資導入自由化を受け入れるという期待が高まった。しかし外資の期待は当面，過大であったことが判明した。ウォルマートなどの外資によるスーパーや量販店への参入禁止は当面維持されることになった。単一ブランド品をあつかう専門店には外資が出資できることになっているが，スウェーデンの家具資本イケアは 2009 年 6 月インド出店計画を白紙撤回した[3]。選挙の勝利と経済自由化の加速化を短絡的に結びつける見方は，インド社会と政治が置かれている条件を見落としている。常に選挙による洗礼を受けるインド議会主義の視点からすれば，与党国民会議派は経済危機にある社会の不満に敏感にならざるを得ないからである。国民会議派は企業家の利益を代弁するが，同時に多様

---

2) Pooja Thakur, India Stocks, Rupee, Bonds Surge on Congress Win; Shares Halted, May 18, http://www.bloomberg.com/apps/news.
3) 同上。

な階層の利益を反映させざるを得ない政党でもある。

インドは連邦国家であり，州の権限も農業分野などで大きい。州議会選挙対策も重要な課題である。当面の政策志向は外資自由化よりも，中小企業さらに農業に対する配慮を優先し，社会的安定性の維持などの政治的配慮も重要である。選挙直後から再度インフレ対策を視野に入れた政策がとられ始めたことも注目される。7月28日には金利据え置きを発表しインフレを意識する一方，景気刺激政策は財政政策に依存するという微妙なバランスをとろうとしてきた[4]。

また新たに考慮に入れるべき条件として，今回の経済危機の経験がある。海外からのポートフォリオ投資を特定の証券会社に限定するなど資本短期資本移動の自由化がまだ不十分だったことが，結果としてインドの金融機関とインド経済への打撃を少なくしたという評価は，金融自由化のテンポを緩める方向に政策を誘導している[5]。インドの外為管理制度は柔軟な管理システムといわれる。1992－93年度からは二重為替制度という独自のフロート制度をとっている。これは「公式レート」と「市場レート」の2本立てで，後者によって「公式レート」が規定される関係となっている。しかし完全なフロート制ではなく，必要に応じて当局の介入がある。1994年8月19日からIMF8条国に移行し経常取引における交換性が保障されている。現段階でインド企業は5億ドルまでの対外投資，対外債務の支払いは自由であり，個人では年間20万ドルまで海外資産，株式等を購入できる。金は無制限に輸入が認められている。インド民間銀行に対する外資出資に関しては，準備銀行が指定した民間銀行のみに外資出資を認めていたが，外資系銀行によるインド民間銀行の買収禁止は当面継続されることになった。資本取引に関しては，最終的には完全な交換性を目指してはいるが，そのプロセスは慎重に進められるとみられる。他方，農村・農業の相対的遅れがインド経済の全体的成長のなかで一層の格差拡大をもたらしているという意識も強まっており，性急な規制緩和がもたらす政治的コストに対して政治家は敏感になっている。2009年8月に行われた日本の衆議院選挙において，各政党の「マニフェスト」が従来になく話題を呼んだが，インド的政治風土において選挙綱領に対する関心は，ある意味では日本より深い。公約を実行するかどうかは，時期の選挙に影響するという認識は各政党の間で共有されている。

また，特に2009年はインド各地で干ばつが見られ水不足が心配されており，特にサトウキビ先物価格はICE（ニューヨーク商品先物市場）で69%も上昇

---

[4] *Reserve of India, Annual Survey,* Aug.21, 2009.
[5] 『日本経済新聞』2009年9月21日。

し，インド人の食生活に不可欠な砂糖価格をつりあげている。インドは最大のサトウキビ生産国の一つであるが，同時に最大の輸入国でもある。ゴールドマン・サックスのエコノミストはインフレ対策のためインドはルピー切り上げを容認しており，同年9月18日現在での1ドル＝48.135ルピーからさらにルピー高が進むと推測している。「12億ドルの人口のうち75％が1日2ドルに満たない所得で生活している現状ではインフレ問題は政策当局者にとっては極めて重要な課題である」と指摘される。

3．デカップリング論と農村の社会問題

　経済危機のインドへの影響は相対的に軽微かも知れないが，その影響は階層によって異なる。特に政府が意識するのは低所得層へ与える実質所得減あるいは物価上昇のダブルパンチである。あまり報道されていないが，ナクサライト問題がインド政治のなかで再浮上している。ナクサライトは別名「毛派共産主義者」の諸グループを指し，1967年頃に中国の文化大革命などと時期を重ねる形で活動が始まった。毛派とされるのは毛沢東の「農村から都市を包囲する」という革命戦略を掲げているためで，ナクサライトの呼称はサンタル部族が反乱を起こした西ベンガル州のナクサルバリに由来する。ナクサライトはインド共産党（マルクス主義）やインド共産党の議会重視主義に反対して，農山村を拠点に地主・高利貸しさらに治安当局に対する武力闘争を通じる政権奪取を目標としてきた。

　マンモハン・シング首相はしばしば，「（毛派共産党は）インドにおける唯一のしかし最大の治安問題」と発言している[6]。また「（全般的な）経済成長のなかでの『離れ小島』を拠点としている」と述べている。毛派は2005年には1600件の事件を引き起こしており，699人を殺害している。インド経済でもっともセンシチブな分野が農業・農村問題であるが，毛派の諸グループの活動拠点はインド内陸部の主として部族地域である。インドにおけるこの極左勢力の拡張には3つの要因があると思われる。第1に，農山村，特に山岳地域の部族地域での貧困の問題が強く意識されるようになっている，第2に，ネパールの毛派共産党が10年あまりの武装闘争の結果，08年に王政打倒を実現するとともに政権を獲得したことである。ネパールでの成功がインドの毛派を勇気付けたことは間違いない。冷戦崩壊後において，グローバル経済の「周辺部」に共産主義を掲げる勢力が活動の場を見出しているのである。なおイン

---

6) Ved Marwah, India in turmoil, Rupa Co., New Delhi, 2009, p.93.

ドの諜報組織である RAW（情報・分析部）はインド国内に対する外部の毛派への支援は認められないとして，中国を含む外部勢力の支援の存在は否定している[7]。ただしインドの毛派の活動はネパールとの国境にも展開しており，ネパールの毛派との接触はあり得る。第3に，最近，この多様なインドの毛派諸グループの間の統合・共同行動の動きが強まっていることである。特に2004年9月には，活動地域が異なるMCCI（インド毛派共産主義者センター）とPWG（人民戦争グループ）の二つの主要毛派グループが統一され，指導部の一元化が進み始めた。これが毛派の活動を活発化させている。2008年の内務省報告によると毛派諸グループはインド全28州のうち23州で活動しており，グループ数は39，武装メンバーは総計約10万人と推計されている[8]。主要な活動拠点は，ビハール，チャッティスガール，ジャールカンド，オリッサ，マハーラーシトラ，アーンドラ・プラデーシというインド内陸部諸州である。山岳地域あるいは部族地域が主要な活動舞台であり，部族民や指定カースト（不可触民），零細小作農民，土地なし農業労働者など経済社会的に抑圧されている階層への働きかけと組織化を行ってきた。インド内で鉄鉱石など鉱物資源が集中している地域と重なっており，毛派はしばしば鉄道輸送などを襲撃・妨害して交通網に打撃を与える作戦をとってきた。チャッティスガール州は2000年にマディヤ・プラデーシュ州から分離して別州となったところであるが部族民が多く，そこでのアブジュマード地域ではインド軍も入れない毛派の「解放区」が存在している。また，2000年にビハール州から分離して別の州となったジャールカンド州も毛派の活動が見られるが，そこの人口に占める部族民の比率は27%にも達している。インドの毛派の運動で注目されるは，禁酒運動のような社会浄化運動も同時に展開していることである。インドにおいては憲法上の規定によって「指定カースト（SC）」（不可触民）と「指定部族（ST）」は公務員採用，大学入試，あるいは被選挙権などで特別枠あるいは優遇措置を受けているが，現実には最低賃金法で規定された水準以下の賃金で働く農業労働者も多く，毛派の活動拠点となりうる地域が内陸部に広がっている。インド連邦政府が農業・農村問題を重視するのは，一般的な経済発展の陰で格差拡大によるしわ寄せを受けている階層の利益をある程度考慮にいれざるを得ないからである。インド憲法によれば治安・警察は州政府の管轄事項であるが，毛派勢力の伸張は全インド的規模で取り組むべき課題であるとする認識が強まっている。現段階で毛派がインドの政治体制そのものを転覆する能力を有している

---

7) Ibid., p.141.
8) Ibid., p.146.

とは思われないが、毛派の伸長は政治的警告の意味を持っている。

インドにおいてGDPに占める農業の比重は1950-51年度の55.4%から、2007-08年には18.5%にまで低下している。農産物が輸出額に占める比重は約15%、農産物加工が輸出額に占める比重は約20%である。しかし農業の重要性を示すものは、インド人の65-70%、つまり3分の2が何らかの形で農業に生計を依存していることである。GDPと人口に占める農業部門の比重のアンバランスこそ、インド経済における最大の問題点の一つを示している。換言すればインドの貧困が集中しているのは農業・農村部門ということになる。GDPの産業別構成を見ると、農業部門の低下にもかかわらず工業部門の比重が伸びず、むしろサービス産業肥大化の傾向が見られる。このことは農村における過剰人口を工業分野で吸収する余地があまりないことを意味しており、雇用問題の観点から深刻な問題を提起している。

インド政府は2002年に農業こそインド経済発展の牽引力であると宣言し、「第2次緑の革命」プログラムを発足させるなど、インド農業の質的見直しの方向を模索している。ITなどの輸出牽引型発展とならんで農業の発展による国内需要拡大の重要性を再確認するとともに、「持続可能な農業生産」へと政策的視点を移動させつつある。インド農業において、耕作地の6割の灌漑がモンスーンに依存しており、農業生産、農地の土地生産性、農業従事者の労働生産性が構造的に低水準であるという伝統的構造的問題は引き続き解決すべき問題として残っている。1960年代の「(第1次)緑の革命」は、改良品種の導入、肥料・殺虫剤の投入による大規模経営での生産増加を追求したものであった。この目的は一定程度達成され、インドの食料自給度の達成がうたわれることになった。しかし、水不足・環境悪化問題を含め、「(第1次)緑の革命」の持続可能性が次第に問われるに至っている。「第2次緑の革命」では、化学肥料に換えてバイオ肥料の導入、化学殺虫剤に代わるバイオ殺虫剤の導入、水資源の保全、バランスのとれた作物パタン・組み合わせなど、いわゆる有機農業の導入を重視している。インドの独立運動を社会改革と結合させて大衆的基盤に置こうとした故マハートマ・ガンディーは、その「建設的プログラム」のなかで、農村における衛生概念の普及と人糞の肥料化を結合させようとした。その意味で、有機農業の考え方はガンディーの農村復興思想の再現という側面を持っている。インド農業は「第2次緑の革命」を通じて、農村での雇用拡大、都市と農村の格差是正を求めている。他方、農村・農業が相対的に遅れているといっても、農村でも購買力は全体としては徐々に高まっていることも事実である。輸出志向発展では吸収・解決し尽くせない農業・農村問題は、イン

表1　中国経済とインド経済の比較

	中　　国	イ ン ド	摘　　要
人　口	約13億人	約11億人	
面　積	960万平方 km	329万平方 km	
GDP	約3兆4,000億ドル	約1兆661億ドル	2007年
一人あたり GDP	2460ドル	823ドル※	2007年
輸　出	1兆2180億ドル	1281億ドル	中国2007年　インド2006年
輸　入	9558億ドル	1913億ドル	中国2007年　インド2006年

※インドは1000ドルを超えたという推計もある。
出所：外務省資料など。

ドの経済発展戦略における大きな挑戦である。

4．中国経済と比較したインド経済

　ここで，「デカップリング論」の主柱である中国とインドを大雑把に比較してみよう。

　上記の表から何を読み取ることができるだろうか。

　第1に，人口規模を見ると中国の方がほぼ2億人程多いが，両国の人口調整政策の相違を見ると，インドの人口は近い将来中国のそれを凌駕すると見られる。それだけではなく，中国の人口構成の老齢化のテンポが速いと見込まれるのに対し，インドでは若年層が今後とも厚く，これが労働力に動員できれば成長にとってプラスであり，動員できなければ経済にとって負担となるという関係になっている。

　第2に，GDP（国内総生産）および一人あたり GDP を見ると，インドは中国の約3分の1となっている。両国の面積比もほぼ3対1となっている。中国の現段階における圧倒的優位性は明らかであるが，問題は今後，経済規模の格差が拡大するのか，縮小するのか，ほぼ現状維持のままで続くのかであろう。

　第3に，貿易額を見ると，輸出においては中国がインドの約10倍，輸入では中国がインドの5倍となっている。これは中国経済の方がそれだけ世界経済に統合されている度合が大きいことを意味している。これはインド経済にとって内需の比重が相対的に高いことを意味し，それだけ内向き経済体制を残している。貿易収支を見ると，中印は対照的であり，中国が出超（輸出超過）であるのに対して，インドは入超（輸入超過）となっている。同時に中印間の貿易額は着実に伸長している。中国の方が外貨準備を蓄積しており，中国の国

家ファンドの役割が非常に大きくなっているのに対して，インドは国家ファンドを設立して本格的に活動させる余地はまだない。人民元は国際通貨の一つとしての潜在的可能性があるが，インド・ルピーは現段階では議論の対象にはなりえない。

以上の数字を見る限り，現時点での中国の優位性は明らかであり，その点から見る限り，インドが一人当たりの所得水準で中国に追いつくのはまだ先の話になる。しかしインド経済がもはや無視できないことは 2009 年 4 月初めの 20 カ国地域諸脳会合 G20 に中国とともに参加し，シング首相は「保護貿易主義台頭に対する懸念」を表明し，世銀，IMF などの運営に対する発言権を強める動きでも明らかである。中印比較経済論は興味あるテーマであるし，政治・国際関係・社会・文化・歴史・価値観まで含めた総合的な課題である。ここでは，両国の比較を考える上で，いくつかの視点を示唆するにとどめる。

（1）政治文化と制度

インドと中国を比較する場合，しばしばインドは「民主主義」，中国は「共産主義」というレッテルで議論されることがあった。しかし政治文化としては，インドは議会制民主主義，中国は共産党一党支配と見るほうが比較し易い。より具体的にいえば，政策決定のプロセスの相違が重要であろう。このプロセスの相違こそ，中印両国の経済政策を比較するうえで有効なキーワードとなる。そのなかで，筆者としてはインドの特徴は，「選挙による定期的な洗礼」，「法的マインドの高さ」，「司法権の独立」，「報道の自由」で説明されるように思われる。これはインドの政治風土の持つ積極的な側面であり，これはある意味では通常の「先進国」と比較しても進んでいる側面を有する。他方，このことはポピュリズムへ堕する危険性，選挙コストの高さ，訴訟過多社会，政策決定にかかる時間など一連のコストがかかるという問題点を随伴している。インド経済の構造的問題としての財政赤字の原因には州政府がかなり関与しているが，これはポピュリズム的政策と無関係ではない。政治文化の積極面に関して言えば，環境問題に関しては住民運動がその悪化をチェックする役割を果たしており，チェック・アンド・バランスの機能が生きている。インドは NGO・NPO 天国といわれているように，民間諸組織の活動も極めて活発である。

それに対して，中国は政治権限が共産党に集中している。しかし現実にはそれほど単純ではなく，党内にも複数の潮流が存在しうるが，概して政策決定，執行などにかかる時間が短いという有利な側面を持っている。しかし大衆運動が抑制されている現状では，環境破壊などに対する住民側のチェック機能はインドなどよりは遅れる可能性がある。どちらのシステムが長期的で「持続可能

な」経済発展にとって有効かの判断は難しいが、重要なことは両国とも独自の政治風土の伝統を有していることである。インドの現在の政治文化も歴史的に形成されてきたものであり容易に変更できるというものではない。端的にいえばインドは、シンガポール、韓国などがとったような「権威主義的」経済発展モデルは、当初から適用できないということである。議会制民主主義を前提としない経済発展モデルを構築することは非現実的であり、その点にインドの独自の発展モデルが存在することになろう。

インド経済を考える上で無視できない重要な事実は、インドの開発戦略、5カ年計画の優先度と問題点など、民族運動時代、独立後の各節々で専門家の間で激しい論争が行われてきたことである。その論争の当事者はインド国内だけではなく海外においても著名なインド人エコノミストを巻き込んだものであり、それは海外のエコノミストをも刺激するという意味で国際的な性格を持つものでもあった。米英で一線に立って活躍しているインド人経済学者ジャグディッシュ・バグワティーやアマルティア・センなどもインドの経済発展戦略に関して発言してきた。経済開発戦略の実施過程で生まれる問題点が、時間がかかっても論争を通じて修正されるという「民主主義」のメカニズムが機能している点が重要であって、それがインドの経済政策とその経済を理解するためのひとつのカギとなっている。

（2）インドにおける経済計画と「混合経済体制」

中国とインドはソ連の計画経済の影響を受けたという点で類似している。インドは強い権限を有する計画委員会（議長は首相）の下で、5カ年計画を実施し、それに基づいて国家資本投資を行ってきた。インドが独自の開発戦略のもとに経済発展を具体的に打ち出したのは、第2次5カ年計画（1955／56年度－1960／1961年度）であり、ネルー首相とそれを理論的に補佐した統計学者マハラノビスの名前をとって「ネルー・マハラノビス・モデル」と呼ばれる。これは国家資本の計画的投入による輸入代替型重工業優先政策であった。この開発戦略が採用されたのには多様な時代的背景がある。ひとつは「自由主義」的経済政策が英国の利益に寄与し、インドの経済発展に結びつかなかったという歴史的経験（特に第1次大戦に至る時期）、ソ連の経済計画、特に第2次5ヵ年計画の成功がネルーのようなインドの独立運動指導者に与えた影響、国家の経済発展における役割の重要性に関して具体的内容に関しては差異があるにせよコンセンサスが存在していたことなどである。現在は第11次5カ年計画（2007－2012年）中であり、年率9％の成長目標を掲げている。

計画委員会を導いてきた輸入代替重工業化戦略に対する評価には否定的な評

価が多い。しかし筆者はインフラ整備など今日の経済発展の基礎を作り上げる上で果たしてきた役割，基礎的科学技術発展など，肯定的な側面を含め，慎重な評価が必要ではないかと考えている。なお 1991 年以降の経済自由化の時期においても，計画委員会の役割は重要で，特に大規模プロジェクト投資を勧告する権限を持っており，遅れている道路，港湾，空港，電力などインフラ部門での国家投資の推進役となっている。もうひとつ計画委員会とならんで重要な経済関連委員会は財政委員会であり，数年に一度，中央と州の財源配分方式などを再検討し勧告案を出すという重要な機能を果たしてきた。インドは連邦政府と州政府の権限分割を憲法によって規定しており，連邦管轄事項，州管轄事項，（連邦・州の）共管事項の 3 分野に分割している。農業などは州に専属し，工業・電力・労働などは共管事項となっているが，州政府の経済発展に果たす役割も極めて重要である。なお，中央・地方関係は中国もインド同様の問題を抱えており，両者の経験交流は双方にとって有益である。

　他方，インドが中国と異なるのは，独立当初から財閥・独占まで形成したインド民族資本の役割の大きさであり，それを前提に公有部門と民間部門が併存するという「混合経済体制」（ネルー首相は「社会主義型社会」と命名）を目指してきた。政府の政策は，金融部門などいくつかの例外を除いて国有化には慎重であり，その結果インド経済においては「市場経済」の論理が相当程度生きてきている。もっとも巨大民間企業は自由に投資計画を実施できたわけではなく，一連の独占規制・投資規制（ライセンス制度）のもとで政府の許認可権の下で一定の制約（官許体制）を受けてきた。しかし民間資本を含む国内市場での競争は，経営改革・技術開発を促し，各資本の独自のカラーと経営ノウハウを生み出してきた。これに対して中国の大企業や同グループは，政府の統制・支援が強いために，政府の経済財政政策との関連が極めて重要である。インドの民間企業は政府との関係を重視しつつも，必ずしもそれに依存せずに独自の発展戦略を展開してきており，新興財閥リライアンス・グループ，ターターなどの老舗財閥，ラクシュミ・ミッタルの国際的鉄鋼資本が，海外企業の買収，海外直接投資などでも，活発な動きを見せている。内外で著名な個別企業名ブランドはインド民間部門での有力企業の強みとなっている。

　他方，インド財閥の急成長の陰に企業ガバナンスの課題も浮上している。経済危機に際して同族企業の杜撰経営が表面化するケースも少なくはない。IT関連有力企業インフォシスでの杜撰ガバナンスはその一例である。家族・親族など閨閥，宗教集団やカースト，出身地域などの共通性などが財閥を形成する上での結束軸となっている。その結束がプラスに働く面がある一方，閉鎖性を

表2　対インドFDI流入額推移（年度ベース，億ドル）

2004—05	2005—06	2006—07	2007—08	2008—09	2009—10※
60.5	89.6	228.2	343.6	351.6	104.9

※2009年4月―同年9月。

　生み出し企業経営の近代化を阻害しているケースも少なくない。また身内争いの結果，巨大企業グループが経済的論理とは異なる理由で分割されるケースもある。最近大きな話題を呼んでいるのが，インド最大の新興財閥で関連企業売上高がインドのGDPの1割にも相当するといわれたリライアンス・グループが，2008年に兄弟間の角逐によって分裂した事件である。1代で巨大財閥をつくりあげてきた創設者の死去に伴い，アンバーニ家一族の内紛が起き，後継者の二人の息子兄弟が遺産相続争いを引き起こした。結局母親の仲裁で同企業グループは二つの企業グループに分割され，兄のムケシュ・アンバーニは，石油と石油化学，繊維，不動産，ベンチャー，小売部門を主として引き継ぎ，弟のアニル・アンバーニは電力，電気通信の分野を引き継いだ。しかし問題はグループ企業の分割だけでは終わらなかった。両グループの間のガス取引を巡る価格争いが起き，ついに紛争は最高裁にまで持ち込まれている。この争いが両企業グループの経営に与えた否定的な影響については言うまでもないが，今日双方とも取り巻きの有力政治家が抱えており，全国的な広がりを持つ政治問題まで引き起こしている。なお，ターター，ビルラーなどの老舗巨大財閥においては，このような問題があっても内部でコントロールすることに成功しており，そこに老舗財閥と新興財閥の相違が示されている。

　インドに対する外国直接投資はインドの優良企業を選別する形で行われているケースが多い。1998年にはインドのFDI受入額は全世界の10％以下に過ぎない110億ドル水準であったが，当時中国はすでに2080億ドルのFDIを受け入れていた。2008−09年度のインドのFDI流入額は352億ドルで2009年には世界全体のFDIの受入国では世界第3位となり，存在感を強めている。

　対インドFDI流入額（2000年4月−09年9月の累積額）を国別比率で見ると，モーリシャス（44％），シンガポール（9％），米国（8％），英国（6％），オランダ（4％），日本（3％），ドイツ（3％），フランス（1％），アラブ首相国連邦（1％）となっている。モーリシャスが突出しているのは，インドとモーリシャスが相互間投資税を無課税にしているためと，在外インド資本がモーリシャスを媒介にして対印投資を行っているためである。英連邦と在外インド人地域が対印FDIで重要な役割を果たしているのがわかる。

（3）統計事情と賃金体系

　途上国経済を分析するうえで直面する問題のひとつは統計数字の信頼性の欠如である。そのなかでインドの経済統計は，他の多くの途上国と比較して信頼性がかなり高いと見られる。これは5カ年計画策定過程が，政治・メディアなど公開の場で統計数字を含めて議論されることが多いこと，統計が賃金体系と連動しており物価など指数に対する一般の関心が高いこと，統計学の分野でインドは先進的であることなどのためである。そのため政治的配慮によって統計を人為的に操作する余地が比較的少ないことを意味する。例えば賃金体系と消費者物価指数の連動性は，統計の正確さを求める社会的圧力を強めている。業種によって異なるが繊維産業などの労働者の賃金は本給と物価手当（DA）で構成されており，DAは消費者物価指数に連動するよう労使間で合意されている。しばしば本給と物価手当額が同じくらい物価手当の比重が大きく，そのため労働者の消費者物価指数に対する関心は著しく高い。労使間で物価手当の算定方式が交渉事項になることも珍しくはない。さらに消費者物価指数を算定する際，階層別消費者物価指数を算定している地域が多い。例えば，消費者物価指数であっても，肉体労働者向け，ホワイトカラー向け，農業労働者向けの3本を算定している州が多い。これは階層によって消費生活が著しく異なるという現実を反映させようとする方向である。

5．社会的流動性とカースト問題

　経済発展と社会変動の関係は，途上国の経済分析において最も複雑な問題の一つである。インドではカースト集団の政治化と宗派的アイデンティティーの先鋭化が問題となっている。インドの経済発展を考察するに際して，カースト制度を障害として指摘されることが多い。その見方は労働市場が技術・産業発展に対応できない硬直的なものであるという認識につながる。この見方が全く間違いであるとは言わないが，インドの現状を誤解に導く非常に固定したステレオタイプされた見方だということは強調した方がいい。これはインド社会と経済の相互関係の動態的理解を妨げる一因となっているように思われる。結論的にいえば，現在のインドの経済発展にとってカーストは主要な障害ではないと筆者は考えている。職業がカースト毎に固定されていて動かせないという必ずしも正しくない理解は，現実の職業選択におけるインド人の行動様式の柔軟性を見る目を曇らせている。

　これはインド社会においてカーストが重要ではないという意味では全くない。カーストが現在のインドにおいて重要な意味を持ってきているのは，カー

ストと職業との関係を過度の固定化ではない。別の意味で重要なのである。カーストが利益集団の単位として利権獲得運動を政治的レベルで展開しており，それが公務員などの労働市場を歪めている点である。利権とは具体的には公務員採用や大学入学に際して特定の割当枠を主として指す。特定の選挙区で立候補権を指定カースト〔不可触民〕や指定部族に限定する制度）の問題がある。この優遇措置は社会的差別を受けてきた不可触民の社会進出を促すうえで，インドの現状からすれば当面不可欠な社会政策として一定の積極的意味がある。しかし問題は不可触民以外の他のカースト集団が同様な優遇措置を要求するようになったことである。不可触民より上に位置づけられる「ヒンドゥー・カースト」のなかで相対的に低いと見られるカースト集団が，自らを「後進カースト」として規定して，指定カースト同様の優遇措置を要求して，それを州政治のレベルである程度実現させてきた。「後進カースト」といっても土地改革などで社会的地位を向上させた村落の支配カーストの場合が少なくない。このような形での「カースト政治」こそ，カースト問題の今日的核心である。社会的差別に対する不可触民の抵抗運動は強まる一方，不可触民以外のカースト集団がカーストを結合軸とする利権獲得運動を拡大してきているのである。カーストと職業との関連性は縮小傾向にある一方，あるいは「平等化」が徐々に進む一方で，利権獲得を巡る集団単位としてのカースト間の対立はむしろ激しくなっている。

　カースト制度のなかで最大の問題は不可触民である。重要なことはかれらが現状と「運命」に甘んじているわけではなく，社会的政治的地位向上を求めるダイナミックな動きを見せていることである。「ダーリット〔抑圧された〕」と自己規定する不可触民のダーリット文学もインド文学の重要なジャンルとして定着している。そこでは現状の告発と改革への強い意志が表現されている。憲法上で指定カーストに対しては法的な優遇措置が与えられており，その中には立候補権を指定カーストにのみ限定する選挙区制度も存在している。それを利用する一部の不可触民出身者の政治進出も見られる。インド最大の人口（1億7000万人）を抱えた政治的には最も重要な州であるウッタル・プラデーシ州で，2007年5月以降州首相をつとめているのは不可触民出身でBSP（インド社会党）党首のマヤワティ女史である。彼女にとって4回目の州首相のポストであるが，BSPは不可触民の地位向上をめざして結成された不可触民を主体とする政党である。マヤワティは将来のインド首相のポストをねらう野心的政治家のひとりでさえある。英フィナシャル・タイムズ紙の過去10年間の世界を動かした17人の有力政治家の一人にマヤワティが含まれている[9]。また

---

9) The Financial Times, Dec.29, 2009.

2007年7月以降，インド大統領の地位にあるのは不可触民出身のプラティバ・デヴィシン・パティル女史である。また仏教徒の比重が極めて低いインドにおいて，新仏教徒といわれる宗派集団が増加しているが，それは不可触民カーストのひとつマハールが，ヒンドゥー教から逃れることによって地位向上をはかろうとした運動の結果である。

だからといって圧倒的多数の不可触民がインド社会で農業労働者など農村での最貧層の重要な構成部分を占めていることもまた事実である。現実的課題は，カースト制度を廃止することではなく，カースト間の不当な差別をなくす，特に不可触民に対する差別をなくすことに置かれている。カーストは何か法律で無効を宣言してなくなるようなものではない。カーストを巡るイデオロギー闘争は長い歴史を持つものであり，インド思想史を貫く一つの赤い糸のようなものとなっている。インドの独立運動の指導者であったマハートマ・ガンディーでさえ，不可触民（彼は「神の子（ハリジャン）」と読んだ）に対する差別撤廃に努力したが，カースト制度を廃止しようと提案したわけではない。またカーストはポルトガル語の「カスタ」から来ているように西欧社会がインド社会を規定した用語であり，インド人が命名したものではない。インドで数千ともいわれるジャーティーという階層区分を指す言葉に相当する。日本でしばしばカースト制度として混同されている4つのヴァルナ（ブラーフマン，クシャトリア，ヴァイシャ，スードラ）制とは別の起源であると見られる。カーストの役割も時代によって変化していると見られ，英国支配時代に以前は流動的であったカースト間関係が，植民地政策のなかで「固定化」が進行したとする有力な学説もある。

あまり知られていないが，カースト的社会秩序（特に婚姻・会食など）が必ずしもヒンドゥー教徒の世界だけではなく，教義的には否定されているはずのムスリム（イスラーム教徒），キリスト教徒，スィーク教徒の間でさえ残存しているケースが多い。それだけインド社会における聖・不浄の観念を軸とするカースト意識が強固であることがわかる。この事実を非ヒンドゥー教徒の当事者たちが隠すことが多いため，日本を含む外国人のなかではインドのキリスト教徒やイスラーム教徒社会はカーストとは無縁のように誤解している者が少なくない。

6．宗派的アイデンティティーの先鋭化と国民統合

カースト問題と全く無関係ではないが，もうひとつ重要な独自の問題として宗派間対立の激化がある。言うまでもないが，宗教が異なると当然対立する

という見方は社会科学以前の俗論である。今日，宗派主義コミュナリズム（自らの宗派的利益を排他的に主張する運動），特にヒンドゥー民族主義の危険性をどれくらい抑制できるかが，インド経済を支える政治的なインフラを左右する重要な条件となっている。それには1991年以降の特別な事情と関連している。規制緩和と門戸開放政策に舵を切り，高成長の道を歩み始めたインドにおいて，そのプロセスと「新たな」政治的宗派主義の台頭が時期的に重複してからである。1992年のウッタル・プラデーシ州アヨーディアでのインド人民党（BJP）系のヒンドゥー過激派のモスク破壊，2002年2月のグジャラート州で列車内でのムスリム殺害事件などは数百人以上の死者を出す宗派間対立を引き起こした。それまで弱小政党の一つであったヒンドゥー主義的民族主義政党であるBJPが大躍進し，1988年には連立政権ではあれ政権を奪う程に成長したことは，独立後のインドの政治における画期的な事件であった。この理由に関しては定説があるとは言えないが，急激な経済発展に伴う社会的変動と関連していることは間違いない。コンピューターのプログラマーなど先進的分野の職種で働く中間層のヒンドゥー教徒の間で宗派的過激主義，具体的にはイスラーム教徒を非インド的として排斥する思考スタイルが支持者を見出している。日本人の間では「近代化」と「脱宗教化」を当然のように考える見方が意外に多い。しかし，実態はそんなに単純ではない。排他的ヒンドゥー主義の台頭はイスラーム教徒やキリスト教徒の間で強い危機感を生んでいる。ここに今日のインドの政治・社会・経済の独特な絡み合いが凝集的に示されている[10]。元英国のフィナンシャル・タイムズのインド特派員（在任期間2001－2005）であったエドワード・ルーチェが著した『神々にもかかわらず―現代インドの奇妙な台頭（－The strange rise of India）[11]』では，経済発展と宗教への帰属意識への強化の併存を非常に鋭い目で現代インドの直面している中心的問題として指摘したものである。従来相互に対立してきた国民会議派を中心とするUPAの第1次マンモハン・シング政権を，インド共産党（CPI-M）を中心とする左翼勢力が閣外から支持するようになったのは，BJPの台頭をインドの国民統合を覆す最大の危機とみなしたためである。インドの国民統合の支柱である「世俗（政教分離）主義」が危機に瀕しているという認識からであった。多宗派集団が存在しているインドにとって「世俗主義」はそれをまとめ上げる

---

10) 近藤光博「インド政治文化の展開―ヒンドゥー・ナショナリズムと中間層」堀本武功・広瀬崇子編『現代南アジア③民主主義のとりくみ』173－194頁。
11) Edward Luce, "In spite of the Gods － The strange rise of modern India" Little Brown Book Group, London 2006.

原則である。その際，二つの誤解を解いておく必要がある。

ひとつはインドの「世俗主義」は，日本などの「政教分離主義」とは異なるインド独特なものだということである。インドの場合は，政治が宗教に関与すること，例えば宗教的偉人の銅像を建てることなどを禁止していない。そうではなく，インドの「世俗主義」は政府が主要な宗教に対して「平等に扱う」ことを求めている。もうひとつは国民会議派が「世俗主義」を掲げてきたのにもかかわらず，実際の政治行動では宗派主義あるいはカースト政治に妥協している会議派の政治家も少なくはないことである。地方政治のレベルではBJPとの境界が明確ではない会議派政治家も少なくはない。

従来，多人種，多民族，多宗教で構成される巨大なインドの国民統合を可能にしようとして試みられてきた政策には，議会制民主主義，インド的世俗主義，言語別州再編成，不可触民・部族に対する優遇措置などであった。インドにおいて西北部のジャンム・カシミール州と東部インドのナガランド，ミゾラム州などに分離主義運動があり，国民統合への挑戦となっていることは事実であるが，独立後のインドは国内の多民族の共存という課題は概して成功してきたといってよい。その主要な理由は1950年代半ば以降採用した言語別州再編成である。言語は各民族にとって根幹に属するアイデンティティーである。言語別州再編成によりインドを構成する民族の言語的要求を満たしたことは事実である。また公用語をヒンディー語に急いで統一しようとしてこなかったことも評価できる点である。多民族の国民国家を一つの公用語の統一させることによって国民統合が促進されるという考え方はインドのような多民族国家では極めて有害であって，国民統合に寄与するのではなくむしろ分裂を内向させる愚策である。特に今日的課題として重要なのは宗派間の対立を煽るイデオロギーを封じ込めること，経済的格差が過度に拡大しないように配慮することである。宗派対立は国内問題にとどまらず，印パ間の対立に連動する危険性に留意すべきであろう。インド内でのテロ問題も，何らかの形で宗派間問題が絡んでいるケースが著しく多いのである。

7．おわりに

インドの社会経済の「後進性」の残存を指摘することは容易である。しかし今後のインドの発展方向を見るためには，次の点に留意すべきであろう。第1に，機能している議会制民主主義の存在である。これは政策決定に時間がかかること，ポピュリズムに堕しやすい面を持っているが，社会的安定性と経済発展をバランスさせる機能を果たしている。第2に，言論の自由は知識集約型

産業の発展にとって有利な社会的インフラだということである。米国の証券業界が企業分析をインドにアウトソーシングしているケースが増えているが，政治的配慮を入れずに客観的に分析しうるインドの社会インフラを考慮にいれた側面がある。第3に，民間企業の長い伝統であり，一部には独自に技術開発を促進できる有名企業が存在していることである。また一部のインド企業は積極的に先進国の企業買収でも活躍している。日本の2008年度の対印直接投資額は8090億円で中国向けの6793億円を超えた。これは日本資本にとっては中国とは異なる独自の経験であると見られる。第4に，海外に開かれたエリートのコネクションである。また世界最大の鉄鋼資本（ルクセンブルク拠点）を抑えるラクシュミ・ミッタル，ペプシ・コーラのCEOインドラ・ヌーイ，米シティー・グループのパンディットはインド生まれのCEOであり，など国際級のビジネスマンを生み出している。第5に，宗派主義による対立を抑え，かつパキスタンとの関係を軸に，地域の政治的安定性の保持・強化の必要性である。

　しばしば中印経済を比較して中国の先進性が指摘される。経済規模，所得水準を含め，現段階において中国に一日の長があることは明白である。しかし，どこの国の経済であれ，現在の成長テンポが長期にわたって維持されることが保証されているわけではない。インド経済は2003年以降，投資の伸びが順調で新たな発展段階に入って来たが，それが世界経済の乱気流に巻き込まれたのが，ここ1，2年の動きである。中印両国とも成熟期に入っているわけでないから，まだ発展の可能性は大きい。しかし日本の高度成長期も一定の期間しか続かなかったように，長期間にわたる高度成長の継続が容易に実現できるほど安易ではない。また長期になればなるほど，政治的なサステナビリティーも重要な要因となってこよう。本稿において国民統合，宗派主義の問題に言及したのはそのためである。中印両国とも「中所得国」への到達までは成功するかもしれないが，さらに「先進国」型高所得国になるためには，経済社会構造の質的な転換を必要とするかもしれない。インドは人口の3分の1とも言われる膨大な貧困層を抱えている。確かにインド経済の全体としての発展が間接的に最貧層の消費水準を引き上げつつ面がある。しかし，貧困層の解消という課題を達成するには，どのような経済的社会的な面での質的変革が迫られているのかという視点がますます重要になってくるように思われる。

第4部　アジアの経済発展と世界経済危機
　　　──外国からの視点

第9章 アジア太平洋の地域統合の進展と世界金融危機（2008－2009年）

Chapter 9 The Progress of Regional Integration in Asia-Pacific and the Global Financial Crisis of 2008 - 2009

Hans C. Blomqvist [*]

Introduction

One of the main underlying reasons for the strong economic performance of the Asia-Pacific region during the last few decades is no doubt the liberalisation of world trade and foreign direct investments and the willingness and ability of most Asian countries to plug into this increasingly globalised economy. Because of this favourable experience, most countries in the region are staunch supporters of continuing multilateral liberalisation according to the principle of "most favoured nation" (MFN). Despite the fact that Asia-Pacific is already highly integrated, the process has been market-driven, however, until recently with little formalised organisation.

The share of intraregional trade of the total foreign trade of the region is now about 50 percent, and in absolute terms it has grown – with few exceptions – by double-digit figures after 1975 and 2001 (Das 2005, Ng and Yeats 2003). According to some measures, the intraregional trade concentration is higher in East Asia than in any other part of the world (Das 2005). Also in terms of foreign direct investment (FDI) the intraregional flows are today of utmost significance, making up about 50 percent of total flows (Hattari and Rajan 2008). The degree of financial integration is much lower than in the leading Western economies, however (see, e.g., Takagi 2009).

Even if de facto integration can be seen as a substitute for a formalised

---

[*] Professor, Hanken School of Economics, Helsinki and Vasa, Finland.

process we have now for some time been observing a clear tendency towards forging regional free trade areas (FTA) in Asia-Pacific, indicating that there is a limit to the benefits of informal integration and that a more institutionalised approach may be needed in order to fully utilise the potential gains from integration. These arrangements vary from very large and loose organisations, such as the Asia-Pacific Economic Cooperation forum (APEC), to bilateral and very specific FTAs, and their number is quite large.

Professional economists usually take a critical view of regional FTAs. Bilateral agreements, in particular, have been severely criticised. Using elementary economic theory, it is not hard to show that discriminating trade arrangements, such as FTAs, can well be inferior even to unilateral liberalization (for a brief summary of the arguments, see Blomqvist (2007)

Even supporters of regional trade agreements usually admit that the final goal is multilateral liberalisation at the global level. This view is predominant also in Asia. The WTO led process has slowed down, however, and encountered increasing resistance. A frequently used argument is therefore that an FTA somehow is a step on the way to multilateral liberalisation or at least a second-best solution if a global agreement is unfeasible. In particular, the growing importance of integrated production networks in the region (see, e.g., Kimura and Ando 2005) makes it difficult to wait for multilateral solutions. Bilateral agreements, in particular, have proliferated as a result. A priori, it is hard to believe that that the trend towards regional agreements would not have good reasons, even if traditional trade theory may not necessarily capture all of them. Moreover, regional agreements are made for many reasons other than trade-related welfare effects. By and large, politicians and many other participants in the public debate tend to be enthusiastic about the expected benefits of such arrangements.

While the economic development in Asia-Pacific has been very impressive it has not come without major hiccups. The Asian financial crisis in 1997−98 represented a serious disruption of a long period of very high growth rates in most of the region. While foreign trade and financial flows decreased during a short period after the crisis, no damage was done in the long term to the integration development. On the contrary, the crisis underscored the need for closer economic co-operation in the region.

The global financial crisis that erupted in 2008 has not, when this was written, had serious effects on the financial system in Asia, perhaps for the very reason that it is less integrated than in the West. On the real side the effect has been significant, though, because of the export-led growth strategy of these economies, but different countries have been hit differently. Overall, 2009 will be a year of slow economic growth, slower than any time since the Asian financial crisis in 1997-98. China, although increasingly dependent on exports, managed to keep up a growth rate of about 7 percent in 2009, while the very open economy of, e.g., Singapore has suffered a big setback, estimated at some 5 percent of GDP in 2009. Malaysia and Thailand, being very export-oriented countries, will also end up with a falling GDP this year. In Japan the GDP was forecast to fall by 3.5 percent (ADB 2009. The figures are forecasts made in mid 2009; the final results may differ from these estimates). The outcome has so far (October 2009) been strongly affected by an extraordinarily expansionary fiscal policy in all industrialised countries, however. This is likely to lead to a degree of recovery in 2010 but whether the world economy can keep up its momentum after the government measures have been phased out remains to be seen. The recovery after the Asian crisis of the 1990s was fairly fast because the rest of the world was not that badly affected. This time around the recession is global and it is not possible for Asia to recover entirely by its own means. Asia has not so far been able to decouple completely from the big Western economies like some observers used to think only a couple of years ago. However, Asia's large and growing share in the global economy makes it a key player in the recovery process.

The objective of this paper is to analyse the driving forces behind the proliferating FTAs in the Asia-Pacific region, and to make an assessment of how the present global recession may affect the developments.

Development of regional integration in Asia

The market driven integration in Asia-Pacific is characterised by the fact that several industries – those where a fragmented production pattern is practical – predominantly function as integrated networks that exceed national borders. This generates numerous trade transactions both between affiliates of multinational companies and between these and independent, local firms, which are often small and middle-sized companies (SMEs). The driving force of market-driven integration thus lies at the micro level, and is directly related to the profit-maximisation efforts of companies (Das 2005).

The networks are not, of course, unique for Asia, but nowhere else are they as prevalent and important as there. Moreover, they have developed very quickly, mainly during the last ten to fifteen years (Ando and Kimura 2003, Kimura and Ando 2005). Ng and Yeats (2003) estimate the intra-network trade in Asia at about one-fourth of total intraregional trade. According to Krumm and Kharas (2003) only four industries account for 38 percent of the intra-industry trade in Asia-Pacific, namely office machinery, telecommunication equipment, electronics and textiles and clothing. These are all industries where the final product can easily be decomposed and where networking in production can be expected to be feasible and advantageous. Kimura and Ando (2005), in turn, show that the trade share of "machinery" is very high in East Asia, and also that the share of components is large, for many countries at least 40 – 50 percent of total trade. They also find, for Japanese affiliates in Asia-Pacific, that over 90 percent of both purchases and sales take place within the region. The Monetary Authority of Singapore, in a study from 2003, arrived at the result that 78 percent of the export value from Asia to countries outside the region was partly manufactured in another country than the official exporter (Das 2005). All these figures are indicators of a large volume of trade in intermediate products across the borders in Asia. In this paper I suggest that the interest and needs of the multinational companies are important driving forces of the integration development in Asia-Pacific. These firms gain from liberalisation, but may have strong preferences as to how exactly this liberalisation should be carried out.

Hence the degree of de facto integration is high in Asia-Pacific. Despite this, Asia-Pacific is one of the least integrated parts of the world from the point of view of formal agreements. The idea of regionalisation took root among decision makers only in the 1990s, and even then the main reason was defensive thinking, a reaction to the integration developments in Europe and North America. The three large East Asian economies, Japan, China and South Korea (hereafter Korea) relied, until very recently, entirely on the multilateral WTO-led process. However, the rapidly increasing intraregional trade now adds to the weight of arguments speaking in favour of more formalised arrangements.

APEC was something of an exception from the general pattern of market-driven but informal integration in Asia-Pacific. Established in 1989 it was conceived in order to put pressure on the multilateral process by proceeding faster than the WTO, but not necessarily discriminating against non-members. The potential for doing this was good in a sense, since the organisation represents a very large part of the global production and trade (about 60 and 47 percent, respectively). APEC has agreed about free trade among the member states by 2010 (for developed countries) and 2020 (for developing countries) but its agenda is vague and the actual content of this commitment is rather diffuse. Partly because this it has not been recognised by the WTO as a formal institution for integration (Voon et al. 2005). Moreover, it has regularly been used as a political forum by the United States which has detracted attention from the economic issues. APEC has been helpful, however, as a forum for continuous dialogue between the members, and has initiated a large number of working groups, committees etc. which, at a general level, has facilitated economic co-operation.

The East Asian Economic Group (EAEG), proposed in 1990 by then Prime Minister Mahathir Mohamad of Malaysia was originally a non-starter. The initiative aimed at creating a counter force to the emerging trade blocs in other parts of the world and a common platform for the member states in e.g. multilateral trade negotiations. The EAEG was to be open and non-discriminating, but non-Asian countries were not to be eligible for membership. At that time it turned out to be impossible to form an organisation along those lines, however, mainly due to resistance from the US, which per definition was excluded from membership. The idea wintered, however, and turned up several years later as a loose grouping called ASEAN+3, to which we will return below.

The foremost example of formalised integration agreements in Asia is the ASEAN Free Trade Area (AFTA), the implementation of which started in 1993. Also in this case the most important driving force was the fear to be left behind in the rapid integration development in America and Europe. Another important reason was the insight that a large unified market is much more attractive for foreign investors than many small national markets with high trade barriers between them. AFTA is still not quite a fully-fledged FTA, since the tariff barriers have not been completely abolished yet. Moreover the bureaucracy involved in the implementation and especially applying rules of origin (ROO) is still an obstacle against realising the full potential of the agreement. Still the result is respectable, considering the political and economic tensions that have prevailed between the ASEAN member countries ever since the organisation was created. ASEAN has also initiated co-operation in foreign direct investment (FDI) and trade with services but much of this is still in its infancy. Moreover, ASEAN has many other goals than integration, and we need to remember that economic co-operation is a much wider concept than integration. In the long run, ASEAN intends to form an economic community, with free movements of goods, services and factors of production (Sen 2004:85-86). The implementation plans are still vague, though. The institutional infrastructure of ASEAN is weak and lacks, for instance, effective mechanisms for solving trade disputes between the member states. This is why the organisation sometimes appears to lack direction.

Besides the attempts at deepening integration in ASEAN, two other important trends have been salient during the last few years. One is the emergence of a larger entity, the so-called ASEAN+3, where "3" stands for China, Japan and Korea. The other one is the bilateral FTAs that are now proliferating in the region at a pace that almost seems to be out of control. ASEAN+3 is not yet an organisation proper but rather a process, which is co-ordinated by a unit in the ASEAN Secretariat and proceeds through meetings at various levels, including summits. To begin with, the grouping concentrated on financial co-operation in the wake of the Asian crisis

1997-98. Other forms of co-operation have gradually been taken up and at a summit in 2001 a working group report, proposing the formation of an "East Asian Community", was endorsed. A part of this vision is a FTA, encompassing the whole group (East Asian Vision Group 2001, Soesastro 2003). Parallel to this, ASEAN approved a programme in 2004 that aims at strengthening its relationships with its major trade partners, both within and outside the region (Killion 2004).

Consequently, the possibility of a large FTA that encompasses the whole East Asia must at least be considered, even if it is hardly imminent. Since an agreement would include several large players, a bloc that controls at least one-fourth of the world's production and trade may eventually emerge (Ng and Yeats 2004). It is important to remember, however, that a FTA is not enough for really "controlling" anything and that a deepening of the integration is difficult, if only for political reasons. It is fairly clear that the political will and the driving force of the initiative emanate mainly from the three Northeast Asian countries, not from ASEAN. The problem is that neither China nor Japan can take the lead, because of political antagonism, and in fact seem to be unable to form even an FTA among themselves and Korea. This is why ASEAN has had to play the role of hub, around which the co-operation evolves. Hence bilateral agreements have been made between ASEAN and each of three other countries, instead of trying to put together one agreement encompassing the whole region. Such a strategy may suggest that those bilateral agreements could be "building blocks" for a future regional FTA (cf. Soesastro 2003, 2006).

The development has been fastest in the case of ASEAN and China, where the parties concerned agreed on a free trade area in 2002 (with a formal agreement in 2004 (Killion 2005)), with a implementation horizon of 2010 (and 2015 for the newer members of ASEAN) (Lim 2003, Antkiewicz and Whalley 2004). The agreement concerns also other issues than trade, such as bilateral investment, simplification of customs procedures and mutual recognition of technical standards. A so-called early harvest clause is included as well, in order to sweeten the agreement for ASEAN. This entails early tariff reductions for agricultural products. Between Japan and ASEAN, an agreement on a "comprehensive economic partnership" took effect in December 2008 (Japan Times 2008) whereas negotiations with Korea were finalised in 2005, with the aim of abolishing or significantly reducing tariffs before 2009 (Asia Times, March 1st, 2005, Bilaterals.org 2009).

All these developments may be seen as a revival of Dr Mahathir's EAEG. Moreover, on the fringes of ASEAN+3 there are other discussions going on as well, more or less behind the scene. Australia and New Zealand both have recently entered a FTA with ASEAN and an agreement between ASEAN and India on trade in goods (TIG) was signed in August 2009 and will enter into force from 2010. Despite all this, and despite the upbeat rhetoric surrounding the discussion on these issues, some anxiousness can be clearly felt in ASEAN, particularly as far as the role of China is concerned. The fear of not being able to compete, given that the export structure of ASEAN and China at least superficially seem similar, and the risk of losing FDI from third countries are factors explaining this uneasiness (Tongzon 2005).

The other important development, besides regionalism, is the increasing proliferation of bilateral FTAs. These agreements are frequently made with trade partners outside the region. Singapore is the country that has taken the lead in this development. Tired of the slow progress of the multilateral and regional integration processes, the country has already concluded FTAs with, among others, Australia, New Zealand, India, Japan and the United States. Furthermore, discussions are going on with several other countries (see, e.g., Govt of Singapore 2009). Also Thailand, the Philippines, Malaysia and China have recently shown interest in bilateral agreements.

Drivers of regional integration

The standard workhorse when analysing welfare effects of regional integration is still the framework developed by Viner some 60 years ago (Viner 1950). The key concepts are trade creation and trade diversion. Regional agreements may create new trade, substituting for inefficient domestic production, between the partners, but they may also replace imports from a more efficient third country with imports from a member country. The outcome then depends on which one of these effects dominates.

If free trade is established between "small" economies trade creation will probably not result from an FTA (Panagariya 1999). This is because the domestic market price will not fall if the country continues to import from third countries. Consumption, domestic production and imports remain unchanged. A larger part of the imports will now emanate from member countries, however, at the expense of more efficient outsiders. The income from tariffs etc will be redistributed, from the government of the importing country to the exporters of the member countries. These effects are likely to be quite large, and certainly larger than the traditional "Harberger triangles" that also will result. The redistribution costs would, moreover, be more problematic the more heterogeneous the member countries are. This may partly explain the difficulties experienced when forming FTAs in Asia.

Unilateral liberalisation would cause no trade diversion, but some inefficient production would be crowded out by imports and the resources could be moved to more competitive production. The tariff income would be captured by a higher consumer surplus, so no income redistribution between countries would take place in this case. Hence this policy would be superior to regional free trade.

In order to work, an FTA must apply rules of origin, defining the share of a product's value that must emanate from within the FTA, to qualify for free trade. Besides introducing a great deal of bureaucracy these rules have other negative effects as well. Imports of components and other intermediate products from member countries is encouraged even though they may not be the best or most efficiently produced. The problems are multiplied if there are overlapping FTAs, which the now prevailing trend towards bilateral agreements leads to (the so-called noodle-bowl effect). Not least the administrative burden required by handling a large number of agreements may be overwhelming for poor countries and certainly uses up resources that could be utilised more productively elsewhere. The repercussions on third countries in the process of negotiating their own agreements are unpredictable and often undesirable.

The welfare effects outlined above may be modified if the assumptions of constant market prices and perfect competition are abandoned. In the former case, the terms of trade are improved by the formation of an FTA, which may lead to trade creation. For this to happen, the FTA needs to be "large" however. Furthermore, in a "large" FTA it is much more likely that the most efficient producer is a member country. For FTAs formed by relatively small, developing countries, this is a much less likely scenario. Abandoning the assumption of perfect competition allows for scale economies, which typically leads to increasing intra-industry specialisation and trade, and also mitigates some of the disadvantage of trade diversion. Thus this is a valid motive for regional integration, although multilateral integration would produce the same result. One may note also that scale economies are a likely reason for the development of the aforementioned production networks, whereas the networks, in turn, are a natural driver of regional FTAs.

Traditional integration theory does not at all take into account spatial consequences of integration. Agglomeration effects are a likely consequence of external economies of scale and lead to a concentration to a limited number of locations where the infrastructure is best developed. Production networks encourage this kind of concentration as well, since the transport and communication facilities that link the various production locations together tend to display external scale economies (Ando and Kimura 2003). Integration means, on the other hand, that countries that specialise in primary products, according to the principle of comparative advantages, may lose, as they may be deindustrialised and then lose their exposure to new knowledge and technologies.

The above discussion gave a rather gloomy perception of what regional integration can achieve. In spite of this, many arguments in favour of FTAs have been presented. Many go far beyond the mainly neoclassical framework of the previous discussion and are often difficult to either prove or reject. Some arguments are non-economic and relate to the countries' political and security situation.

Especially if an FTA is "large" and heterogeneous—like ASEAN+3— and the trade barriers are moderate from the beginning, trade diversion is unlikely to be a big problem. This is because the (approximately) most efficient producer of most goods is likely to be a member of the FTA and the deadweight losses that still emerge are small as long as the original trade barriers are low. Moreover, the above-mentioned terms of trade effect would have a favourable impact. A World Bank study (Krumm and Kharas 2003) concludes that much of the positive effects of trade liberalisation in East and Southeast Asia can be achieved with a regional agreement. The problems with income redistribution and agglomeration effects would remain, though. These could perhaps be taken care of through various compensation mechanisms, but these are not easy to organise in practice. For smaller FTAs, such as AFTA, not to speak of bilateral agreements, the expectations are lower, and possible advantages must probably be found beyond traditional integration theory.

"Dynamic" effects, such as economies of scale, increasing scope for intra-industry trade, increasing FDI from third countries, and technical development and innovation as a consequence of increasing competition are all potential advantages of regional FTAs that have been mentioned. In Asia, the widely differing comparative and competitive advantages in the region have contributed to the formation of production networks, which in turn, are a strong driving force of integration. In this case it is common that the products are tailor-made for the final product. If so, the concept of trade diversion is rather irrelevant. Trade facilitation, such as upgrading of infrastructure, and improved institutional frameworks, such as streamlining of customs procedures, mechanisms for resolving disputes etc, are increasingly important for smoothly functioning trade and may be a strong incentive towards formalised regional and bilateral agreements. More integration on the financial side would serve the same purpose.

The existing industrial structure in Asia is often heavily affected by trade related investment measures (TRIMS), that is combinations of incentives and regulations introduced in order to help creating an industrial structure deemed desirable by the authorities. Chase (2004) points out that TRIMS give the firms a strong incentive for lobbying in favour of regional and bilateral arrangement instead of multilateral solutions. This is the case not least in Asia, because the multinational firms usually are present in many countries, where they form networks between its own affiliates or together with domestic subcontractors. TRIMS affect in what countries the investments are made and sudden policy shifts are undesirable because of the "sunk" costs involved. The fact that subcontractors today produce much more than just simple standardised components, but also design, systems and technical solutions (Das 2005), implies that there are large "sunk" costs also in the form of human capital. Liberalisation is therefore problematic for a firm that has already invested under an assumption that the conditions of today will prevail also in the future. An FTA, and especially a bilateral agreement, gives the politicians more leeway than a multilateral agreement to customise special conditions for "sensitive" industries, at least for a transitory period. According to Chase (2004) the restructuring costs that a change of policy entails for the firms may be avoided or reduced through regional or bilateral agreements. Thus one may assume that the more mobile, "footless", real capital is, the faster liberalisation will proceed (cf. Maggi and Rodrígues-Clare 2005).

Regional agreements are considered a way of "locking in" liberalisation measures and insulate the reforms against protectionist special interests. International commitments are also a way of handling domestic lobby groups and their resistance to further reforms (see, e.g., Chase 2004, Whalley 1996). While multilateral commitments, in principle, could achieve the same thing, the WTO process is slow and its outcome uncertain.

A regional FTA may be a useful first step if the member countries wish to "deepen" the integration. Such deepening has frequently been proposed in Asia, especially after the financial crisis of the late 1990s when the need for more regional co-operation became evident. Other types of co-operation may be easier to bring about if there is already some kind of organisation, such as an FTA. Many regional public goods, such as water resources and environment also must be handled in a regional context, and then an already existing organisation may be taken advantage of. Trade facilitating, as well as improving transport and communication facilities and harmonisation of customs procedures, has been part of the agenda of many FTAs.

An important driving force as far as bilateral agreements are concerned is securing trade relations with particularly important partners. In Asia, for instance, it is of vital interest to have a secure access to the Japanese market, still the biggest and most sophisticated one in Asia. A secure market access improves the possibilities for investing in order to capture scale economies, which improves the efficiency of production. The FTAs between Singapore and the US and Japan, respectively, are a case in point. An agreement gives a certain degree of security in the trade relations as well as an instrument to deal with trade disputes. A bilateral agreement may also be seemingly attractive because it can be customised for special preferences of the partners and may also encompass many things apart from commodity trade.

Eruption of the financial crisis

The present crisis had been fermenting in the global financial system for some two years before it erupted in a full-scale disaster in September 2008, when investment bank Lehman Brothers went bankrupt. While the reasons for and proceeding of the crisis is now relatively well understood, few people, including professional economists had been able to foresee the full force of the coming crash. As well known, the origin of the crisis can be found in the American housing market. Borrowers with questionable creditworthiness could borrow 100 percent of the market value of their homes, even without any down-payment. This was the so-called sub-prime segment of the housing market. The strong loan-fed increase in house prices allowed people to borrow even more using their homes as collateral. However, house prices stopped increasing in 2006 and as the general economic situation also started to weaken, borrowers started defaulting on their loans, creating increasing problems for the lenders. Some of them failed or had to be bought up by other players in order to survive. Worse still, large amounts of "toxic" loans had been resold and repackaged into derivatives sold to investors all over the world. The risk involved in these derivatives was not properly understood; the credit rating institutes typically gave them high marks. When the true risk was understood the acute crisis broke out, as nobody knew exactly how much of these toxic assets the financial institutions held and what exactly they were worth, if anything. This, in turn, caused the interbank market to stop functioning and led to an almost complete standstill of the credit market in the last quarter of 2008. Due to the difficulties of obtaining credit the goods markets were quickly affected as well.

Impact of the international financial crisis in Asia

Asia, taken together, today accounts for close to 40 percent of world GDP and thus plays a crucial role in how the global economy will recover from the financial crisis of 2008 – 2009. Many Asian economies have been less affected by the crisis than the Western countries and could therefore help pulling the global economy out of the recession. To some extent Asia's relative financial isolation and less developed financial markets, in fact, protected the regions from the worst direct effect of the financial near-collapse of 2008 (Takagi 2009). The integration of the Asian market has also helped softening the direct and indirect impact from the financial crisis.

The lesson from the Asian crisis of the 1990s is still well remembered in Asia, which has protected the firms and governments in the region from taking on excessive debt obligations. (Watanagase 2008) A weakness of the region is the lack of a common strategy and response to the crisis, however, despite the increasing degree of regional integration as described above. There has been some development in the arrangements organised under the so-called Chiang Mai initiative after the crisis of the 1990s – in particular the bilateral currency swap facility has recently been multilateralised. However, more could be done in terms of reserve pooling and governance of the reserves, according to some observers. The financial intermediation system, and its regulatory framework is not yet efficient enough (Drysdale 2008). A recent report by the Asian Development Bank (ADB) arrived at the same result.

While trade integration was, at least until recently, driven by market forces, financial integration needs a stronger input from the governments. This is because the development of domestic financial markets depends on the regulatory framework to a great extent. This is even more so when international financial transactions are concerned. Takagi (2009) shows, using correlation analyses between saving and investment, that although the degree of financial openness in Asia has been on the increase after 1990 its absolute level is still well below that of Europe or the OECD.

Asian economies also appear to be more connected to international financial centres outside the region than they are with each other (see also Wataganase 2008). They are, as a whole, more restrictive in terms of capital controls and exchange regulations than other industrial countries, even if they are exceptions from that rule. By and large, they also have less developed internal financial markets, with a relative lack of, e.g., a corporate bond market.

The financial sector in Asia has done better than in most other parts of the world during the crisis (ADB 2009). For one thing, it was in better shape to begin with. But it was also less integrated than that sector was in the West. Although the relative isolation of the Asian financial markets helped protecting the region against the worst onslaught of the financial crisis of 2008, a case can be made for further developing these markets, according to, e.g., Takagi (2009). One reason is that more developed financial markets are needed in order to secure smooth availability of local funding for investment projects. Another one is that financial integration facilitates further deepening of real market integration, as more integrated financial markets reduce cross-border transaction costs. A stronger financial environment in Asia would probably also contribute to stabilising the global market, making it less dependent on a small number of major financial centres.

However, increasing sophistication of financial markets and lower barriers to cross border capital flows also entail an increasing systemic risk. In order to cope with that risk the governments should build adequate institutions for supervision. Regional and international co-ordination of those efforts would be of utmost importance.

Conclusions

There is no reason to slow down the process of regional integration because of the present financial market problems. On the contrary, the Asian economies will stand stronger and more resilient the more integrated their markets are. There are no signs that the regional economies would be inclined now to renege on earlier commitments as to market integration. Instead, the faltering of the region's traditional trade partners in the West has underscored the need to find new engines of growth. Finding a way out of the chronic excess saving in East Asia, which of course is a manifestation of the existing global imbalances, would be part of the solution.

Dobson (2009) points at the significance of the so-called G20 meetings in 2009 as a catalyst for deeper regional integration. But there is still the risk that the process slows down or stalls for a while as the relevant authorities are now occupied with more pressing short-term issues and may not be able to devote enough of their efforts to issues more important in the long term. This is worrying, especially as the recovery from the crisis may be slow, according to leading international institutions (see, e.g., ADB 2009). Still, in spite of the fact that some protectionist measures were taken at the height of the crisis, the Asian countries however have declared their determination not to resort to protectionism (Dobson 2009). The integration process is likely to go on, slowly but surely. Bringing on board countries like Australia and India is important, too, and those countries are increasingly involved in the ongoing process. As emphasised in this paper, integrated industrial networks are a strong driver of economic integration in Asia. Financial crisis or not, they need a smoother trade environment. They are also powerful lobby groups, since the networks tend to be centred on large multinational companies.

References

Ando, Mitsuyo and Kimura, Fukunari (2003): The Formation of International Production and Distribution Networks in East Asia. NBER Working Paper No. 10167, National Bureau of Economic Research, Cambridge, MA.

ADB (2008): Emerging Asian Regionalism: A Partnership for Shared Prosperity. Asian Development Bank, Manila.

ADB (2009): Asian Development Outlook 2009. Asian Development Bank, Manila.

Antkiewicz, Agata and Whalley John (2004): China's New Regional Trade Agreements. NBER Working Paper No. 10992, National Bureau of Economic Research, Cambridge, MA.

ASEAN Secretariat (2009): ASEAN and India Sign the Much Awaited Free Trade Area. http://www.aseansec.org/PR-ASEAN-India-Sign-Much-Awaited-FTA.pdf (accessed 9.9. 2009).

Asia Times (2005): "ASEAN, Korea Move on FTA", Asia Times Online, March 1st, 2005 (accessed 4.3. 2005).

Bilaterals.org (2009): http://www.bilaterals.org/rubrique.php3?id_rubrique=142&lang=en (accessed 9.9. 2009)

Blomqvist, Hans C. (2007): "Regional Integration in Asia-Pacific: Rhetoric and Reality", in Onishi, Takehito and Teh, Cheng Guan Benny (eds): The Shape of the East Asian Economy to Come. Cambridge Scholars Publishing, Newcastle.

Chase, Kerry A. (2004): "From Protectionism to Regionalism: Multinational Firms and Trade-Related Investment Measures", Business and Politics, Vol. 6.

Das, Dilip (2005): "Market-Driven Regionalization in Asia", Global Economic Journal, Vol. 5.

Dobson, Wendy (2009): The Financial Crisis and East Asia. East Asia Forum. http:// www.eastasiaforum.org/2009/07/26/the-financial-crisi-and-east-asia (accessed 25.9.2009).

Drysdale, Peter: East Asia and the Global Financial Crisis. East Asia Forum. http://www.eastasiaforum.org/2008/12/25/east-asia-strategic-interests-in-fixing-the-global-financial-crisis/ (accessed 16.9. 2009).

East Asia Vision Group (2001): Towards an East Asian Community: Region of Peace, Prosperity and Progress. http://www.mofa.go.jp/region/asia-paci/report2001.pdf. (accessed 9.3.2006)

Government of Singapore (2009): Singapore's FTA Network: Expanding Markets, Connecting Partners. http://www.fta.gov.sg/index.asp (accessed 15.9. 2009).

Hattari, Rabin and Rajan, Ramkishen S. (2008): "FDI Flows to Developing Asia: Triad versus Intraregional Sources". Asian Development Bank Institute, Tokyo.

Japan Times (2008): "ASEAN-Japan FTA to take effect Dec. 1". October 22, 2008.

Killion, M. Ulric (2005): Chinese Regionalism and the 2004 ASEAN-China

Accord: The WTO and Legalized Trade Distortion. Working Paper, Shanghai International Studies University.

Kimura, Fukunari and Ando, Mitsuyo (2005): "The Economic Analysis of International Production/Distribution Networks in East Asia and Latin America: The Implication of Regional Trade Arrangements", Business and Politics, Vol. 7.

Krumm, Kathie and Kharas, Homi (eds) (2003): East Asia Integrates: A Trade Policy Agenda for Shared Growth. World Bank, Washington, D.C.

Lim, Hank (2003): "Structural Changes and Domestic Reforms in Singapore: Challenges and Implications to Regional Co-operation in ASEAN and East Asia", in Hirono, Ryokichi (ed): Regional Co-operation in Asia. Institute of Southeast Asian Studies, Singapore.

Maggi, Giovanni and Rodrígues-Clare, Andrés (2005): A Political-Economy Theory of Trade Agreements. NBER Working Paper No. 11716, NBER; Cambridge, MA.

Ng, Francis and Yeats, Alexander (2003): Major Trade Trends in East Asia. World Bank Policy Research Working Paper 3084, World Bank, Washington, D.C.

Panagariya, Arvind (1999): Essays on Preferential Trading. World Scientific, Singapore.

Sen, Rahul (2004): Free Trade Agreements in Southeast Asia. Southeast Asia Background Series No. 1, Institute of Southeast Asian Studies, Singapore.

Soesastro, Hadi (2003): "Asia-Japan Co-operation Toward East Asian Integration", in Hirono, Ryokichi (ed): Regional Co-operation in Asia. Institute of Southeast Asian Studies, Singapore.

Takagi, Shinji (2009): Financial Integration in Asia: A Medium-Term Agenda. Paper presented at a conference on financial sector reforms and economic integration in Asia, Beijing, 14–15 May, 2009.

Tongzon, Jose L. (2005): "ASEAN-China Free Trade Area: A Bane or Boon for ASEAN Countries?" The World Economy, Vol. 28.

Viner, Jacob (1950): The Customs Union Issue. Carnegie Endowment for International Peace, New York.

Voon, Jan P., Chen, Edward K.Y. and Bridges, Brian (2005): "ASEAN Plus

Three: Rethinking Asian Cooperation", Asian Profile, Vol. 33.

Watanagase, Tarisa (2008): Global Financial Crisis and Economic Integration in Asia. Adress at the TU-JBIC International Conference on "The Future of Economic Integration in Asia", Bangkok, 21 November 2008. http://www.bis.org /review/r081128c.pdf (accessed 24.9.2009).

Whalley, John (1996): Why Do Countries Seek Regional Trade Agreements? NBER Working Paper No. 5552, National Bureau of Economic Research, Cambridge, MA.

第10章 インドと日本——新しい状況と機会

Chapter 10 India-Japan: New Situation and New Opportunities

H.S. Prabhakar [*]

The world is about to emerge from the bottom of a global recession that caused widespread business contraction, increasing unemployment and shrinking government revenues. Although recent data indicate the large industrialized economies may have reached bottom and are beginning to recover, unemployment is still rising. A number of small banks and households still face considerable problems in restoring their balance sheets. Nearly all industrialized countries and many emerging and developing nations have announced economic stimulus and/or financial sector rescue packages.

Many Asian developing economies have been through financial crises in the past as well. Although most observers say the region's economic fundamentals have improved greatly in the past decade, this crisis has provided a worrying sense of deja vu, and an illustration that Asian policy changes in recent years—including Japan's slow but comprehensive structural and banking reforms, Korea's opening of its financial markets, China's dramatic economic transformation, and the huge buildup of sovereign reserves across the region—have not fully insulated Asian economies from global contagion.

However, in the second quarter of 2009, there were signs that many Asian economies were rebounding sharply from the slowdowns and contractions they suffered in the previous months. Many observers have attributed this recovery to the rapid implementation of large fiscal and monetary stimulus programs that were possible because of the comparatively strong fiscal positions that most Asian governments were in. Also, the large amount of foreign exchange surplus of China, Japan and India has been one reason for the buildup of enormous government reserves

---

[*] Associate Professor in Japanese Studies, School of International Studies, Jawaharlal Nehru University, New Delhi, India.

in the region, including China's $2.1 trillion, Japan's $996 billion and India's $270 billion — together comprising a large reserve stockpile in the world. Such reserves have given these governments resources to provide fiscal stimulus programs, inject necessary capital into their financial systems, as well as provide backstop guarantees for private financial transactions.

The most important challenge will be to maintain the progress of the world economy, which is mainly possible only through the mutual cooperation between Asia's three biggest economies along with United States. It is very important for Japan, China and India to manage their relationship well because of their impact on the world economy.

Japan's "two lost decades"

The financial market turmoil has changed the global economic landscape including the economy of Japan. Like all countries, Japan has taken the current crisis seriously and recognizes that this crisis cannot be overcome without global cooperation. Against this backdrop, Japan's responsibility to the world as the second-largest economy was to think and act globally in cooperation with the rest of the world. Japan has been at the forefront in addressing the problem and was determined to make its utmost contribution to the international community under the global initiatives.

Although Japan was not at the epicenter of the crisis, its export-dependent economy was vulnerable to the collapse in world trade, which resulted in its most severe recession of the post-war era. By March 2009, the confidence of large manufacturing firms had plummeted to its lowest level since 1975, causing a major retrenchment in their investment plans. Headline inflation has turned negative and by mid-2009 prices were down around 2% year-on-year. Output is projected to drop by around 6% by the end of 2009, following a 0.7% decline in 2008.

Despite the relative soundness of the financial system, the Japanese economy has experienced a severe slump because exports shrank dramatically to almost half of the pre-crisis level due to the contraction of external demand. This has caused closure of several manufacturing facilities across Japan as well as an increase in unemployment (currently

5.1%). The Japan Business Federation mentioned that the average bonus paid by 164 major companies was down 15.01 percent from a year earlier to 755,628 yen, the sharpest drop since Japan's largest business lobby, known as Nippon Keidanren, began surveying bonuses in 1959.

In response, the government has been implementing economic policy packages which will total around 5 percent of the GDP in aggregate, and increasing the public debt to GDP ratio to almost 190%. Years of deficit spending to finance economic stimulus packages put together by the Liberal Democratic Party predecessors has left the Hatoyama administration with an unprecedented level of government debt.

By the end of fiscal 2009 in March, the outstanding balance of central government bonds is projected to top 600 trillion yen for the first time. The figure is the highest among advanced economies. Massive public spending programs to pump up the economy since the late 1990s have led to a doubling of the outstanding balance of government bonds in about a decade.

The huge increase in the outstanding balance is also due to a drastic decrease in tax revenues caused by the global economic recession. The debt dependence began to accelerate in the 1990s after the collapse of the asset-inflated economy. With tax revenues declining due to a stagnant economy, the central government relied on debt to pay for large public works projects and tax cuts as part of a series of economic stimulus packages.

The last LDP government headed by Taro Aso compiled the largest ever economic stimulus package in fiscal 2009, piling on further debt. The successor DPJ government has set a target of limiting central government bond issuance in fiscal 2010 to under 44 trillion yen, but it has yet to draw a road map for cutting into the outstanding balance of government bonds. While the massive debt accumulated by successive LDP governments has been described as a negative legacy by the Hatoyama government, his administration has delayed setting its own goal of improving the fiscal situation until fiscal 2010 or later. Wages and bonuses have also been cut across the board.

Concern about the economy falling into a second bottom in the face of deflation and a soaring yen, coupled with the People's New Party leader

Shizuka Kamei's insistence on larger fiscal spending, pushed up the final figure to a whopping 7.2 trillion yen. Business confidence among large manufacturers increased for the third consecutive quarter, but the improvement rate shrank and overall sentiment remains low, the Bank of Japan's Tankan survey for December revealed.

Japan suffered from a stock price crash in the early 1990s and people became very pessimistic. They reduced consumption and expanded money holding in preparation for a sudden wage cut or job loss. The demand for imports also decreased and the current account improved, which in turn caused the yen to appreciate. Eventually, both exports and imports decreased and the current account returned to its trend level. Thus, the strong yen was evidence of people's pessimistic economic outlook and low consumption. It arose together with deflation and decreases in employment and national income.

The financial turmoil that started in Dubai in late November 2009 also has shaken the Hatoyama Cabinet sufficiently to decide to focus more on increasing the size of this budget, instead of its substance. The package now includes allocations of 500 billion yen for public works projects.

Since the 1990s, successive administrations led by the Liberal Democratic Party relied excessively on public works projects to stimulate the economy--only to expand fiscal deficits, which later squeezed social security expenditures. In order to end this vicious cycle, the Hatoyama administration vowed that its economic policy would "put people's lives first" and de-emphasize big construction projects. The recent measure of 7.2 trillion Yen is not enough for the administration to offer stopgap measures.

An economic stimulus package is meant to serve as the government's message of reassurance to people who are worried about their future. This is all the more reason why it should be designed to cleverly stoke private-sector consumption and investment, not to merely cover demand deficiency with fiscal spending.

Due mainly to the above measures, the level of Japan's GDP growth in FY 2009 will remain at minus 3.3 percent, a level equivalent to those of other major developed countries. Through these measures, the aim is to keep the unemployment rate below 5.5 percent, the worst level that Japan has experienced in decades. Japanese shares also suffered their biggest yearly decline, with the Nikkei dropping 42% as the world's second-largest economy slid into recession.

According to Tatsuya Tanimoto, Senior Vice Minister of the Cabinet Office, there are three main characteristics of Japan's contribution in response to the financial crisis. The first was Japan's economic policy packages, including its fiscal measures, in order to lead the world economy back to a steady growth path.

The second was Japan's cooperation in the arena of international finance, including through the IMF, the World Bank and the Asian Development Bank. The third is its efforts to prevent protectionism so that world trade flows would not be hampered (Tatsuya Tanimoto, 2009).

In the financial sector, policies are aimed at sustaining credit flows and stabilizing markets. On the fiscal front, the government has launched four crisis-driven stimulus plans since August 2008, amounting to 4.7% of the 2008 GDP, above the average of 3.9% for OECD countries adopting stimulus programs. Increased spending, at 4.2% of the GDP, accounted for the bulk of the stimulus in Japan. As a result of the stimulus and the severe recession, the government budget deficit is projected to reach 10% in 2010. Output is projected to continue increasing in the second half of 2009. However, the pace of recovery is likely to be restrained by subdued export growth, as world trade picks up only gradually and the appreciation of the yen over the past year reduces Japan's market share. Consequently, output growth is projected to remain below 1% during 2010, resulting in entrenched deflation and a continued rise in the unemployment rate. A stronger pick-up in world trade, meanwhile, could lead to a faster rebound in Japan.

Nearly 190 listed companies have solicited almost 23,000 voluntary or early retirements, according to Tokyo Shoko Research. The report further mentions that 186 companies had announced from the beginning of this year that they wanted a total of 22,713 employees to quit.

It is the first time that such a figure has exceeded 20,000 since 2002, when financial institutions accelerated bad debt disposal under deflation and listed companies sought 39,732 voluntary and early retirees. The latest figure marks 2.5 times the total figure--8,979--during the whole of 2008, a drastic increase that indicates the severity of the nation's employment situation.

Moreover, in order to maintain capital flows to Asia's developing countries that are temporarily unable to raise funds through international bond issuance due to market disruptions, Japan has decided to provide guarantees by the Japan Bank for International Cooperation of up to 500 billion Yen on Yen denominated bonds, or Samurai bonds, issued in Japanese markets by such developing countries (Tatsuya Tanimoto, 2009).

There are still many risks along the way to recovery from the global financial crisis. The American economy remains weak, with unemployment at 10 percent, and Europe and Japan remain in the doldrums. China's powerful recovery and India's return to normalcy with exports growing at a pre-crisis level and hope for 7% growth next year are bull elements for the world economy.

Japan and India at COP-15

Along with its efforts to save the domestic economy, Japan was instrumental in assisting the emerging and developing countries in order to mitigate the negative impact of the precipitous drop in capital flows that had been driving economic growth in those countries. In the context of bilateral assistance, Japan has pledged 5 billion US dollars in support for environmental investment in developing countries for the next two years. At COP-15 in December 2009, Japan announced that it would provide as much as US$ 19.5 billion assistance to help reduce emission levels in developing countries. Japan's offer to developing nations under a climate deal thereby created a major boost to the summit in Copenhagen.

The figure amounts to more than half of the money as part of a plan to assist developing nations, a key sticking point at the COP-15 conference. Japan was making the pledge "all on the premise that a fair and effective international framework should be built and that this framework should involve all major countries".

It marks the biggest contribution yet to the so-called fast-track fund aimed at helping developing nations cope with climate change through 2012. Prime Minister Hatoyama's government has ramped up pledges by Japan to battle global warming and to find a successor to the landmark Kyoto Protocol. Japan earlier said it would also take part in a six-nation, 3.5 billion-dollar fund to address deforestation, a major source of climate change.

World pledges on cutting greenhouse gas emissions by 2020 are nowhere near enough to keep global warming in check, a UN report mentions. What is important is the world's long term emissions path, rather than a make-or-break figure in 2020.

The text, circulated by environmental groups, came on the eve of the last day of UN talks on fighting global warming in Copenhagen, as world leaders were expected to push for a final deal.

The analysis, carried out by the UN's climate secretariat, says that "unless the remaining (emissions-reduction) gap ... is closed and parties commit themselves to strong action prior to and after 2020, global emissions will remain on an unsustainable pathway" that could raise global temperatures by up to 3 degrees by 2100. UN scientists say that an increase in world temperatures of more than 2 degrees could lead to catastrophic climate change.

In a last minute attempt to achieve a breakthrough at the UN climate summit, Japan and the United States announced short and long-term financial pledges for developing countries to mitigate the effects of climate change over the next three years and to adapt to the future effects of global warming by 2020.

Japan's Environment Minister Sakihito Ozawa mentioned that Japan would provide about 1.75 trillion yen over the three years through 2012 to support efforts by developing nations to fight global warming, if the major powers at the ongoing UN climate change conference all agree on fair, ambitious targets for reducing greenhouse gases. Japan planned to push for fast-growing economies such as China and India to commit to binding targets for reducing greenhouse gas emissions at the UN climate change conference in Copenhagen.

Tokyo has maintained that a post-Kyoto Protocol framework should impose obligations on the United States, which withdrew from the 1997 protocol, as well as China, India and other "key developing nations" not currently bound to meet specific targets.

The Japanese government proposed that a table of midterm targets for emissions reduction for 2020 for all countries, excluding the least developed, be attached to the political agreement. Tokyo will not accept the argument that targets set by those nations are mere voluntary goals and nonbinding.

If an extension of the Kyoto Protocol is presented as an alternative, the Japanese government would not agree to write its 25 percent reduction goal into the revised protocol.

As negotiators struggled to finalise a draft for the climate summit, India's Prime Minister Manmohan Singh and his Chinese counterpart Wen Jiabao on 18 December held talks in a bid to consolidate the position of developing countries ahead of the world leaders' meeting in Copenhagen.

Singh recalled that the two countries have been cooperating at various fora, including the G-20. The developing countries have been resisting attempts by the rich nations to set aside the Kyoto Protocol, which sets legally binding greenhouse gas emissions reduction targets for industrialised nations.

India and other emerging economies prepared a Copenhagen accord late on the evening of 18 December in association with the US, to be presented to an overnight plenary session of the UN climate summit. The accord came under attack from the Group of 77 almost at once, though it was unclear if it would carry its opposition into the plenary session.

In a dramatic development earlier, US President Barack Obama attended a meeting of the heads of government of BASIC countries - Brazil, South Africa, India, China - and held an hour-long meeting. The demand by rich countries was that emerging economies should not only take steps to control emissions of greenhouse gases that are warming the earth, but that their actions should be verifiable by the international community. India and China have opposed this earlier, saying this would impinge upon their sovereignty.

Obama admitted that there was a "fundamental deadlock in perspectives" between developed and developing countries on how to tackle climate change. "Both sides have legitimate points." He said a legally binding treaty to fight climate change was necessary but would be "very hard" to get. "If we just waited for that then we would not make any progress." Applauding India for the steps it had voluntarily taken to control greenhouse gas emissions, Obama said: "a more binding agreement was not achievable at this conference".

The 1997 protocol also had contained a strong compliance mechanism which penalises the rich nations if they do not meet emission reduction targets they had agreed upon. Besides, an additional 22 billion US dollars was allocated over the same period to support trade finance, in order to reduce risk and facilitate trade with developing countries. Furthermore, Japan has pledged to scale up its ODA to the Asian region to 2 trillion yen where India receives the largest share.

The member nations of the European Union reluctantly agreed to sign up for the accord worked out at a summit of 120 leaders by the United States, China, India, South Africa and Brazil - meant as the first UN climate pact since the 1997 Kyoto Protocol.

The deal sets an end-January 2010 deadline for all nations to submit plans for curbs on emissions to the United Nations. A separate text proposes an end-2010 deadline for transforming the non-binding pledges into a legally binding treaty. Even backers of the accord conceded it was imperfect and fell far short of UN ambitions for the Copenhagen talks, meant as a turning point to push the world economy towards renewable energy and away from fossil fuels.

The climate change conference, which had been billed as the most important postwar international gathering and perhaps the world's last chance to halt global warming, ended with a vague, non-legal agreement that few delegates enthusiastically supported.

The effectiveness of the Copenhagen Accord contains very few specific figures, commitments or timelines in the global fight against climate change. The accord promises a mobilisation of $100 billion in annual funding for developing countries to meet the challenges of climate change from 2020.

Global Crisis and the Indian Economy

It is impossible to ignore India today as it was decades before, though India still finds it difficult to fully perceive itself as a world power. One of the indirect consequences of the rise of China and India and their privileged relationship with the West, however, might be seen as one of the concerns of Japan's identity crisis.

Decades before, Japan represented the "Asian West." Nevertheless, the emergence of Chinese-style and Indian-style modernity may be worrying Japan. After all, if China becomes America's main economic partner in Asia, and similarly India is America's main diplomatic partner, what role is left for Japan? Its aging population watches resignedly as the new, younger Asia becomes as important for the US as Europe was during the Cold War, so opines Domique Moisi.

There is, at least in some quarters, dismay that India has been hit by the crisis. When the crisis first broke internationally, within official circles in India there was a perception that the Indian economy would be less affected and the Indian financial sector would be relatively immune to the winds from the international financial implosion. The presence of a large nationalised banking sector and a somewhat more stringent regulatory regime for real estate lending by banks were seen to protect the Indian financial system from harmful contagion from abroad. But this was proved to be wrong.

The economic boom in India that preceded the current downturn was dependent upon greater global integration in three ways: greater reliance on exports, particularly of services; increased dependence on capital inflows, especially of the short-term variety; and the role these played in underpinning a domestic credit-fuelled consumption and investment boom (Jayati Ghosh and C. P. Chandrasekhar, 2009).

India's main stock market index, Sensex, plunged nearly 50% during the year. All global markets saw record falls in 2008 as the financial turmoil and economic slowdown ended the stock market boom with the onset of the crisis. Trade to GDP ratios in India increased from 11% in 1995 to

23% in 2006. However, unlike China, where much of the export expansion was on account of manufacturing, export growth in India was principally due to services. In the merchandise trade area, India's export success was restricted to a few sectors such as garments, chemicals, pharmaceuticals and metals and engineering goods.

While the first three categories of exports grew because of dynamism in the global market, the latter two were largely driven by increased demand from China in the period since 2002. In services, however, India emerged as the largest exporter of computer and information services in the international economy in 2005, and its share in world exports of computer and information services was 17% in 2006. Services in general have come to dominate the Indian economy contributing an overwhelming share to its recent relatively high rate of growth.

As might be expected, the main impact of the global financial turmoil in India has emanated from the significant change experienced in the capital account in 2008-09 so far, relative to the previous year. Total net capital flows fell from US$ 17.3 billion in April-June 2007 to US$ 13.2 billion in April-June 2008. Nonetheless, capital flows are expected to be more than sufficient to cover the current account deficit this year as well. While Foreign Direct Investment (FDI) inflows have continued to exhibit accelerated growth (US$ 16.7 billion during April-August 2008 as compared with US$ 8.5 billion in the corresponding period of 2007), portfolio investments by foreign institutional investors (FIIs) witnessed a net outflow of about US$ 6.4 billion in April-September 2008 as compared with a net inflow of US$ 15.5 billion in the corresponding period last year (Rakesh Mohan, 2008).

A CII (Confederation if Indian Industry) analysis of quarterly performance of 2661 companies clearly shows that the growth in their net profit has fallen sharply from 22 percent growth in December 2007 to 18 percent in December 2008. For the first time in five years, India's export growth has turned negative during the crisis period. Exports for October 2008 contracted by 15% on a year-on-year basis. This should not be surprising as the OECD economies that account for over 40% of India's export market have been slowing for months.

Given the above forms of integration through trade, the global slowdown had directly affected exports and economic activity in India. Merchandise trade was the first to be affected. Merchandise exports in October-December 2008 were more than 10% lower than their value a year earlier. Import values on the other hand continued to increase, albeit at a slower rate because of falling world oil prices. As a result, the trade deficit for the period from October to December 2008 widened to $36.3 billion, 40% higher than a year earlier and estimated to be as much as 12.6% of the GDP (Reserve Bank of India, 2009A).

A decelerating export growth has implications for India, even though the economy is far more domestically driven than those of East Asia. Still, the contribution of merchandise exports to India's GDP has risen steadily over the past six years—from about 10% of the GDP in 2002-03 to nearly 17% by 2007-08. If one includes service exports, the ratio goes up further. Therefore, any downturn in the global economy will hurt India. A slowdown in export growth also has other implications for the economy. Close to 50% of India's exports—textiles, garments, gems and jewelry, leather and so on—originate from the labour-intensive small- and medium-enterprises.

The initial responses of the government focused on the financial side of the current crisis, with three major components to the first stimulus package adopted in late 2008. These included measures by both the Reserve Bank of India and the government aimed at reducing interest rates and increasing the access to credit of large and small firms, state governments and individuals. At the same time, access to credit from foreign sources was sought to be enhanced through measures that lifted the remaining constraints on external commercial borrowing. The ceiling on FII investment in rupee-denominated corporate bonds was more than doubled. The slogan appeared to be, "if domestic credit is unavailable or expensive, borrow from abroad." While the overall fiscal deficit (of central and state governments together) in the fiscal year 2009-10 is likely to increase to around 12% of the GDP, a large part of it is likely to be the result of tax cuts and subsidies rather than direct spending.

A recovery in the US from the current crisis, though slow, is bringing into India IT transactions worth billions of dollars. The outlook for India moving forward is mixed. The index of industrial production registered a growth of 11 percent in the month of August 2009. This was higher than the growth of 6.8 percent registered in July 2009 and also from the 1.7 percent growth registered in the same month last year. This indicates that the economy is back on the recovery path and the stimulus packages are slowly working at the ground level. All the three sub sectors, that is, mining, manufacturing and electricity recorded an improvement, with their respective growth rates being 11 percent and 10.6 percent. An improvement was indicated in the stock market on account of some recovery taking place in the global economy and stability in the world markets. The sensitive index of Mumbai stock exchange crossed 17000 points by the end of September 09 (FICCI, 2009).

India- Japan Partnership

While efforts to establish political and strategic ties are visible in India-Japan relations, one can certainly see Japan's rationale behind delaying the seeking of closer ties with India, especially at a time when Japan-US relations are set to be reviewed by the new government in Japan. India's proactive regional diplomacy in East Asia notwithstanding, the change that the Hatoyama government seeks for Japan will also include new possibilities for improved relations with India. In this process, the emergence of India as a future global player is acting as an additional structural factor.

As a result of the growing engagement profile between the two countries, the year 2007 was declared the Indo-Japan Friendship Year. Going by the number of Japanese delegations visiting India in the near past, it is evident that India figures as a significant spot on the Japanese investment radar and with its growing economic strength, India too has adapted its foreign policy to increase its regional as well as global influence. Thus, Japan figures importantly in India's "Look East Policy" as well.

It is an impressive change from a situation where India was merely a potential market for Japan while Japan's importance for India was that of being the most important purveyor of bilateral ODA and foreign direct investment. There has been remarkable progress on the political/strategic, economic and cultural fronts, including the fact that Japan's de facto definition of Asia is no longer limited to Japan and East Asia. It now includes the whole of South Asia. A robust trade partnership between the two has also created the possibility of a viable security cooperation in the Indian Ocean and Southeast Asia, where Indian and Japanese interests converge, which could protect against Chinese economic hegemony in Southeast Asia.

Bilateral trade between Japan and India has been rising steadily since 2003, increasing from US$ 3.7 billion in 2002-03 to US$ 6.5 billion in 2005-06, and rising further to US$ 7.5 billion in 2006-07. While Japan ranks 10th among India's export destinations, India stands 26th among Japan's export destinations. During April−February 2007−08, Indo-Japan bilateral trade rose to US$ 7.01 billion compared to US$ 5.33 billion in the same period in the last fiscal year. Japanese exports to India have grown 28 percent in 2008 and imports rose 26 percent. This rise saw the trade between the two countries top $13 billion which put them on course to hit the target of $20 billion by 2010 as outlined under former Japanese Prime Minister Shinzo Abe. Japan is amongst India's top five trading partners −with a potential to reach US$ 14 billion by 2012−as both countries are involved in several developmental projects.

The Japanese net foreign institutional investors (FII) inflows into India have also progressively increased. After the first set of "India Investment Funds" from Japan to India include funds such as Nomura India Securities up to 2004, the number of such funds has doubled from 8 in November 2005 to 16 as of March 2007 with net assets worth US$ 8.2 billion. India's popularity with Japanese investors can also be gauged from the fact that many new India retail funds have been launched in Japan, which by the end 2007 were worth US$ 4.05 billion.

Such has been the growth in Japanese investment in India that as much as US$ 1.9 billion foreign institutional investment inflow came from Japan alone. Some of the portfolio investors are Investment (US$ 920.5 million), Shinko Pure India Equity Fund (US$ 617.1 million), JF India Fund (US$ 142.7 million), Black Rock India Equity Fund (US$ 929.1 million) Mitsui-Sumitomo India-China Equity Fund, HSBC India Open Fund (US$

1033.3 million) from HSBC Investments (Japan) K. K, Sumitomo Mitsui Asset Management Co., Ltd. (US$ 264.1 million) and Shisei Investment Management Co., Ltd (US$ 241.9 million), among others.

As far as Japanese Foreign Direct Investments are concerned, a 2008 survey conducted by the Japan Bank for International Cooperation (JBIC) revealed that India has become the most favored investment destination for long-term Japanese investments. While nearly 70 percent of Japanese manufacturers regarded India as the most attractive country to do business in over the next 10 years or so, only 67 percent preferred China. Russia came in third, with a 37 percent rating, followed by Vietnam at 28 percent. Japan ranked sixth in terms of cumulative foreign direct investment (FDI) in India worth US$ 3,047 million in April 2000 to July 2009, of which US$ 517 million came in the period April-July 2009, according to the latest data released by the Department of Policy and Promotion (DIPP).

Some of the Japanese flagship investment projects to India include the following: Maruti Suzuki India Ltd (MSIL) plans to invest US$ 2.25 billion, mostly in research and development (R&D), warehousing, marketing, logistics and design. Suzuki has planned an additional investment of US$ 2.03 billion by 2010 to increase production and sales. Toyota Motor Corporation has planned to set up an assembly plant for low-priced compact cars in southern India by 2010. Zentek Technology, a digital consumer electronics software maker, is going to set up a development base in Gurgaon. Kyushu Electric Power Co. has signed an MOU with NTPC Ltd. to promote technological and environmental expertise exchanges.

In June 2008, Japanese pharmaceutical company Daiichi Sankyo bought a 34.8 percent controlling stake in India's largest pharmaceutical firm, Ranbaxy Laboratories. A few months later, Japanese telecom giant NTT DoCoMo bought a 26 percent stake in Tata Teleservices Ltd. (TTSL). Honda, the Japanese auto giant planning its foray into the compact car segment in India, will expand its dealership network across 90 cities in the country and its production capacity to 160,000 units. Canon, Japan's digital imaging technology giant, is set to roll out its global flagship stores. Nissan, yet another Japanese auto giant, is working on an "entry car strategy" to build its mass presence in India and select overseas markets. The sectors that attract Japanese investment include transportation (28 percent); telecommunications (18%), fuel (13.5%), chemicals (12.17%) and trading (6%).

The above examples point to a singular fact that Japanese presence in India through more than 600 companies is on the rise. However, the corollary is also true. Indian companies are exploring opportunities to invest in Japan. Around 70 Indian IT companies have already established their offices in Japan though only about a dozen or so are making good profits. In fact, in a bid to encourage more investment in India, Japan has decided to open its second business support centre in Mumbai which would become operational in the year 2010. Collective figures from 1991 to 2008 exhibit that Japan ranks third in terms of technology transfers to India. Between 1991 and 2008, Japan contributed to 10.92 percent of the total technological transfers to India.

Furthermore, India may also see an investment of US$ 10 billion from Japanese companies alone in the Delhi-Mumbai Industrial Corridor (DMIC) belt, where several Japanese small and medium enterprises (SMEs) in diverse sectors like electronic components, banking, water treatment, logistics and education among others are seriously considering long-term investments.

The reasons behind this sudden Japanese interest in India are obvious. First, India offers a large domestic market base. Besides, mutual synergies between businesses in the two countries are driving initiatives. Japan is a relatively labour-scarce, capital and technology abundant country that complements India's rich spectrum of human capital. India's prowess in the software sector lends synergy to Japan's excellence in the hardware sector. India's abundance of raw materials and minerals matches well with Japan's capabilities in technology and capital to produce knowledge intensive manufactured goods. India's large domestic market has been the main factor for investments by Japanese companies. The majority of investments are in traditional fields like automobiles and auto parts and electronics. However, some companies have invested in businesses like pharmaceuticals (EISAI), health drinks (Yakuruto), pulp (Nihon Koso) and rice processing (Yanmar). Japanese small and medium enterprises have also begun to discover India as a new growth market. Hence, there is no dearth of business delegations visiting India.

The Government of Japan has committed to provide US$ 2.18 billion to India to undertake nine new infrastructure projects in different parts of the country. This is the highest ever Official Development Assistance (ODA) committed by the Japanese government to India, an increase of 22% over the previous year. India has continued to be the highest recipient of ODA from Japan in the last few years. Among the new projects approved with Japanese assistance and signed recently are the Kolkata Metro Project, the Hyderabad Outer Ring Road Project, the Hogennakal Water Supply Project, the Tamil Nadu Urban Infrastructure Project, the Haryana Transmission System Project and the Uttar Pradesh Forestry and Poverty Alleviation Project. Moreover, the Government of Japan has also committed to fund Phase II of the Delhi Metro Project. In 2008, the Government of Japan also committed to funding the Goa Water Supply and Sewerage Project and the Maharashtra Transmission System Project.

Potential Areas for Future Collaboration

Another area of collaboration between India and Japan is the energy issue. Japanese leaders have frequently stated that one of their primary foreign policy objectives to promote energy conservation. International Energy Agency (IEA) statistics indicate that to produce one unit of GDP, India needs 9.2 times as much energy input as Japan does. India is open to technologies that curb emissions and is currently pursuing alternative energies including wind and hydropower. Collaboration with Japan, including technology transfers, would allow India to improve its energy efficiency, thereby positively affecting global energy security and climate change. There is also need for private sector cooperation on energy initiatives. Private sector cooperation will require India to reform its regulatory environment and enforce intellectual property rights.

Unless reorganized, India's multiple energy bureaucracies and its lack of a centralized energy policy will be impediments to energy cooperation with Japan. It is evident that successful energy cooperation would require both India and Japan to make large fiscal and governmental commitments. However, it is also clear that in pursuing the common objectives of energy efficiency and security, India and Japan could meet their respective goals of economic growth and lead the fight against climate change.

Bilateral civil nuclear cooperation between India and Japan will provide an important link between India's concerns about energy security and economic growth and Japan's desire to be a leader in addressing the challenges of global climate change. For example, if India adds 20 gigawatts of new nuclear power capacity by 2020, the globe would benefit from 145 million tons in carbon dioxide savings; this would equal the entire European Union reduction of greenhouse gases under the Kyoto Protocol. Moreover, Japanese companies could stand to gain a great deal by helping India to implement the requisite technology to achieve these savings.

As space-faring nations, India and Japan must lay the foundation for deeper cooperation in the peaceful use of outer space. This includes cooperating on commercial space launch vehicles, satellites for environmental monitoring, arms control, and missile defense. Although both nations have been cooperating with the United States on civilian space mechanisms, their own collaboration has been lagging.

Conclusion

Japan has just experienced a major political power shift. The long-ruling Liberal Democratic Party (LDP) has been replaced by the Democratic Party of Japan (DPJ) in general elections for the powerful Lower House held in August 2009. It is too early to predict what effect this change will have on relations with India. Prime Minister Hatoyama recently said, "although it was necessary for the government to act in line with key policies pledged in the Democratic Party of Japan's campaign manifesto, it also was important to flexibly respond to situations," hinting he was ready to drift from the promises in the party manifesto when necessary. Support for Japan's three month-old government has dipped to 48 percent for the first time, according to a late December 2009 opinion survey in which many voters complained that Prime Minister Hatoyama lacks clear leadership with reference to relocation of the US base from Okinawa.

The combination of a new government coupled with the familiar risks of coalition governments and the precarious position of Japan's economy may lead to postponing some significant investments in India and other locations. The DPJ appears to be less pro-American than its predecessors and hence has opposed the dispatch of the Japanese Navy (refueling) to the Indian Ocean to participate in international naval operations; has yet to make a decision on the relocation of US forces from Okinawa to Guam, and above all now on the concept of flexibility in the DPJ election manifesto.

If DPJ continues to pursue this type of elastic policy, relations with India will not improve greatly, either. On the other hand, if Japan focuses and advances on strengthening its partnerships in Asia as seen in most of PM Hatoyama's speeches hitherto, India could be an attractive partner and an appealing destination for Japanese technology transfer and investment. Immediate action is pending on this count due to the slow decision making process in Japan, though it has only been three months since the DPJ has come into office. Nevertheless, many are certain to view an extension of the India-Japan tie-up as an evolving front against the 'peaceful rise' of China, if not anti-Chinese. India and China have also emerged strong in their understanding gained at the COP-15 meeting.

India and Japan had cordial relations until the year 2000 which were undoubtedly assisted by the following mechanisms: Treaty of Peace (1952), Agreement for Air Service (1956), Cultural Agreement (1957), Agreement of Commerce (1958), Convention for the Avoidance of Double Taxation (1960), and Agreement on Cooperation in the field of Science and Technology (1985).

Nevertheless, it is only in the period since former Japanese PM Yoshiro Mori visited India followed by his successors − Koizumi Junichiro and Abe Shinzo − that the bilateral relations has seen the fast forward movement. Especially appreciated by Japan are India's economic liberalistion in the wake of globalisation, privitisation, as well as deregulation to facilitate the flow of FDI and allow development. Realising the potential of India emerging as a future global force coupled with an idea of taking advantage of economic opportunities that exist in India, Japan allowed for more investment and ODA. These measures matched perfectly with the political understanding and cooperation.

The bilateral relations evolved to cover today such areas as defense and security, joint naval exercises, parliamentary exchange, and business and cultural delegations. There exist enormous opportunities for cooperation, as reflected in several joint statements issued by Indian and Japanese PMs during their annual summits, both at Asian regional as well as global levels in resolving global knotty issues including expansion of the UN Security Council, securing energy and the environment. Nevertheless, they lack considerable will to forge a common strategy at vital forums such as global meetings on climate change.

References:

Asia Economic Policy Conference organized by the Federal Reserve Bank of Opinion Survey on the Image of Japan in India May 8, 2009.

Business confidence up, but gloom remains, *The Asahi Shimbun*, 14 December 2009.

Chellaney, Brahma, 'Dancing with the dragon', *Japan Times,* June 25, 2009.

Chellaney, Brahma, Security and Strategic Challenges in Asia − Prospects of Japan-India Cooperation, *Proceedings from Observer Research Foundation, Chennai India Symposium,* August 2008.

China View (2009), Survival from financial crisis highlights 2009 www.chinaview.cn, 9 December 2009.

Chu, Shulong, The East Asia Summit: Looking for an Identity, *Brookings Northeast Asia Commentary,* Number 6 February 2007.

Community Building, *Japan Center for International Exchange,* No. 1, January 2006.

Desker, Barry, Why the East Asia Summit matters, PacNet, No. 55B, Pacific Forum/CSIS, Honolulu, Hawaii, 19 December 2005

Domique Moisi, Recognizing confident India as indispensable, *The Japan Time,* 22, December 2009

Economic stimulus plan ── *The Asahi Shimbun,* AsahiIHT: December 10, 2009.

Economic Survey of Japan: overcoming the global crisis-the need for a new growth model, 30 September 2009.

Emmott, Bill, *Rivals: How the Power Struggle Between China, India and Japan Will Shape Our Next Decade,* (London; Allen Lane, 2008).

Eric Johnston, Divided Climate Summit ends with Deal, *Japan Times,* 20 Dec 2009.

Expanded stimulus package, *The Japan Times*: Friday, Dec. 11, 2009.

FICCI, "Current state of Indian Economy" 2009, http://www.ficci.com/indian-economy-Sept_2009.pdf, October 2009.

Ghosh J and C. P. Chandrasekhar (2009), "The costs of 'coupling': the global crisis and the Indian economy" *Cambridge Journal of Economics* 2009, 33, 725–739 doi:10.1093/cje/bep034.

Gov't employee winter bonuses fall significantly, December 9 2009 /Eastern *(Breitbart.com).*

Hassan, Mohamed Jawhar, Strengthening Cooperation in East Asia: Towards an East Asian Community, *Paper presented at the 1st Korea-ASEAN Cooperation Forum,* 10-12 November 2006.

Hogg, Charu Lata, India and its Neighbours: Do Economic Interests have the potential to build peace? *Chatham House Report,* (October 2007). http://www.atimes.com/atimes/South_Asia/IF09Df03.html.

Hughes, Christopher W, Japan's response to China's rise: regional engagement, global containment, dangers of collision, *International Affairs* 85: 4 (2009) pp. 837–856.

Inamori Kazuo, Finally a Trrue Change of Government, *Japan Echo,* Vol. 36, No. 6, December 2009.

India elsewhere: A special report on India, *The Economist,* December 11, 2008..

Japan's Active Engagement in Business Cooperation with India II, *Embassy of Japan,* New Delhi, April 2007, http://www.in.emb-japan.go.jp

Japan's response to current crisis, Tanimoto Senior Vice Minister of Cabinet Office, June 8, 2009, International Monetary Fund Conference, Kyoto.

Jiang Guopeng, Survival from financial crisis highlights 2009, Chinaview.cn, 09 December 2009.

Kitaoka Shin'ichi and Mikuriya Takashi, Starting Point for a Transformation, *Japan Echo,* Vol. 36, No. 6, December 2009.

Kojima Akira, Japan as Number Three, *Japan Echo,* Vol. 36, No. 6, December 2009.

Masaaki Shirakawa: Coping with financial crisis—Japan's experiences and current global financial crisis, Address by Mr Masaaki Shirakawa, Governor of the Bank of Japan, at the Fourth Deposit Insurance Corporation of Japan Round Table, Tokyo, 25 February 2009.

Nariai Osamu, Short comings in the DPJ's Economic Policies, *Japan Echo,* Vol. 36, No. 6, December 2009.

'New East Asia, old enmities' *The Economist,* October 6, 2005.

Opinion Survey on the Image of Japan in India, *Ministry of foreign Affairs,* Govt of Japan, May 8, 2009.

Outstanding balance of government bonds to top 600 trillion yen, *The Asahi Shimbun,* 12 December 2009.

Panda, Rajaram and Yoo Fukazawa (eds.) *India and Japan: In Search of Global Roles.*

Rakesh Mohan (2008), "Global Financial Crisis and Key Risks: Impact on India and Asia", IMF-FSF High-Level Meeting on the Financial Turmoil and Policy Responses at Washington D.C. October 9. http://rbidocs.rbi.org.in/rdocs/Speeches/PDFs/87784.pdf

Ryou, Hayoun, India-Japan Security Cooperation: Chinese Perceptions, *IPCS Issue Brief,* No 89 (January 2009)San Francisco Santa Barbara, CA, United States October 20, 2009.

Sakakibara Eisuke, A Golden Opportunity for the Japanese Economy, *Japan Echo,* Vol. 36, No. 6, December 2009.

SASAKI Takeshi, The End of Two Eras, *Japan Echo,* Vol. 36, No. 6, December 2009.

Satu P. Limaye, Tokyo's Dynamic Diplomacy: Japan and the Subcontinent's Nuclear Tests, *Contemporary Southeast Asia,* August 2000.

Subbarao D (2009), "Impact of the Global Financial Crisis on India Collateral Damage and Response" at the Symposium on *"The Global Economic Crisis and Challenges for the Asian Economy in a Changing*

World" organized by the Institute for International Monetary Affairs, Tokyo, 18 February 2009.

http://www.bis.org/review/r090223b.pdf

Suri, Anirudh, India and Japan: Congruence, at Last, *Asia Times Online,* June 9, 2007.

Tadashi Isozumi, economic recovery slower than expected, *The Daily Yomiuri,* 11 December 2009.

Tanaka, Hitoshi, The ASEAN+3 and East Asia Summit: A Two-Tiered Approach to Community Building, *Japan Center for International Exchange,* No. 1, January 2006.

Tatsuya Tanimoto (2009), "Japan's contribution in response to the current crisis" speech by senior vice minister of cabinet office, International Monetary Conference Kyoto, Japan June 8, 2009.

Terashima Jitsusro, Time for a Mature Foreign Policy, *Japan Echo,* Vol. 36, No. 6, December 2009.

Tomoki Matsubara, Hatoyama vows support for democracy in Asia, *The Daily Yomiuri,* 11 December 2009.

World Economic and Financial Crisis－Japan and The Asia Pacific, *The Asia-Pacific Journal* : Japan Focus Luke Nottage, Lessons from Japan for the US financial crisis *East Asia Forum.*

第11章 大きすぎて助けられない世界の金融メルトダウン

Chapter 11 Too Big To Bail: The "Paulson Put," U.S. Presidential Politics, and the Global Financial Meltdown

Thomas Ferguson and Robert Johnson*

In March 2008 the Death's Head suddenly appeared over the offices of Bear Stearns, the giant brokerage house, in lower Manhattan.[1] To the astonishment of the world, U.S. Treasury Secretary Hank Paulson and Federal Reserve Chair Ben Bernanke−both Republicans nominated to their positions by President George W. Bush−and then New York Federal Reserve Bank President Timothy Geithner responded by introducing a visionary single payer government insurance scheme−not for sick Americans, but for ailing financial houses. Stretching both law and precedent, they threw open the Federal Reserve's discount window not only to commercial banks, but also to investment banks that were

---

* Thomas Ferguson is Professor of Political Science at the University of Massachusetts, Boston. Robert Johnson was formerly Managing Director at Soros Funds Management and Chief Economist of the United States Senate Banking Committee.
1) This paper draws liberally from Thomas Ferguson and Robert Johnson, "Too Big To Bail: The 'Paulson Put,' Presidential Politics, and the Global Financial Meltdown, Part I: From Shadow Banking System To Shadow Bailout," *International Journal of Political Economy* 38 (Spring, 2009), 3-34; and Thomas Ferguson and Robert Johnson, "Too Big To Bail: The 'Paulson Put' Presidential Politics, and the Global Financial Meltdown Part II: Fatal Reversal− Single Payer and Back," *International Journal of Political Economy* 38 (2009), 5-45. These essays are extensively documented; given their ready availability, this paper trims references to a minimum. Unless specifically noted, citations to newspapers and magazines are normally to their internet sites, not the printed edition. We cite specific URLs only if confusion seems likely. Note that many daily papers post articles late on the night before the print edition appears.
We thank Jane D'Arista, William Black, Jan Kregel, Gerald O'Driscoll, Mario Seccareccia, Peter Temin, and the editor of this book for comments and assistance. We owe special debts to Joseph Stiglitz and Walker Todd for very extensive comments and discussions. Our study started out as a chapter in a projected book on the economic crisis being put together by Stiglitz with Jose Antonio Ocampo and Stephany Griffth-Jones for Oxford University Press. The chapter we submitted was heavily praised, but we were asked to shorten the essay and specifically to remove the names of a series of Democratic party political figures now in power. We were agreeable to shortening, but not to air brushing the names and instead published with the *IJPE*.

primary dealers in government securities. By special agreement with the Treasury, the New York Fed also took on to its books $30 billion dollars of Bear Stearns' bad assets so that J. P. Morgan Chase could take over what remained of the Bear.

On September 7, Paulson and Bernanke dramatically confirmed the new collectivist course by taking over Fannie Mae and Freddie Mac, the two gigantic Government Sponsored Enterprises (GSEs) that support mortgage markets. At a stroke the government acquired new gross liabilities equal to 40% of US Gross Domestic Product.[2]

But on September 15 — a date that will be forever emblazoned in the financial history of the world, alongside that fatal 5th of June, 1931, when German Chancellor Heinrich Brüing repudiated Reparations and precipitated chain bankruptcy in Western Europe the reluctant revolutionaries suddenly had second thoughts.[3] They decided to cross up markets and do what free market conservatives had been demanding since the beginning of the crisis: let a giant financial house — Lehman Brothers — go bankrupt.

The result was catastrophic. Gigantic runs began on money market funds, commercial paper, and many banks. Stock markets everywhere went into free fall as panicky investors drove yields on safer government securities down practically to zero — in effect signaling a preference for government bonds to all other assets in the world. As inter-bank markets ground to a terrifying halt, Paulson, Bernanke, and Geithner borrowed another page from Lenin (or, more accurately, Mussolini, for their clear intention was to support, not replace, private markets) and effectively nationalized AIG, the giant insurer. Then Paulson and Bernanke raced to Congress to confront it with a stunning choice: Pass at once a gigantic, ill-defined $700 billion asset buying program that the Treasury would

---

2) Formally the Federal Housing Finance Authority took them into conservatorship. For the gross liabilities, see Martin Wolf, "No Alternative To Nationalization," *Financial Times* (September 8, 2008).

3) Cf. Thomas Ferguson and Peter Temin, "Made in Germany: The Germany Currency Crisis of July 1931," in Research in *Economic History 21*, ed. Alexander J. Field (Oxford, 2003), 1-53 and Ferguson and Temin, "Comment on The German Twin Crises of 1931," *Journal of Economic History* 64 (September, 2004), 872-76

administer with no review or accountability or else bear responsibility for a real life financial Armageddon.

With the public seething and elites bitterly divided, the American political system seemed for a few vertiginous days on the verge of melting down itself. In the end an amended bailout bill passed, larded up with more pork than a runaway Oscar Mayer refrigeration car.

Shockingly, however, world markets just shrugged. They continued melting down. Eventually British Prime Minister Gordon Brown stepped in. Openly deriding Paulson's vague asset-buying proposal as a clueless giveaway of taxpayer money, Brown focused on recapitalizing British banks at a relatively stiff price. The amount injected was too small to solve the problem, and the government did not take the bad assets off the banks' books or force the banks to write them down; but next to the pathetic U.S. effort, Brown's plan almost glowed. Along with the Irish government's decision to guarantee all deposits, it set off a competitive scramble among the G7 countries to ring fence their financial systems from total collapse via partial nationalizations, state loan guarantees, and extended insurance on bank deposits.

The swift creation of relative safe havens in the big core capitalist countries triggered an enormous inflow of capital from developing countries into first world financial centers. Many investors dumped assets indiscriminately in their haste for safety. Financial systems in the developing world, including Eastern Europe, teetered on the brink of collapse. The U.S. Federal Reserve, which had already opened unlimited swap lines with several first world central banks, brushed aside concerns about multilateralism and opened new $30 billion swap lines for central banks in Mexico, Korea, Brazil, and Singapore.

As this paper goes to press, the usual suspects — finance ministers, heads of state, leading bankers — are, like Humpty Dumpty's men, struggling to put all the pieces back together again. But a jumble of discordant viewpoints and the changeover of the American Presidency in the midst of the crisis have made it hard to come to grips with what has happened and why.

Some key points are obvious. The widely touted American investment banking-led model of global finance has plainly collapsed. All major American investment houses have either gone bankrupt or defensively transformed themselves into commercial bank holding companies. Out of the debris a new, universal bank based financial system appears to be taking shape, one in which preferential access to government aid and the Federal Reserve's discount window is likely to be pivotal.[4] The place of money market funds, hedge funds, and non-banks in this new system is murky. What is clear is that a new round of "corporatism" in which the state moves more deeply into the day to day functioning of markets is taking shape.

But the giant, ever-swelling tide of bailouts has done little more than stave off complete collapse. While officials and business leaders celebrate the "green shoots" of recovery (principally rises in share prices and declines in risk premia on some financial instruments), unemployment rates around the world remain stubbornly high. Mortgage defaults and bankruptcies are still running at high levels, while private consumption in the US and elsewhere stagnates. Financial markets have still not returned to "normalcy." Banks are not lending—though many are paying bonuses, lobbying, and making political campaign contributions—and most private credit markets remain at least semi-frozen. The so-called "shadow banking system" of so-called "non-banks" that formerly lent prodigiously almost literally to all comers has collapsed, while the rest of American business is engrossed in "deleveraging" (paying down debt). The U.S. Treasury is plainly "picking winners" in finance as other sectors of the economy queue up for bailouts of their own. With a new round of staggeringly expensive bank bailouts looming, the Federal Reserve continues not only to support the banking system but in many instances to replace it via the myriad "special lending facilities" that it set up earlier in the crisis.

Clearly, the long running debates about the future of the international monetary system badly missed the mark. These all focused on the likelihood that foreign dollar holders—possibly China, or Japan, or major

---

4) Universal banks should not be confused with financial supermarkets, as the recent split up of Citigroup suggests; cf. Peter Thal Larsen, "Death Call On Universal Banking Premature," *Financial Times, January* 14 2009.

Arab oil exporters — might some day ring down the curtain on the system by dumping their holdings in response to unsustainable current account deficits.[5] This crisis, however, has "Made in America" stamped all over it; a complete breakdown of financial regulation lies at its heart.

Yet not only the public, but many participants in financial markets continue to shake their heads about precisely what happened and why nothing seems to be working very well, even though the Federal Reserve's balance sheet more than doubled in size between the start of the crisis and Spring, 2009.

This paper distills parts of our longer analysis of the world financial meltdown from its origins to Election Day 2008. We suggest that the serial disasters had little to do with conventional "policy errors" or, as many have increasingly wondered, sheer incompetence, though both were plentifully in evidence. Instead, what we term the "Paulson Put" (on par with the fabled "Greenspan Put" that implicitly promised Fed action in cases of steep stock market declines) is key to understanding what happened.[6]

The original idea of the Paulson Put was to stave off high profile public financial bailouts until after the election, when they were less likely to trigger a political firestorm that could threaten existing wealth holders by opening up a Pandora's Box of reform demands. The key expression here is "high profile," for the Paulson Put had two distinct policy faces. One, already alluded to, embraced the highly visible adoption of "single payer"

---

5) See, e.g., the gigantic literature on the "New Bretton Woods System" spawned by such papers as Michael P. Dooley, David Folkerts-Landau, and Peter Garber, "The Revived Bretton Woods System: The Effects of Periphery Intervention and Reserve Management on Interest Rates and Exchange Rates," National Bureau of Economic Research (Cambridge, 2004), Working Paper 10332.

6) When someone buys a "put" he or she purchases the right to sell an asset at a specified price. In effect, one is buying insurance against price declines. By extension, the "Greenspan Put" referred to the market's belief that the Fed Chair would steer the Fed to counteract large declines in the market. The existence of a "Greenspan Put" was widely acknowledged within financial markets for excellent reasons: Greenspan, in speeches, left no doubt about his intentions. See the discussion in Gerald O'Driscoll, "Money and the Present Crisis," manuscript, (2008). But various scholars have questioned the evidence about the Fed's actual behavior. A good review is Willem Buiter, "Central Banks and Financial Crises," a paper presented at the Federal Reserve Bank of Kansas City Symposium on "Maintaining Stability in A Changing Financial System" (Jackson Hole, Wyoming, Aug. 21-23, 2008). As O'Driscoll, "Money," observes, the put is entailed by Greenspan's (and Bernanke's) insistence that the Fed could clean up asset bubbles after they burst.

government insurance for banks, investment houses, and Government Sponsored Enterprises (Fannie and Freddie). The second was a much less heralded "shadow bailout" designed to prop up the financial system in ways that would attract as little attention as possible. This latter effort knit together another emergency safety net for banks in trouble out of separate threads that were each by themselves all but imperceptible: Assistance on a gigantic scale to banks and thrifts from the obscure Federal Home Loan Bank System, a concerted effort to play down eventual taxpayer liabilities for Federal Deposit Insurance payouts, emergency purchases by the GSEs, especially Fannie Mae, of home mortgages and mortgage bonds to stem declines in those markets; finally, unconventional expansions of the Federal Reserve's balance sheet.

Unfortunately, bursting asset bubbles nourished on high leverage are reverse Cinderella stories on steroids. At midnight the transit is not from beautiful dream to drab reality, but to the very gates of hell itself, as whole economies and credit systems crash for years.[7] By striving to put off a reckoning as long as possible, the Paulson Put guaranteed that the final cleanup bill would rise astronomically. In a political system in which "no new taxes" is an axiom of political life for both political parties, it also set off a desperate search for short cuts that would not work, such as turning the Federal Reserve's balance sheet inside out, to avoid going to Congress.

Eventually the Paulson Put collapsed under the weight of all these contradictions. As Bear Stearns vividly illustrated, there was no unobtrusive way to stretch the Put to cover investment banks. That could only happen during a cataclysm. No less fatefully, involving the GSEs in the shadow bailout was quixotic. Already compromised by political pressures and past accounting scandals, the GSEs were too financially fragile to be used as safety valves. Paulson & Co.'s efforts to use them for this purpose pushed them over the edge, leading anxious foreign investors to dump their bonds and forcing their de facto nationalization.

The reaction to the takeover of Fannie and Freddie, in turn threw the switch on the doomsday machine—the disastrous series of actions and

---

7) The best discussion of the macroeconomics of bursting bubbles is Richard Koo, *The Holy Grail of Macroeconomics: Lessons From Japan's Great Recession,* Revised ed. (Singapore, 2009).

reactions that destroyed the (first) Paulson Put as well as all chances Republican Senator John McCain had of winning the presidency: First, the unpopular GSE bailout in the midst of the election campaign. Then, in convulsive reaction to furious critics in and out of the Republican Party, the decision to let Lehman Brothers go bankrupt—in effect, the definitive expiration of the original Paulson Put. The final part of our discussion traces how the original Paulson Put morphed into a newer, chastened version fixated on protecting existing shareholders in America's leading financial firms from dilution—a preoccupation that led directly to the meltdown of the whole world financial system, since it fatally compromised any chance of a serious bailout. As a result, the banking system remains under pressure. With the Federal Reserve continuing to make markets for many classes of assets, the serious work of reconstructing the financial system has barely begun.

The Paulson Put is Born

The "Paulson Put" was a response to the problems growing out of the more famous "Greenspan Put" and the deregulatory bacchanal that it supported. But that story, along with its relation to global imbalances, is too complex to trace here. We, accordingly, present that discussion elsewhere.[8] Here it is necessary to begin with the situation in early August, 2007, when the Fed was still acting as though inflation was the biggest threat to the American economy.

Market reaction to the Fed's refusal to cut rates on August 7 was brutal. The stock market swooned; the dollar fell. A broken trail of evidence suggests that neither Bernanke nor Paulson fully appreciated the danger to the economy as a whole, but they quickly got the message that Wall Street and America's greatest banks were in peril. Both the Fed and the Treasury abruptly switched gears. Still cautioning against proposals from

---

8) Ferguson and Johnson, "'Paulson Put' Part I"; the campaign mounted by the Fed under Greenspan to shuck its traditional responsibility for regulating primary dealers in government securities has still not received the attention it deserves. This striking case of a government agency lobbying to shrink its mission should be a yellow flag in the face of the current push to make the Fed responsible for monitoring the stability of the U.S. financial system.

the Democratic Congress to bail out homeowners, Bernanke and Paulson now began improvising a strategy for getting help to the banks that would not attract attention.

From the Greenspan to the Paulson Put.

The Treasury secretary and the Fed chair knew, like everyone else in the markets, that chances for success hinged on cooperating with each other. If markets sensed that their two institutions were working at cross-purposes, the response would be swift and disastrous. But their positions were not institutionally equivalent. The Secretary of the Treasury was part of the president's team, formally partisan, and by design responsive to direct political pressures. By contrast, the Fed had a more restricted range of action and was formally nonpartisan. Indeed, in the mythology, it was nonpolitical. Although the president could fire Paulson at any time, he could not dismiss Bernanke once he had appointed him. Traditional banking crisis doctrine assigned to the Treasury chief the responsibility for bailing out banks, on the excellent grounds that backdoor bailouts by central banks were hard to police and even harder to stop before they started inflating the currency. The traditional view thus insisted that Congress and the president, acting through the budget process, shoulder responsibility for bailouts.[9]

This defined the problem that the "Paulson Put," as we call it, was designed to overcome. For the president and Congress to assume responsibility for bailouts was fine in theory. But the Republicans had only recently been mauled in the 2006 midterm congressional elections. Having lost control of both Houses of Congress, they now faced a housing crisis of their own: losing the White House. The Republican Right was on a

---

9) See, e.g., Walker Todd, "Lessons of the Past and Prospects for the Future of Lender of Last Resort Theory," Federal Reserve Bank of Cleveland (Cleveland, 1988), Working Paper No. 8805 and Todd, "History of and Rationales For the Reconstruction Finance Corporation," *Federal Reserve Bank of Cleveland Economic Review* (1992) Q IV, 22-35. Our own approach would stress more strongly public goods aspects of the problem. The Reconstruction Finance Corporation, it is important to note, was in fact the creation first of all of the largest US banks. See the detailed account, based on extensive archival research in Gerald Epstein and Thomas Ferguson, "Monetary Policy, Loan Liquidation, and Industrial Conflict: The Federal Reserve and the Open Market Operations of 1932," *Journal of Economic History* 44 (1984), 957-83. We regard the Swedish bailout as superior to the RFC, which looks good mostly by comparison to the Bush or Obama administrations' approach.

tear about spending. Even more seriously, income distribution had at last emerged as a public issue. In the face of years of propaganda about the "magic of the marketplace," the spectacle of the U.S. government pouring in large sums of money to rescue institutions controlled by America's most affluent citizens promised to be toxic. Neither party's leaders were likely to be enthusiastic; but because Republicans would be making the key decisions in the White House and Treasury, the brunt of the blame figured to fall on them.

The Shadow Bailout: Federal Home Loan Banks

Paulson and Bernanke, accordingly, evolved a two-track strategy for getting out of the crisis or, to be precise, for rescuing Wall Street and the banks. The Fed, whose every move in money markets was closely scrutinized, at once took measures that were customary for central banks, or at least the U.S. central bank, in these situations. It cut rates sharply —once even by a startling three quarters of a point—and talked up cooperation with other central banks, which were now discovering that many financial houses in their own countries had also been drinking the Kool-Aid of "riskless" collateralized debt obligations (CDOs).

Paulson's moves, by contrast, were much more circumspect. Indeed, at times he virtually disappeared from public view. Behind the scenes, however, he was very much engaged. Formally or informally, the Treasury Department was the dominant force in a network of lesser-known financial agencies that collectively commanded massive financial and regulatory resources that could help distressed financial houses. Paulson, as head of Treasury and—in this case perhaps more importantly—informal chief of the administration's economic policy making apparatus, could thus preside over a gigantic Shadow Bailout of the shadow banking system with public money that almost no one tracked. With most of the media and even the markets fixated on the Fed, his first move was simple: Sit back and watch quietly while regional federal home loan banks shoveled billions and billions of dollars out to banks and mortgage companies, including many of America's largest.[10]

---

10) The Treasury Secretary's formal authority over the various agencies we discuss here varies; his real influence is also subject to informal pressures and suasion. In practice, however, we agree with Barton Gellman, *Angler* (New York, 2008) that Paulson had taken over the reins of economic policy from Vice President Cheney.

Figure 1 The Shadow Bailout:
Total Outstanding Federal Home Loan Bank System Debt

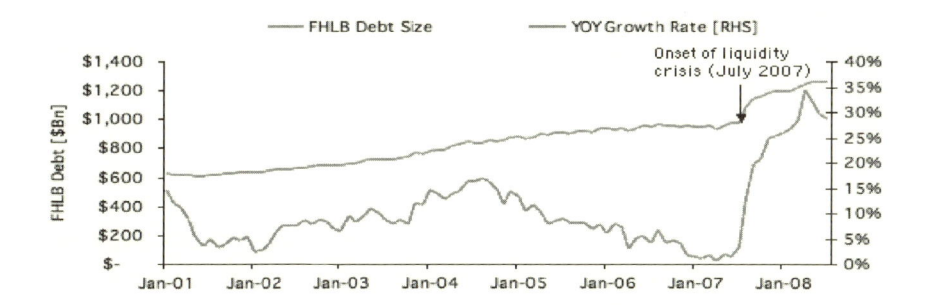

Sources: Citigroup, From Federal Home Loan Bank (FHLB) and Federal Deposit Insurance Corporation (FDIC) Data

Figure 1, with its associated table, tells the story. In the late summer of 2007, as the housing crisis snowballed into the credit crunch, the balance sheet of the federal home loan bank system exploded. As Figure 1 indicates, lending in the form of advances and other purchases of mortgage-related securities increased sharply. The aid went not only to the small banks or thrifts that were traditionally regarded as the system's clients but also — as the table shows — many of the very largest financial institutions in the United States (Table 1).

Table 1 Advances to 7 Large Banks

Year	Total	Subtotal Large	Large %
2005	619880	127096	20.50
2006	640681	178874	27.92
2007Q1	624418	190724	30.54
2007Q2	640035	191630	29.94
2007Q3	824000	263545	31.98
2007Q4	875061	261753	29.91
2008Q1	913104	265922	29.12
2008Q2	913897	256424	28.06

Source: FHLB and FDIC

The colossal dimensions of this Shadow Bailout, which drew little notice in the national press (and no discussion in presidential campaign coverage), are tellingly illustrated by a single comparison. In March 2008, the Fed rocked the world by advancing $30 billion to subsidize JPMorgan Chase's takeover of Bear Stearns. By contrast, in the third quarter of 2007, Countrywide Credit, the nation's largest mortgage institution, borrowed $22.3 billion from the Federal Home Loan Bank of Atlanta. This was on top of $28.8 billion that it already owed the Atlanta Regional Bank.[11]

Most American banks are members of the Federal Deposit Insurance Corporation (FDIC), which insures their deposits. Funds for paying out on that insurance come from charges on banks that the FDIC sets. Amounts vary by need, rising when bank failures proliferate. It is thus the banks themselves that are first on the hook for bank failures.

Since the 1990s, bank failure rates have generally been low; but as housing markets tanked in 2007, it became obvious that they were going to rise. This quickly raised concerns about the adequacy of the FDIC's "insurance fund." The obvious answer—raise assessments on banks—was not politically appealing. They are, after all, massive contributors to political campaigns at all level.[12] On the other hand, if they did not pay, someone else eventually would have to. Who was obvious—the public—just as it had after the last election in which waves of banks failed: in 1988. Public discussion of this eventuality, however, was precisely what the Shadow Bailout was designed to avoid.

Paulson and Co.'s solution was to try to slide through the campaign on the audacity of hope and let the FDIC spend down its reserves, while letting current and former FDIC officials explain that the "insurance fund" was backed by the Treasury, which would provide whatever sums were needed. Lost in the shuffle was the potential shift in the burden of

---

11) Calculated from statistics presented in James Hagerty and Joann Lublin, "Countrywide Deal Driven by Crackdown Fear," *Wall Street Journal*, January 29 2008. The Treasury established a temporary expanded credit line for the Federal Home Loan Bank System, with essentially no publicity, the day after the takeover of Fannie Mae and Freddie Mac.
12) See, e.g., Thomas Ferguson, *Golden Rule: The Investment Theory Of Party Competition And The Logic Of Money-Driven Political Systems* (Chicago, 1995 or Ferguson, "Blowing Smoke: Impeachment, the Clinton Presidency, and the Political Economy," in *The State of Democracy in America*, ed. William Crotty (Washington, D.C., 2001).

paying, from banks to taxpayers. When everyone's attention focused on the GSE bailout, discussed in the second part of this paper, the Treasury quietly inserted language into the bill removing penalties on Fed loans to failed banks. This was widely regarded as "a backdoor way to shore up the FDIC" by making it easier to tap the Fed for support.[13]

Eventually, snowballing bank failures (some very large) forced the FDIC to raise charges on the banks. In the bailout legislation, however, the Treasury included not only a much ballyhooed provision raising limits on deposit insurance from $100,000 to $250,000 but also a proviso permitting unlimited loans from the Treasury to the FDIC. The American public, which knew nothing of the "Ricardian Equivalence" beloved by conservative economists, according to which people immediately start saving to pay taxes they know are coming, was left in blissful ignorance, even as bank stock prices fell off a cliff.

By tapping the Federal Home Loan Bank Boards and blurring who would pay when the FDIC ran through its funds, the Shadow Bailout seemed for a time to be succeeding spectacularly. The press, scholars, and the Washington community let down their guard. Instead of following the money, they focused on the pageantry and drama of the presidential campaign. But even as the Republican candidates cut each other up and Barack Obama started to whittle down Hillary Clinton's seemingly insurmountable lead, Paulson made a fatal miscalculation: He decided to impress Fannie Mae and Freddie Mac into the Shadow Bailout.

The Shadow Bailout: Freddie and Fannie

In January 2008, the Republican administration and the Democrat-controlled Congress agreed that modest fiscal stimulus through tax rebates would be good public policy in an election year. Some Democrats, mostly in the House, appear to have favored a larger stimulus. Most Democratic leaders, however, were at best lukewarm to this, whereas Republican congressional leaders were actively hostile. Proposals for mortgage relief provoked additional discord. Representative Barney Frank (D-MA),

---

13) Yves Smith, "Housing Bailout Bill Also Eased Having Fed Rescue Banks," *Naked Capitalism*, July 31 2008.

chair of the House Financial Services Committee, talked up a plan to let bankruptcy judges modify mortgage terms — normal American legal practice for everything but mortgages.

Other Democratic leaders in both houses shied away from forcing the issue in the face of intense opposition from banks and the mortgage industry. In the end, the Democrats settled on a plan for mortgage relief originally promoted by Credit Suisse, Bank of America, and other financial institutions. Although decidedly more aggressive than the administration's, it did not include the bankruptcy language. The Democrats also embraced a proposal supported by the Mortgage Bankers Association that expanded the size of mortgages the two GSEs, Fannie Mae and Freddie Mac, could purchase. Both choices limited mortgage relief because few banks saw any reason to make concessions while the jumbo provision aided primarily affluent neighborhoods.[14]

Because the GSEs were, along with the Home Loan Banks, the instruments most perfectly adapted for use in a bailout intended to stay below the radar scan, they were swept up in the Shadow Bailout. Bending them to this purpose, however, was fraught with political peril and economic risk. Because of the clouds of sometimes partisan misinformation that now swirl around the GSEs, some clarification is necessary about exactly what they were and how they figured in the debacle that unfolded.

The Federal National Mortgage Association ("Fannie Mae") was founded during the high tide of the New Deal. For decades, it was the only game in town when it came to secondary mortgage markets; because of defaults and prepayments, making markets in secondary mortgages was just too

---

14) For Frank and the mortgage provisions, cf. James Politi and Krishna Guha, "Bush Attacks Democrats Housing Crisis Plan," *Financial Times* (February 29, 2008).; for Credit Suisse, Bank of America, and the Democrats, cf. Reuters, "Mortgage Bailout Plan Gains Traction in Congress," *Reuters*, March 13 2008. Compare this last with Atif Mian, Amir Sufi, and Francesco Trebbi, "The Political Economy of the U.S. Mortgage Default Crisis," National Bureau of Economic Research (Cambridge, 2008), Working Paper 14468, a paper we otherwise much admire. For the jumbos, see Krishna Guha and Jeremy Grant, "Analysts Predict Wave of Home Refinancing," *Financial Times* (January 25, 2008). For the Mortgage Bankers Association support, see Lindsay Renick Mayer, "Update: Fannie Mae and Freddie Mac Invest in Lawmakers," in *Center for Responsive Politics* (2008), The jumbo provision and a small provision for expanding Federal Housing Administration lending made it into the economic stimulus bill. Wider mortgage relief without the bankruptcy provision came later in the year.

risky for private lenders. In 1968, President Lyndon Johnson wanted to get as much debt as possible off the government's books. So Fannie Mae was privatized. In 1971, Congress chartered a similarly structured competitor: the Federal Home Loan Mortgage Corporation ("Freddie Mac" －both corporations eventually became known by their nicknames). Various administrations kept repeating the mantra that the GSEs were private corporations without full government backing.

Markets, however, mostly disbelieved this. Possibly, in the end, widespread confidence that the GSEs would be bailed out stemmed as much from their sheer size as from any putative moral obligation. In any case, once foreign central banks began buying large amounts of their bonds, perhaps on assurances of government guarantees offered by individuals who may not have had authority to make such commitments, Fannie and Freddie evolved into American originals: semipublic institutions too big and complicated to fail without international ramifications.

The spectacular growth of mortgage lending in the 1980s fundamentally altered the GSEs' environment. They were allowed to buy only medium-size ("conforming") mortgages from high-grade credit risks. Unlike the much smaller Government National Mortgage Association ("Ginny Mae"), whose obligations were carried on the books of the Treasury and were therefore backed by the "full faith and credit" of the U.S. government, Fannie Mae and Freddie Mac remained privately run and owned. But the presumption that they could count on a government bailout allowed them to raise money more cheaply than private firms. The latter thus had little prospect of competing in market segments the GSEs dominated.

As mortgage companies proliferated and secondary mortgage markets boomed in the 1980s, increasing numbers of banks and other potential competitors began to lobby Congress and successive administrations to prune back or even eliminate Fannie Mae and Freddie Mac. Wells Fargo Bank, General Electric (GE) Finance, Household Finance, and other large firms all became players in one or another of these efforts. GE even tried to persuade a group of Wall Street firms to form a direct competitor to the GSEs.[15] Prominent business－supported thinks tanks on the political

---

15) Paul Muolo and Mathew Padilla, *Chain of Blame* (Hoboken, 2008).

right took up the cause of abolishing the GSEs; the notion became a staple of media commentators who wanted to appear sophisticated and curry favor.

The GSEs defended themselves by spending more and more money on political contributions and lobbying. A conservative analysis limited to GSE contributions flowing only to sitting members of Congress in 2008 from 1989 onward reported total donations of just under $5 million. Another 2008 study that included lobbying totals as well as contributions suggested that "over the past decade" the two GSEs had spent almost $200 million "to buy influence." Through foundations they controlled, Fannie Mae and Freddie Mac also distributed millions of dollars more in grants, which, reporters have suggested, were sometimes awarded as favors to influential political figures.[16]

The subtlety of the GSE's maneuvering has been insufficiently appreciated by their myriad critics, in part because of the serpentine ways political money flows in the American political system. The New Deal legacy ensured that the two GSEs had a natural elective affinity with Democrats. Their political contributions reflect this: By one reckoning, between 1989 and 2008, they channeled 57 percent of their political funds to Democrats, with the three biggest recipients being Senate Banking Committee Chair Chris Dodd (D-CT) ($165,400) and Senators Barack Obama (D-IL) ($126,349) and John Kerry (D-MA) ($111,000). But they also maintained strong ties with a succession of "moderate" Republicans and lobbyists linked to the highest levels of the GOP, including Kenneth Duberstein, Frederick V. Malek, and Robert Zoellick.[17]

In the meantime, Fannie Mae and Freddie Mac mirrored with special force the Democratic party's broad "right turn" after 1980.[18] Many "New

---

16) For the contributons, see Lindsay Renick Mayer, "Seeking Stimulation," *Center for Responsive Politics* (2008), January 31 and Mayer, "Update: Fannie Mae and Freddie Mac Invest in Lawmakers," Center for Responsive Politics, Sept. 11; for the lobbying, cf. Lisa Lerer, "Fannie, Freddie Spent $200 Million To Buy Influence," *Yahoo.com* (July 16, 2008); for the foundations, see *Wall Street Journal*, "Fannie Mae's Political Immunity," July 29, 2008.

17) For the contributions, see Mayer, "Update," and the discussion in Ferguson and Johnson, "'Paulson Put,' Part II"; for the Republicans, see Jack Shaffer, "Fannie Mae and the Vast Bipartisan Conspiracy," *Slate* (September 16, 2008)..

18) Thomas Ferguson and Joel Rogers, *Right Turn: The Decline Of The Democrats And The Future of American Politics* (New York, 1986).

Democrats" gravitated naturally to the GSEs, which were, after all, exactly what New Democrats professed to admire: big, highly profitable businesses. Gradually, the GSEs began to function as a kind of political machine for this wing of the party. As Bill Clinton left office as president, for example, he appointed several top staffers to the boards of the GSEs, including Rahm Emmanuel and Harold Ickes.

In the 1990s, long-time Democratic operative Jim Johnson ran Fannie Mae before moving on to the compensation committee of Goldman Sachs, where he helped set the remuneration of Hank Paulson, then head of the firm. (In 2008, Democratic presidential nominee Barack Obama picked Johnson to vet possible running mates; he was forced to step aside when it came out that he, along with many other political figures, including Senate Banking Committee Chair Dodd, received a sweetheart loan from Countrywide Credit, long a staunch GSE ally).[19]

The GSE's political evolution affected their business strategies as the housing boom took off in the new millennium. By then they ranked among the largest enterprises in the United States. Like the rest of corporate America, remuneration of their top officers and advisers had spiraled upward, despite all the talk about their public service mission. An indulgent Congress also permitted the concerns to behave like most private companies and conceal or camouflage much of that compensation. Individual members of Congress who inquired about these arrangements were sometimes bluntly threatened.

Developments in mortgage markets after 2001, however, made traditional GSE rhetoric about their unique role in promoting homeownership ring hollow. Nothing Fannie Mae or Freddie Mac had to offer could top privately offered NINJA (no income, no job, no assets) mortgages that — as long as they lasted—funneled home loans to people

---

19) For Johnson, Paulson, and Obama, see Bethany Mclean, "Fannie Mae's Last Stand," *Vanity Fair*, February 2009, which records Johnson's denial when he left the Obama campaign that he had received favors from Countrywide. But see Zachary Goldfarb, "House GOP Report Details Countrywide's Efforts to Benefit VIPs," *Washington Post* (March 19, 2009) on the House Republican investigative study on Countrywide's "special loans." Note that a number of prominent McCain backers also had ties to the GSEs, though links to the Democrats generally ran somewhat tighter. See, for the Republicans, e.g., Jonathan Weisman, "Figures in Both Campaigns Have Deep Ties to Mortgage Giants," *Washington Post* (July 17, 2008).

who would otherwise not qualify. In the meantime Franklin Raines, who left the job as budget director in the Clinton administration to take over as Johnson's successor at Fannie Mae, and other GSE executives continued steering the two giants in what was sometimes described as more business-like directions—or, in other words, on a trajectory embracing many of the shenanigans other financial houses engaged in to inflate reported profits. Not because of any "dual mandate" Fannie Mae had to serve the public interest and also make profits, but because the top management would then become fabulously rich and share the wealth with friendly members of Congress and allied community groups.

Soon after he took the helm of Fannie Mae in 1998, Raines explicitly set a target of doubling earnings per share. William Black has shown that suborning the audit department's internal controls through high pressure and a munificent new bonus scheme appear to have been critical to his success.[20]

The explosive boom in collateralized debt obligations (CDOs) gave the GSEs a new, crucial, and hugely remunerative role: They provided guarantees that helped secure AAA ratings for the top tranches of the CDOs rolling off the assembly lines of Wall Street. Eventually, however, the

---

[20] This point is worth emphasizing, considering studies such as Peter J. Wallison and Charles Calomaris, "The Last Trillion Dollar Commitment: The Destruction of Fannie Mae and Freddie Mac," in *Financial Services Outlook*, American Enterprise Institute (Washington, D.C., 2008). As Black shows, it was the bonus and executive compensation systems modeled on those that were then proliferating in the private sector that created the incentive structures that led to the accounting debacles:
Raines learned that the unit that should have been most resistant to this 'overwhelming' financial incentive, Internal Audit, had succumbed to the perverse incentive. Mr. Rajappa, Senior Vice President for Operations Risk and Internal Audit, instructed his internal auditors in a formal address in 2000 (and provided the text of the speech to Raines): 'By now every one of you must have 6.46 [the earnings per share target] branded in your brains. You must be able to say it in your sleep, you must be able to recite it forwards and backwards, you must have a raging fire in your belly that burns away all doubts, you must live, breath and dream 6.46, you must be obsessed on 6.46. . . . After all, thanks to Frank [Raines], we all have a lot of money riding on it. . . . We must do this with a fiery determination, not on some days, not on most days but day in and day out, give it your best, not 50 percent, not 75 percent, not 100 percent, but 150 percent. Remember, Frank has given us an opportunity to earn not just our salaries, benefits, raises, ESPP, but substantially over and above if we make 6.46. So it is our *moral obligation* to give well above our 100 % and if we do this, we would have made tangible contributions to Frank's goals' (William Black, "Expert Witness Statement William K. Black in the Matter of Raines, Howard, and Spencer —Notice No. 2006-1," *Office of Federal Housing Enterprise Oversight*, [2008], emphasis in original).

GSE's emulation of Wall Street's business models caught up with them. To increase earnings, the firms took on more leverage. Along with the additional risk, they also tried smoothing earnings, just as many American businesses did during the stock market boom. They were caught and eventually forced to restate earnings.

Raines, an African American who was by then co-chair of the Business Roundtable, lashed back at his critics in a stormy congressional hearing. The hearing transcript reveals that he was vigorously assisted by several members of the Congressional Black Caucus who had supported Raines and the GSEs for years. They sought to deflect critics by drawing attention to the campaign business interests that had been mounting against the GSEs. One, Representative William Clay (D-MO), compared the attacks to a "witch hunt" and a "lynching." Eventually, however, mounting evidence of accounting irregularities and disclosures of bonuses and pension benefits of almost Medician proportions to Raines and other executives soured the mood. Representative Barney Frank labeled Raines's compensation and pension benefits "inappropriate," and members of Congress started demanding the money be returned.[21]

Although there was talk of indictments, no one was charged, though the Securities and Exchange Commission (SEC) sued Raines and two others. The case was settled after Raines departed Fannie Mae in December 2004 amid a chorus of promises of sweeping reforms by politicians in both parties.

At the time, the GSEs' prospects looked dire. But in fact their position was not as bleak as it seemed. With the housing boom cresting, homeownership as a political goal was irresistibly attractive, even to Republicans, who might normally be sympathetic to the idea of cutting the

---

21) For Raines, Clay, Democrats, and bonuses, see Lucian Bebchuck and Jesse Fried, "Executive Compensation at Fannie Mae: A Case Study of Perverse Incentives, Nonperformance Pay, and Camouflage," *Journal of Corporation Law* 30 (2005), 807-822; Stephen Lebaton, "Chief Says Fannie Mae Did Nothing Wrong," *New York Times*, October 7 2004; for the reaction, see Stephen Lebaton, "Shakeup at Fannie Mae: The Overview Assessing What Will Now Happen To Fannie Mae," *New York Times*, December 17, 2004 2004. For the transcript, see U.S. Congress, House (2004), "The OFEHO Report: Allegations of Accounting and Man- agement Failure at Fannie Mae." *Subcommittee on Capital Markets, Insurance, and Government Sponsored Enterprises, Committee on Financial Services.* Available at http://commdocs.house.gov/committees/bank/hba97754.000/hba97754_0f.htm.

GSEs down to size. In addition, the administration, like the Fed, warmly approved of subprime or any other kind of lending "free markets" threw up.

In a speech in Arizona in 2004, for example, President George W. Bush proclaimed, "We want more people owning their own homes." Yet, the president lamented, "Not enough minorities own their own homes. And it seems like to me it makes sense to encourage all to own homes. And so we've done some interesting things. Again, I want to thank Congress. But we passed down payment assistance programs that will help low-income folks buy their own home. . . . I proposed that mortgages that have FHA [Federal Housing Administration]-backed insurance pay no down payment." Just in case that was not enough, however, the housing boom cheerleader in chief also averred that "I've called on private sector mortgage banks and banks to be more aggressive about lending money to first-time home buyers. And the response has been really good."[22]

At just about that moment, the chief executive officer (CEO) of the most aggressive mortgage bank in the United States—who, not coincidentally, happened to be a prominent financial supporter of the president's reelection bid—was cranking up a broad national campaign in favor of exactly what the president professed to want: "homeownership for all." But Angelo Mozilo, Countrywide Credit's visionary founder, was also a long-time supporter of Fannie Mae and Freddie Mac. He and his now gigantic concern were also anything but doctrinaire: Although he supported Bush for reelection, along with many other Republicans, Mozilo and his firm had also maintained close relations with many Democrats in Congress and the GSEs, from Fannie Mae's Jim Johnson on down. The mortgage giant quickly reached across the aisle to Democrats for help with its homeownership campaign—and to shield Fannie Mae and Freddie Mac in their moment of maximum vulnerability.[23]

The campaign to save the GSEs enjoyed a singular advantage: It could tap a broad, preexisting network of allies for help. For many years, a network of community organizations including parts of ACORN (the

---

22) Floyd Norris, "Who's To Blame," *New York Times Floyd Norris Blog* (October 8, 2008).

Association of Community Organizations for Reform Now) and small, local businesses had functioned as a loose, decentralized, and pluralistic support network for the GSEs. The original inspiration for many participants appears to have been the cause of low-income housing. But as the neoliberal Democratic tilt in the GSEs increased, the network's uses for broader campaigns that profited the GSEs and allied mortgage bankers became apparent.[24]

The result was a political movement and ideological syncretism that has not received the attention it deserves. The mostly neoliberal business executives and their friends in Congress reached out to community activists who were hungry for funds and meaningful roles in a social system that

---

23) Mozilo himself donated at least $5,500 to the 2004 Bush campaign, narrowly defined to exclude donations to the Republican National Committee. He was not the only executive from the firm who personally contributed. Countrywide's political action committee also donated $5,000. Note that total political contributions by the firm and its executives ran substantially larger, and some party contributions should perhaps be reckoned in. But the subject is too complicated for this paper. It is enough to say that Countrywide's donations in 2004 definitely tilted toward Republicans, though, as discussed below, the firm had important Democratic allies even that year, making smaller contributions even to John Kerry's campaign. The campaign finance data come from the Federal Election Commission, as presented by Political Money Line

24) The *Wall Street Journal*, in its editorial and op ed pages, along with many analysts from think tanks in Washington, D.C., have encouraged notions that the subprime crisis was somehow integrally related to earlier battles over the Community Reinvestment Act (CRA). See Robert Gordon, "Did Liberals Cause the Subprime Crisis?," in *American Prospect*, Sept. 16, 2008; this viewpoint was also represented at the 2008 Jackson Hole Conference sponsored by the Kansas City Federal Reserve Bank; cf. Gary Gorton, "The Panic of 2007," in Paper Presented at the Federal Reserve Bank of Kansas City Symposium on "Maintaining Stability in a Changing Financial System," (Jackson Hole Wyoming, 2008), Aug. 21-23. But the evidence is overwhelmingly against this claim: Most lenders that were enthusiastic users of mortgage bonds in the 1980s strongly supported Reagan administration efforts to trim back the CRA. It is true that in the mid-1990s, the Clinton administration sought to link fulfillment of CRA requirements by banks to purchases of GSE bonds, but that effort was watered down by the Bush administration after 2001, just as subprime lending exploded. Even more to the point, though, most subprime loans were made by finance companies and mortgage banks that were not subject to the CRA or by banks that only partially were (Gordon, "Did Liberals"). It is also clear that institutions not subject to the CRA afforded notably worse loan terms to their clients; cf. Janet Yellen, "Opening Remarks to the 2008 National Interagency Community Reinvestment Conference," Federal Reserve Bank of San Francisco, March 31, 2008, http://www.frbsf.org/news/speeches/2008/0331.html. Analyses such as Wallison and Calomaris (2008) neglect the context of private sector interests that are the real roots of the GSE's wreck. The story is really another variation on Epstein and Ferguson, "Monetary Policy." Of course, such accounts also omit all mention of the Shadow Bailout, which, as described below, was directly responsible for pushing Fannie and Freddie over the edge.

increasingly exalted business as the speculum mentis, the highest activity of the human mind. As they became comfortable with casual references to "working-class housing," mortgage bankers often joined the GSEs in picking up the tab for community "housing campaigns."

Countrywide's drive on behalf of "home ownership for all" brought this impeccably politically correct movement to a new level of refinement. Fannie Mae, Fred- die Mac, Countrywide, Washington Mutual, Ameriquest, New Century Financial, HSBC, and other mortgage firms joined leaders from nonprofits and the Hispanic Political Caucus to support an organization to promote homeownership called Hogar (Spanish for "home"). Mozilo himself actively preached the gospel, and his activities were widely appreciated. In 2004, the National Housing Conference declared him "Person of the Year" for his efforts to advance homeownership among minority and low-income families. As the Bush administration moved to cut the GSEs down to size in the wake of the scandals, Mozilo and like-minded private sector supporters closed ranks with the network to beat back attacks on the GSEs.[25]

Democratic congressional leaders were willing to consider certain reforms, but they wanted safeguards on subprime mortgages. They

---

25) For the campaign, see, e.g., *Mortgage Banking*, "Countrywide Announces $1 Trillion Commitment," *Mortgage Banking*, February 5, 2005 or Jeffrey Lubell, "Homes For Working Families: Increasing the Availability of Affordable Homes," Center for Housing Policy (Washington, D.C., 2006). One vehicle for the effort was an organization called Homes for Working Families. Mozilo chaired its board, on which sat the CEOs of both Fannie and Freddie. Lubell, "Homes." Lubell's report was issued for this group by the Center for Housing Policy, which described itself as "the research affiliate" of the National Housing Conference. For Hogar, cf. Susan Schmidt and Maurice Tamman, "Housing Push For Hispanics Spawns Wave of Foreclosures," *Wall Street Journal*, January 5, 2009. LatinoPoliticsBlog.com, "The Great American Mortgage Scam and the Latino Community," *LatinoPoliticsBlog.com*, March 15 2009, notes how, since the mortgage bubble burst, the Hispanic Congressional Caucus has distanced itself from even the memory of the effort. For Fannie and Freddie's support of ACORN and the Citizenship Education Fund, which grew out of the Reverend Jesse Jackson's Operation PUSH (People United to Save Humanity), see *Wall Street Journal*, "Fannie." For Mozilo's award, see "National Housing Conference to Honor Angelo Mozilo for Lowering Homeownership Barriers." *Nation's Building News* (May 17). Available at http://www.nbnnews.com/NBN/issues/2004-05-17/ Housing+Finance/2.html, accessed October 10, 2008. This is the newspaper of the National Homebuilders Association; it was sponsored by Countrywide. The attack on Freddie and Fannie is the real context of the story related in Charles Duhigg, "Pressured To Take More Risk, Fannie Hit A Tipping Point," New York Times, October 4 2008 and explains by Daniel Mudd was so eager to please Mozilo.

also drew a line at eliminating GSE support for programs promoting public and low-income housing that nourished the activist network. The administration, the financial industry, and the Federal Reserve all strongly opposed restrictions on subprime mortgages. Indeed, though the point vanished in the heat of the 2008 presidential campaign, at the time the administration wanted even more subprime lending. Eventually Bush and Greenspan concluded that the game of reforming the GSEs was not worth the candle. With mortgage markets booming, they left House Republican leader Michael Oxley of Ohio in the lurch after he had promoted reforms at their urgings.

Ironically, given what the private mortgage firms were up to, in the short run the failure to rein in the GSEs came with a silver lining. Although they, too, eventually started playing with lower-grade mortgages, they mostly maintained their traditional lending standards. Wider private sector expansion into the GSE's terrain would surely have brought more of the saturnalia that marked the privates' move into subprime.

Fannie Mae and Freddie Mac never truly recovered from the scandals. Conscious of their political weakness, they deliberately allied themselves with Countrywide, IndyMac, Washington Mutual, Lehman Brothers, and other private firms that would find expanded GSE lending and guarantees useful.

This led the GSEs to buy more and more mortgages for resale or their own accounts and eventually to move heavily into lower-grade (Alt-A) mortgages. It appears that the GSEs never really sorted out their accounting issues and, indeed, considered these a distraction from their main mission of sustaining themselves by supporting homeownership (and short-term profits). Critics continued to complain that the firms were undercapitalized, taking on too much debt, and were extravagantly rewarding top management while lining the pockets of politicians and lobbyists. They were right on all counts, even if the claims many also advanced about how private markets had rendered Fannie Mae and Freddie Mac unnecessary were about to be spectacularly shown up.

As private lenders withdrew from the market in 2007, Fannie and Freddie Mac became virtually the sole sources for mortgage refinancing,

Figure 2
The Shadow Bailout 2007-08: Lending and Guarantees from GSE's Advance as Private Sector Mortgage Flows Retrench

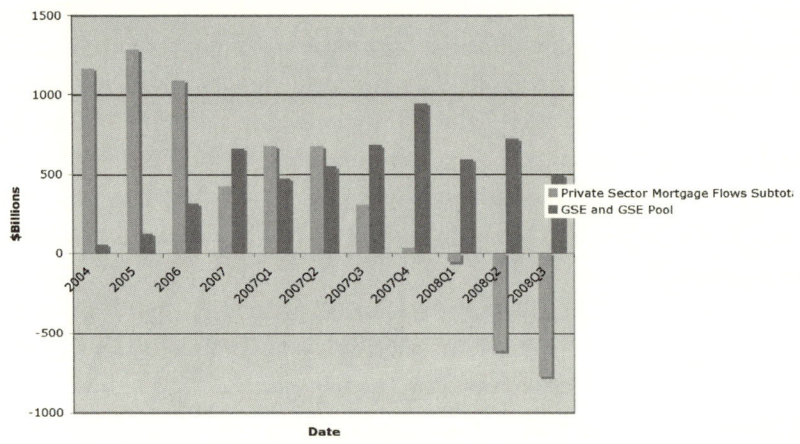

Source: US Federal Reserve Flow of Funds Data

as Figure 2 shows. In the face of mounting deterioration in subprime markets, the Bush administration, with the acquiescence of congressional Democrats, pushed to loosen standards. A new phase of the Shadow Bailout began: "Paulson wanted to use the troubled companies to unlock the frozen credit market by allowing Fannie and Freddie to buy more mortgage-backed securities from overburdened banks." (Becker et al. 2008). Accordingly, "the White House pitched in. James B. Lockhart, the chief regulator of Fannie Mae and Freddie Mac, adjusted the companies' lending standards so they could purchase as much as $40 billion in new subprime loans" (Duhigg 2008).[26]

Annual reports and the firms' accounting statements indicate that

---

26) The first quotation is from Jo Becker, Sheryl Gay Stolberg, and Stephen Lebaton, "White House Philosophy Stoked Mortgage Bondfire," New York Times, (December 20, 2008); the second is from Duhigg, "Pressured.". This latter adds considerable detail that illustrates the real relationships between the GSEs and private lenders. The article also relates a story according to which Paulson later sent a deputy, Robert K. Steele, to urge restraint on the GSEs. But for reasons unexplained, Steele failed to convey the message. This part of the story has all the earmarks of a precautionary memo for the files. It is unlikely in the extreme that Steele, who worked closely with Paulson, would have failed to convey a message his boss thought was important. As Becker et al. (2008) demonstrate, the priority just then was the Shadow Bailout.

Freddie Mac's financial position was substantially weaker than Fannie Mae's. Their quarterly reports show both buying mortgages and issuing guarantees in the face of the steep market fall, when from a business standpoint they should have pulled back. But Fannie Mae's response was much more extensive.

The End of the Shadow Bailout

For Paulson to engineer all this in the midst of a presidential election was quite a featsas well as an eloquent warning about the state of financial journalism in America. But prodigious as it was, the Shadow Bailout was simply not enough. As markets for mortgages and housing collapsed in the late summer of 2007, demand for commercial paper backed by CDOs or mortgages also dried up. Conduits and structured investment vehicles (SIVs) that relied on this "asset-backed commercial paper" market for refinancing now faced a new crisis. They accordingly pressed banks that had sold them the toxic junk to take it back by exercising "liquidity puts" they held on the parent banks.

Because this threatened to push some of America's largest banks over the edge, Paulson commenced another search for rescue funds that did not require going hat in hand to Congress.

He located two. For a while the Treasury and many others on Wall Street excitedly talked up possibilities that Sovereign Wealth Funds (SWFs) might provide the necessary funds. These were investment arms of countries that had accumulated hoards of dollars, from either selling oil or pegging their currencies and exporting back into the United States. The notion of buying big blocs of shares in leading U.S. banks clearly attracted some of these. Critics, including some skeptical investment bankers, suggested that was because owning banks carried with it the prospect of substantial political power.

Former Treasury secretary Lawrence Summers, a prominent Democrat who had parachuted from the presidency of Harvard University into a large investment fund, advised overseas investors to work with American financiers in evaluating possible acquisitions. Citigroup's Robert Rubin and other American financiers also made strong pitches to various

SWFs. Several eventually made substantial investments in Citigroup, Merrill Lynch, UBS, Morgan Stanley, and a few other firms. But as the crisis deepened, and bank stocks sagged, fears of emulating Mitsubishi's legendary purchase of Rockefeller Center at the top of the last great real estate bubble overcame every other emotion. After investing some $38 billion, the SWFs listened, occasionally talked, but effectively withdrew from the market.[27]

Paulson groped in desperation for another solution that did not put the government visibly on the hook. He proposed that the big banks organize a "super SIV" (or "master liquidity enhancement conduit" as the Treasury styled it) into which they would pour their toxic junk. What was to happen then was murky, but the idea appears to have been to slowly liquidate the mess over time. The proposal, reminiscent of the scheme for a "National Credit Corporation" briefly floated by bankers and President Herbert Hoover in the early stages of the Great Depression, was widely mocked, even by financiers.[28] In principle, however, it contained the germ of a good idea, one of the few with real prospects for helping to resolve the crisis. If implemented early, on a sufficiently vast scale, the plan would have kept money markets functioning normally, because traders could be confident that the institutions they were dealing with were in fact solvent once the toxic assets were gone. For financial houses, however, the scheme promised less exalted benefits: Warehousing toxic assets would stop fire sales that kept driving down asset prices.

The scheme had obvious drawbacks. It was in effect a "bad bank," a superfund for banks. At what price were bad assets to be transferred to the bad bank? Too low would leave huge holes in banks' balance sheets. Too high would overwhelm the superfund with certain losses. Most urgent of all, however, was the question of where the money would come from, because the whole point of the exercise was to avoid going to Congress in the midst of the election.

---

27) Estimates of SWF investment differ, at least in part because they count slightly differently. This estimate can be compared with those proffered by Brad Setser on his blog at the Council of Foreign Relations. For our purposes, the differences make no difference.
28) Epstein and Ferguson, "Monetary Policy."

The only plausible private sources of new cash were the banks themselves. Not surprisingly, they found this prospect daunting. Institutions with large exposures to conduits, such as Citigroup, JPMorgan Chase, Bank of America, or Wachovia, were reported to be intrigued. Other banks, with less exposure, were more skeptical, whereas foreign financial institutions, like the governments that were in several instances bailing them out, wanted no part of what was obviously a U.S.-centered scheme. So the banks dithered, as did Fidelity, Pimco, and other investment companies.

Paulson, a former Goldman Sachs CEO, neither could nor would force them to do what they did not want to do. The proposal died when HSBC and a few other institutions made a show of putting their conduits and SIVs on their balance sheets. Citigroup thereupon quickly and visibly reorganized. Rubin's choice to run the bank, Vikram Pandit, was announced on December 11. The next day the Fed quietly opened a new special facility expressly designed for distressed banks and stated its readiness to engage in swap agreements (for dollars) with foreign central banks. Citi then announced it was moving $49 billion of SIV assets onto its balance sheet.

Abandonment of Paulson's superfund proposal left all the toxic waste in place, with more showing up every day. Because no one knew what anyone's balance sheet was really worth, including his or her own, banks hesitated to lend to anyone, including other banks ("counterparty risk"). They also doubted their own ability to refinance in a timely fashion, which encouraged them to hoard resources. As a result, the financial system started locking up. With consumers stressed out and actual costs of credit rising as banks, struggling to digest bad assets, ceased making anything but super-safe loans, Fed rate cuts did not filter down to borrowers. They simply fattened banks' otherwise thinning margins by lowering their cost of funds.

Desperate banks also socked customers with all sorts of new charges and fees. Meanwhile the tide of foreclosures overwhelmed Fannie Mae and Freddie Mac's efforts while igniting fears about their own financial positions. Anxieties about possible insolvency of bond ("monoline") insurers added to all these pressures because many institutions could legally hold only insured bonds. Such insurance, for example, was critical for the functioning of the market for "floating rate notes" that many institutions, including hospitals and other nonprofits, used to raise funds. Repeated Fed rate cuts did little to relieve the situation. Downward pressures on the economy, accordingly, intensified, though at first the rate of growth declined surprisingly slowly. In the midst of all this, a scandal over a call girl abruptly drove from the scene Governor Eliot Spitzer (D-NY), the only public official actively challenging the notion of simply handing out long-dated bills for the bailout to the public. His dizzying fall triggered a media firestorm.[29]

It was almost at once eclipsed by the even more sensational story that Bear Stearns had suddenly become Bare Stearns. Bear had been a major player in the market for mortgage-backed securities for many years. Two of its hedge funds had been among the first casualties of the break in mortgage markets the previous year. In addition, Bear was a major holder of GSE debt and creditor to an Amsterdam hedge fund that was itself heavily invested in GSE paper. As spreads widened between Treasury notes and GSE paper—an inevitable consequence of the Shadow Bailout—holders of that paper suffered losses. For the Amsterdam hedge fund, the shock was too great. When it failed to meet margin calls, its collateral was seized and partially sold, further depressing GSE securities prices and putting yet more pressure on firms that held large blocs of these instruments, such as Bear.

As an investment bank, Bear was not normally eligible to borrow from the Fed or receive cash infusions from Federal Home Loan Banks. But like all investment houses and primary dealers in government securities, the

---

29) Some of the many twists in the Spitzer saga are discussed in Note 24 of Ferguson and Johnson, "'Paulson Put,' Part II." An early effort to explain the significance of the monolines to Congressman Barney Frank, Chair of the House Financial Services Committee, did not fare well. See Ferguson and Johnson, "Britney and the Bear: Who Says You Can't Get Good Help Anymore?," *Huffington Post,* March 27 2008.
30) Gretchen Morgenson, "In the Fed's Crosshairs: Exotic Game," *New York Times,* March 23, 2008. The next few paragraphs cover very controversial ground. Readers are once again referred to our *International Journal of Political Economy* essays, which sift through the claims and counter-claims.

firm had borrowed massively on its own account. It also owed millions of dollars to clients whose money it invested. Perhaps scariest of all, however, was the Bear's ubiquitous status as a "counterparty" in the dense web of credit default swaps that radiated out from the principal Wall Street houses.[30]

The specter of chain bankruptcy, derivative counterparty default, and a consequent run on the dollar plunged the Fed and the Treasury into something very much like a religious crisis. As citadels of market fundamentalism, their leaders clearly found it hard to accept that sticking to the old-time religion and letting Bear go bust would likely bring down the whole system. After Bear's fall, many analysts, including former company executives, also suggested that the Fed and other financial houses, notably Goldman Sachs (which, of course, Paulson had previously headed), may have been out to get the firm. To be sure, resolutions of past financial crises, such as those of the New Deal era, were crucially affected by efforts of stronger rival financial houses to enhance their positions.[31] But given the fragmentary state of the documentary record, assessments of such claims in Bear's case have to be provisional and tentative.

Our reading of the evidence is thus deliberately cautious. Bear had famously declined to join the syndicate of investment houses that the New York Fed organized in 1998 to save Long Term Capital Management (LTCM). That mockery of the Fed's leadership and refusal to join peers certainly left a legacy of persistent bad feeling. But there is no particular reason the lingering bitterness from that episode should have uniquely affected Paulson, even though he had been involved in the LTCM negotiations. In truth, as even Bear executives admit, the house was widely detested.[32]

The apparent leak to the cable business news channel CNBC of an email to clients by Goldman's derivatives department indicating that the

---

31) See the discussion in Thomas Ferguson, "From 'Normalcy' To New Deal: Industrial Structure, Party Competition and American Public Policy in the Great Depression," in *Golden Rule: The Investment Theory of Party Competition and the Logic of Money-Driven Political Systems*, ed. Thomas Ferguson (Chicago, 1995), 113-72.
32) Bill Bamber and Andrew Spencer, *Bear Trap The Fall of Bear Stearns and the Panic of 2008* (New York, 2008). Bamber was a senior managing director at Bear.
33) Bamber and Spencer, *Bear*, Chapter 6.

firm would no longer accept Bear as a counterparty was disastrous to Bear's effort to portray itself as still open for business.[33] It is also true that throwing wide open the Fed's discount window to primary dealers in government securities before, rather than just after, JPMorgan Chase purchased Bear might well have kept Bear in business, at least for a while. Instead, the announcement by the Fed on March 11, 2008, of another special facility, the $200 billion Term Securities Lending Facilities, was widely taken by markets as a signal that the Fed suspected one or more large investment banks were in trouble.

In the end, however, judged by the standards of past bailouts, the disposition of Bear itself was unremarkable. Whether run by the FDIC or the Fed, bailouts and forced mergers of banks normally resulted in total losses to stockholders. By contrast, the fates of bondholders and other creditors were negotiable, but, typically, most were rescued. The wrinkle in Bear's case was its stockholders' success in bidding up the share price they were originally offered from $2 to $10 a share.

What startled the world were the parts of the bailout that touched JPMorgan Chase and the wider financial world. Paulson and then New York Fed President Timothy Geithner, with broad support from Greenspan's successor at the Fed Ben Bernanke, brought in the single-payer insurance scheme discussed at the beginning of Part I. Stretching both law and precedent, they decided to extend the Fed's safety net to cover all primary dealers in government securities, even investment banks. Armed with an unheralded letter from Paulson agreeing that losses by the New York Fed could be deducted from monies the bank annually remits to the Treasury (thus putting taxpayers directly on the hook for losses), the New York Fed took over $30 billion of the worst junk in Bear's portfolio for its own account. Then the Fed hired BlackRock, a large investment fund, to run these assets. This allowed JPMorgan Chase to buy out Bear and save itself billions of dollars in losses it would have been hit with if Bear had simply declared bankruptcy.[34]

---

34) The New York Fed lent $29 billion against $30 billion in assets; the loan was formally to a Delaware corporation set up to hold the assets. JPMorgan Chase contributed $1 billion in the form of a note subordinated to the Fed's. For Paulson's letter to Geithner, see http://online.wsj.com/public/resources/documents/Treasuryletter0308.pdf.

Financial markets jubilated both the rescue and new safety net for investment banks. Stocks rose smartly, led by financials. For the Fed and Treasury, however, the downside was profound. Though the Paulson Put was still alive, the Shadow Bailout was over. Henceforth, Paulson, Bernanke, and Geithner would have to work in a glare of publicity, even as they fought to withhold details from the public, whose money was financing the whole thing.

The heightened scrutiny emerged very quickly as a towering problem. Squirreled away in custodial accounts at the Federal Reserve were over $900 billion of GSE paper belonging to other central banks. SWFs—funds controlled at least nominally by foreign governments—probably held almost as much for their own accounts outside the Fed. With criticism running high of the Fed's policy of holding down interest rates, foreign holders of the GSE securities needed reassurance about the safety of their holdings—or else both the market for GSE paper and the dollar itself could crumble.

Few foreign holders appreciated the subtleties of the Shadow Bailout, if they knew about it at all. But what was happening on the GSE's balance sheets was easily tracked. In the unlikely event foreign creditors missed the signs of deterioration, the din raised in the U.S. press by domestic critics of Fannie Mae and Freddie Mac, such as William Poole (by then retired from the St. Louis Fed) could hardly escape their attention. (Kopecki 2008). Barron's began asking if the two firms were "toast" (Laing 2008). A run began on both GSE stocks and, especially, their debt. Spreads between the agency debt and Treasury notes ballooned, especially after the FDIC took over giant IndyMac, a major mortgage institution in July 2008.[35]

Paulson and Bernanke simply could not permit a GSE collapse. By July 2008, private mortgage firms had all but melted away. Fannie Mae and Freddie Mac were virtually the only players left in the U.S. secondary mortgage market. If they went south, no one would step up to take their place. Primary mortgage markets would soon lock up, bringing housing

---

35) For Poole, see Dawn Kopecki, "Fannie, Freddie 'Insolvent' After Losses Poole Says (Update 1)," *Bloomberg.com*, July 10 2008; for Barrons, see Jonathan Laing, "Is Fannie Mae Toast?," *Barron's* (March 11, 2008), available at http://www. smartmoney.com/investing/economy/is-fannie-mae-toast-22694/.

sales across the United States to a screeching halt. Housing prices, already falling like a runaway elevator, would go into a steeper tailspin, pulling national income — and the dollar — down with it.

Not surprisingly, Paulson and Bernanke lunged once again for single-payer insurance, though it was sure to stir up a hornet's nest. Claiming that "if you've got a bazooka and people know you've got it, you may not have to take it out," Paulson asked Congress for standby authority to inject federal money into the GSEs as capital and, if necessary, to take them over. In effect, he was offering federal guarantees to GSE debt holders. In return, he agreed to support modest bank-inspired proposals for mortgage relief that congressional Democratic leaders had been elaborating since the late winter As a precaution, the Federal Reserve also granted Fannie Mae and Freddie Mac the right to borrow from the New York Fed.[36]

Senator Dodd has stated subsequently that when he agreed to support Paulson's quest for new powers, he believed Paulson's assurances that they would never be used. He and the Democrats mostly went along, though coming on the heels of the Bear bailout, the prospect of nationalization flabbergasted many in both parties.

To many Republicans, the combination of big bailouts for two more giant financial institutions and even modest government help for ordinary Americans with bad mortgages was too much. Many went ballistic, including some Republican House leaders. The Bush administration had no choice but to stand with Paulson on the GSEs, but it could not stomach some of the housing provisions. The president threatened a veto. Anxious foreign holders thereupon accelerated their selling. GSE paper in Fed custodial accounts started dwindling fast. As spreads widened between GSE debt and Treasury notes, the administration had to back down.

The veto threat was withdrawn when it became clear that the bill would not pass without additional Democratic votes to steamroll the raging opposition of congressional Republicans. For a few weeks after passage of the rescue bill, Paulson put on a brave face. He acted as though the crisis had been surmounted. Few agreed. Critics on the right called for breaking

---

36) The "bazooka" quotation comes from Andrew Ross Sorkin, "Paulson's Itchy Finger on the Trigger of A Bazooka," *New York Times Deal Book,* September 8 2008..

up the GSEs. Others railed against the notion that the government would actually use the authority it now possessed to take over the firms. In the meantime, a team of analysts from Morgan Stanley that Paulson had engaged poured over the GSEs' books. Foreigners steadily sold GSE securities, while stocks of Fannie Mae and Freddie Mac fell. Chinese spokespersons issued barely veiled warnings that something had to be done to guarantee the GSEs.[37]

As the New York Times recognized, "the bailout became inevitable when central banks in Asia and Russia began to curtail their purchases of the companies' debt, pushing up mortgage rates and deepening the economic downturn." Even as delegates to the Republican National Convention dispersed from their celebration of free markets and the minimal state, Paulson exercised his authority under the new legislation. Surprising both managements, he took both Fannie Mae and Freddie Mac into conservatorship. At a stroke, the federal government was now in charge of financial institutions with gross holdings of securities equivalent to 40 percent of the gross domestic product (GDP). To guarantee GSE solvency, the Treasury also agreed to purchase up to $100 billion dollars worth of additional preferred stock in each. It also committed to purchasing mortgage-backed securities from them—effectively circumventing legal restrictions on their total lending that the bill also contained—and opened short-term credit lines for both with the Federal Reserve Bank of New York.[38]

Fatal Reversal

Reaction was intense. "Comrade Paulson" jokes punctuated late night television and radio and even some newspaper columns. Yet almost immediately alarm bells started ringing about an even bigger crisis. The venerable investment banking firm of Lehman Brothers was on the edge of bankruptcy. Several firms—U.S. and British press accounts dwelt on Barclays, HSBC, and Bank of America, though Deutsche Bank and BNP

---

37) For the Chinese warnings, see, e.g., Kevin Hamlin, "Freddie, Fannie Failure Could Be World 'Catastrophe' Yu Says," *Bloomberg.com,* August 22 2008.
38) The *Times* quotation is from "The Bailout's Big Lessons," *New York Times*, September 8 2008.

Paribas were also mentioned—were interested in buying Lehman. But like JPMorgan Chase earlier, would-be buyers claimed that any deal would require subsidies or guarantees of some kind from the Fed.

Paulson, Bernanke, and Geithner began another round of meetings stretching into late night with heads of leading private banks and investment houses. In the end, they decided to do what free market conservatives had been demanding since the beginning of the crisis: Let a giant financial institution fail.

They thereby turned a desperate situation into a world historical disaster.

Because, as Napoleon famously remarked, victory has many fathers, but defeat is an orphan, pinning down how the trio arrived at their position is even more difficult than in the case of Bear Stearns. At the time, the decision to let the firm go down was presented as a group product in which all three concurred. Both the Fed and Treasury also claimed that they had a much better feel for the markets than they did in March and expected that the fallout could be contained. As Bernanke related to Congress the following week, "We judged that investors and counterparties had had time to take precautionary measures."[39]

Later, as the debris scattered around the world, however, stories began to appear that the Fed—presumably Bernanke—had wanted since July (about the time the GSE legislation passed) to approach Congress for legislation sanctioning a broader bailout. The implication was that Paulson's role was critical—an emphasis that Paulson did not dispel in several interviews he gave.

The Treasury secretary's own rationales for refusing aid to Lehman have been confusing and contradictory. On some occasions he has claimed that

---

39) Cf. U.S. Congress. Senate. 2008. Chairman Ben S. Bernanke, Testimony Before the Committee on Banking, Housing, and Urban Affairs, on September 23, 2008. Available at www.federalreserve.gov/newsevents/testimony/bernanke20080923a1.htm, accessed July 29, 2009.
40) The Paulson quote comes from Joe Nocera and Edmund Andrews, "Struggling To Keep Up As The Crisis Raced On," *New York Times*, October 22 2008. This article indicates clearly that Paulson in fact considered some form of assistance. Krishna Guha, "Paulson Rues Lack of Tools As He Stared Into the Abyss," *Financial Times* (December 31, 2008) is a specific and important confirmation.

he "never once considered it appropriate to put taxpayer money on the line in resolving Lehman Brothers." The evidence is overwhelmingly against this claim, because some of the private bankers involved in the negotiations talked to the press. Indeed, on at least one occasion Paulson himself indicated that he was open to government assistance and, according to the reporter, other officials involved corroborated those claims.[40]

On the key question of what made Lehman different from Bear Stearns, Paulson later asserted that existing law made it impossible for the government to help the former. Bear, he claimed, had good collateral, but not Lehman. Bernanke echoed this line on several occasions. But the story is flimsy indeed. The $30 billion worth of CDOs and similar instruments that JPMorgan Chase persuaded the Fed to absorb were obviously not AAA paper, whatever their ratings. For a long time, the New York Fed fiercely resisted calls for transparency, but it is now clear that Bear's collateral depreciated substantially since the deal went through (Y. Smith 2009a).[41]

The most compelling reasons for regarding the lack of legal justification as a fairy tale, however, are three simple facts. First, just days after Lehman blew up, Treasury and the Fed collaborated in the de facto nationalization of AIG, the giant insurer. The law had not changed and in this case, the collateral was clearly worthless, as AIG's repeated trips back to the well since attest more eloquently than any accounting statement. Even more devastating was the belated revelation that, in fact, the Fed did make two gigantic loans to Lehman—for $87 billion and then, after the first was repaid, for $51 billion—after it went bankrupt, to help wind down its affairs. Even if these were so-called conduit loans formally through another

---

41) For Paulson's claims about collateral, see Nocera and Andrews, "Struggling"; for Bernanke's, see, e.g., his speech to the Economic Club of New York in *Wall Street Journal Economics Blog*, "Fedspeak Highlights: Bernanke on House Prices, Lehman, More." *Wall Street Journal Economics Blog* (October 15). Available at http://blogs.wsj.com/economics/2008/10/15/fedspeak-highlights-bernanke-onlehman-house-prices-more/, accessed July 29, 2009. For the collateral depreciation, see Yves Smith, "The Fed's Bear Stearns Assets: "No Prospect For A Profit"," *Naked Capitalism*, February 5 2009.

42) The loans and the AIG case are discussed in Ferguson and Johnson, "Paulson Put,' Part II"; for Paulson's pride in pushing the limits of the law, see David Cho, "A Skeptical Outsider Becomes Bush's 'War Time General'," *Washington Post*, November 19 2008; for the contrast with Bernanke on whether to go to Congress shortly later, see John Hilsenrath, Deborah Solomon, and Damian Paletta, "Paulson, Bernanke Strained For Consensus in Bailout," *Wall Street Journal*, November 10 2008.

bank (that passed the money through to Lehman), the collateral for them cannot have been any better following bankruptcy than it was before. It is also embarrassingly plain that, in other contexts, Paulson trumpeted the need for and his personal willingness to push the limits of the law in emergencies. Indeed, as discussed below, it appears that only a few days later, as world markets melted down, his preference, in sharp contrast to Bernanke's, was to push on and avoid going to Congress (Hilsenrath et al. 2008).[42]

The most convincing explanation for the decision begins by recognizing that sometimes the order of events matters. And the commanding fact about the Lehman decision is that it happened only days after the GSE bailouts, as the firestorm their nationalizations triggered still blazed. Though the GSE controversy pales by comparison with the tumult engendered a few weeks later by Paulson and Bernanke's bailout proposal to Congress, statistical indicators of media attention confirm our qualitative judgment about the fierceness of the reaction to the earlier decision (Figure 3).

Figure 3 While Not As Large As That Over TARP, Excitement Over GSE Nationalization Ran High

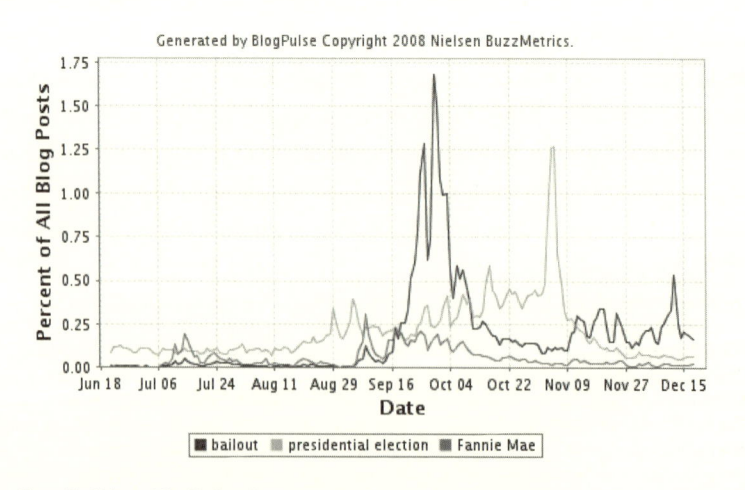

Source: Compiled From BlogPulse, Dec. 18, 2008, http://www.blogpulse.com

Although expressions of dismay erupted across the political spectrum, the most vehement responses came from Republicans, where faith in markets was virtually a litmus test for party membership but where frustration had been building since the Bear Stearns bailout. The weathervane most sensitively registering all these tensions was hard to miss: It was Senator John McCain (R-AZ), who had clinched the Republican presidential nomination well before Bear Stearns went down. In March, only days before Paulson and Co. bailed out Bear, McCain had proclaimed: "It is not the government's role to bail out investors who should understand that markets are about both return and risk, or lending institutions who didn't do their job" [43]

For McCain, the sudden embrace of single payer by Paulson, Bernanke, and Geithner was acutely embarrassing. Nevertheless, he gamely climbed aboard; his rationale throughout the campaign was that allowing Bear to go bankrupt would have had catastrophic consequences. [44] But he obviously found the episode painful and intensely felt the pressure from the party base. Less than two weeks later he went back to preaching the old-time religion. Rejecting government help for Americans with troubled mortgages, McCain declared that "it is not the duty of government to bail out and reward those who act irresponsibly, whether they are big banks or small borrowers." [45] Paulson's appeal to Congress for legislation allowing him to take over the GSEs gave McCain a new headache at a moment when he trailed in the polls and his campaign was sputtering. In the run up to the convention, he was desperate to court the right wing of his party, which took the hardest line against bailouts. But an open breach with the Bush administration was a practical impossibility. The administration still controlled the party machinery. Its assistance remained vital for fundraising (which was increasingly channeled through so-called joint committees with the national party that the administration also controlled,

---

43) For McCain's statement, see John McCain, "Statement by John McCain on America's Credit Crunch," *www.johnmccain.com*, March 13 2008.
44) Steven Lee Myers, "Bush Backs Fed's Actions, But Critics Quickly Find Fault," New York Times, March 18 2008, for McCain's support for the Bear bailout; see also his continued defense in "The Times Interviews John McCain," *New York Times*, July 13 2008.
45) Larry Rohter and Edmund Andrews, "McCain Rejects Broad US Aid on Mortgages," *New York Times,* March 26 2008.

because McCain had earlier accepted public financing out of desperation).

McCain thus fell in line behind Paulson's request for standby authority to seize the GSEs but took pains to register his distaste for bailouts. He justified his position by saying that it was too risky to leave the government without authority in case the worst happened. He did express some hope that perhaps the problem would go away. Though in other contexts he claimed early familiarity with the GSEs' problems, he doubted that it would be necessary to take them over.

Haunted by continuing dissension, McCain returned to the question less than two weeks later. In late July, he released a new position statement. It began by reassuring doubters yet again that he was really on their side. "Americans should be outraged at the latest sweetheart deal in Washington. Congress will put U.S. taxpayers on the hook for potentially hundreds of billions of dollars to bail out Fannie Mae and Freddie Mac." Then, after reiterating reluctant support for the legislation, he added several sentences whose explosive import was widely missed:

> If a dime of taxpayer money ends up being directly invested, the management and the board should immediately be replaced, multimillion dollar salaries should be cut, and bonuses and other compensation should be eliminated. They should cease all lobbying activities and drop all payments to outside lobbyists. And taxpayers should be first in line for any repayments.[46]

The place of preferred stockholders in a GSE takeover was just then emerging as an issue. It was obvious that common stockholders would suffer if Paulson took the GSEs over. The government's new equity rights would leave little for them, even if they were not formally wiped out. Saving debt holders, of course, was the point of the whole exercise; they were supposed to emerge whole. Preferred stock, however, lay in a gray zone intermediate between debt and common stock. Its owners had rights to income but no voting rights. Much of the preferred stock was in the hands of financial institutions. These had strong reasons for expecting to be

---

46) John McCain, "Taxpayers on Hook to Bailout Fannie, Freddie," *www.johnmccain.com* (July 24, 2008).
47) John Dizard, "This Short Term Fix Creates A Long Term Problem," *Financial Times* (September 16, 2008).

treated like debt holders: Paulson was actively encouraging banks to buy GSE preferred stock as a way to shore up both the GSEs and themselves because regulators allowed GSE preferred shares to be counted as part of banks' capital.[47]

In the end Paulson essentially wiped out holders of both common and preferred stock. The decision left many banks' capital adequacy ratios precariously exposed and engendered a widespread feeling of betrayal. But the step made perfect political sense: By heavily diluting the preference shares, it met the test laid out by his party's nominee.

Nevertheless, not only McCain but much of the party was clearly taken aback by the decision to emulate Mussolini (their usual comparison was Lenin). Although Senator Barack Obama and most Democrats said little beyond signaling general support, McCain and his controversial new running mate, Alaska governor Sarah Palin, felt obliged once again to take a strong stand. They published a high-profile attack on bailouts in what was virtually a Republican house organ, the Wall Street Journal's Op-Ed page. Although they again repeated McCain's reluctant support for the takeover, they ratcheted up the vehemence of their language. They also flatly promised to break up and privatize Fannie Mae and Freddie Mac if elected.[48]

Between the lines, it was obvious that McCain was close to being fed up. This is not an inference. Only days later, as the financial world melted down in the wake of the Lehman decision, McCain stood up and denounced Paulson's nationalization of AIG (Chipman and Nichols 2008). He also drafted a statement attacking the Bush administration's bailout policies. That was not released until many frantic hours later, after it had been watered down beyond recognition, and McCain had done another 180-degree turn. Returning to the administration's fold, he now grudgingly supported the nationalization (Chipman and Nichols 2008; Stein 2008).

---

48) John McCain and Sarah Palin, "We'll Protect Taxpayers From More Bailouts," *Wall Street Journal* (September 9, 2008).

49) For McCain's somersaults, see, e.g., Kim Chipman and Hans Nichols, "McCain, Obama Blame Regulators; McCain Shifts on AIG (Update 3)," *Bloomberg.com*, September 17 2008 and Sam Stein, "McCain Removed Bush Criticism From Wall Street Statement," *Huffington Post*, September 18 2008. For the GOP leadership, see Ted Barrett, Diana Walsh, and Brianna Keilar, "AIG Bailout Upsets Republican Lawmakers," *CNN.com*, September 17 2008..

But the point is clear: As Lehman slid to the brink, Paulson and Bernanke, who both enjoyed solid links to the Bush administration, could hardly expect McCain and an indefinitely large bloc of the rest of their party (including many congressional Republican leaders, who also denounced the AIG rescue [Barrett et al. 2008]), as well as many Democrats, to take yet another giant bailout lying down.[49]

Bernanke was in addition just back from an almost Dickensian encounter of his own with the ghost of bailouts past. At the annual conclave in Jackson Hole, Wyoming, sponsored by the Federal Reserve Bank of Kansas City, his conduct had been roundly criticized to his face. In front of other central bankers, economists, policymakers, and financiers, a raft of critics assailed him for betraying free market principles and capitulating to demands from the financial sector for bailout. A paper by Willem Buiter accused the Fed of falling victim to "cognitive" interest group capture and specifically referenced historical studies of similar Fed behavior in the Great Depression. Some press accounts claim that Bernanke was exhausted and hint that he was demoralized, but there is no question that he appreciated the gravity of the charges, which received wide publicity in the Financial Times and other major media.[50]

The Put Is Dead; Long Live the Put

If the extinction of preferred shareholders in the GSE bailout was an unheeded warning shot that the days of the Paulson Put were numbered, the decision to let Lehman go bankrupt marked the Put's definitive expiration. Thereafter so much happened so fast that it is easy to lose sight of the disastrous new course that Paulson was now charting, with Bernanke and Geithner assisting.

The trio's first problem was simply to try to keep up with the dizzying

---

50) Buiter, "Central Banks and Financial Crises," 102, citing Epstein and Ferguson, "Monetary Policy." There was more irony than Buiter could know: As Gerald Epstein and Thomas Ferguson, "Answers to Stock Questions: Fed Targets, Stock Prices, and the Gold Standard in the Great Depression," *Journal of Economic History* 51 (March, 1991), 190-200, went to press, Bernanke offered collegial advice and comments. He understood the problem very well.

51) John Taylor, "The Financial Crisis and the Policy Responses: An Empirical Analysis of What Went Wrong," National Bureau of Economic Research (Cambridge, 2009), Working Paper 14631, presses this case and has recently repeated it in numerous forums.

Figure 4 Credit Default Swap Prices: It Was Lehman
J P Morgan Chase and Goldman Sachs

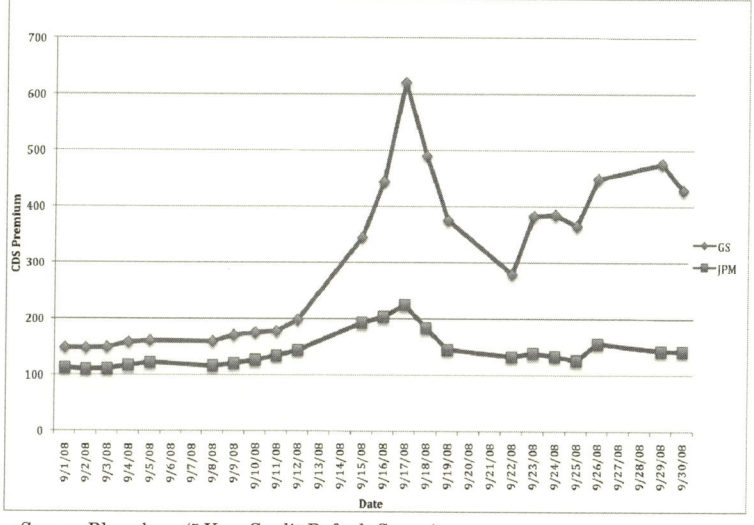

Source: Bloomberg (5 Year Credit Default Swaps)

scale and pace of devastation. Contrary to claims recently advanced by revisionists who argue that the real break in world markets came more than a week later when Paulson and Bernanke approached Congress with their broader bailout proposal (Taylor 2009), the evidence that the Lehman bankruptcy sundered world markets is overwhelming.[51]

Every direct indicator of financial risk we have examined explodes, in some cases a day or two in advance of the actual declaration of bankruptcy: Prices of credit default swaps on the four largest American banks, controlling some 40 percent of all deposits, for example, all rose like rockets before falling back when Paulson, Bernanke, and Geithner reversed course two days later and once again embraced single payer by bailing out AIG. The same holds for credit default swaps of Goldman Sachs and Morgan Stanley, the two most important remaining investment banks. (See Figure 4, which shows credit default swap prices for Goldman Sachs and JPMorgan Chase.) Another excellent general indicator of stress, the "option adjusted" spread on broad investment grade bank debt—what banks had

Figure 5   Spreads On Bank Debt Blow Out As Lehman Collapses

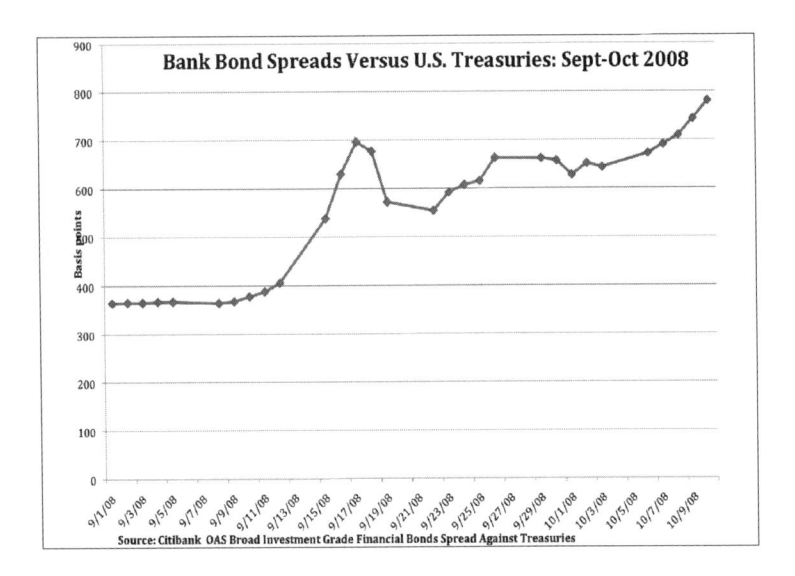

Bank Bond Spreads Versus U.S. Treasuries: Sept-Oct 2008

Source: Citibank OAS Broad Investment Grade Financial Bonds Spread Against Treasuries

to pay to raise new capital—also shows a sharp rise as Lehman gave up the ghost (Figure 5).

Default on Lehman's bonds and subsequent fire sales of assets staggered many firms, including a substantial number of European houses (Larsen 2008). Hedge funds that used Lehman as their prime broker lost access to their funds (Mackintosh and Hughes 2008), while losses on Lehman's commercial paper caused some money market funds to "break the buck"

---

52) Cf. Peter Thal Larsen, "Shockwaves That Took Europe By Surprise," *Financial Times*, October 4 2008; James Mackintosh and Jennifer Hughes, "New York Steals UK Hedge Fund Business," *Financial Times*, October 17 2008; and the fine discussion in Sam Jones, "Why Letting Lehman Go Did Crush the Financial Markets," *Financial Times FT.com/Alphaville* (March 12, 2009).

53) For the refinancing fears, see Gavin Finch and Kim-Mai Cutler, "Money Market Rates Double Amid Global Credit Squeeze (Update 4)," *Bloomberg.com*, September 16 2008; for the doubling, see Jones, "Why." The Fed's H.4.1 statistical release, available on the Federal Reserve Board Web site for the seven days ending September 17, 2008, shows that borrowing from the Primary Dealer Credit Facility, which carried a clear stigma, jumped sharply, as indeed, did the whole category of "other loans." The former had been zero the week before then jumped all at once to an average of $20.268 billion. The use of weekly averages disguises the dimensions of the explosion that followed Lehman's bankruptcy, because the Wednesday total is $59.78 billion.

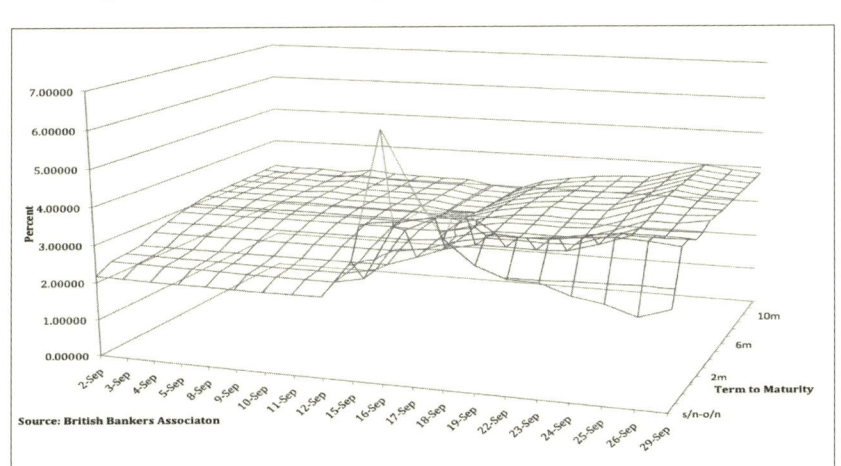

Figure 6 Lehman's Collapse Inverts the LIBOR Yield Curve

[Chart: 3D surface plot showing LIBOR yield curve from 2-Sep through 29-Sep across maturities (s/n-o/n, 2m, 6m, 10m). Y-axis: Percent, 0.00000 to 7.00000. Source: British Bankers Associaton]

(Jones 2009). In a matter of hours—not pace John Taylor—markets for both regular and asset-backed commercial paper dried up, and an awesome run began out of money market funds altogether, as panicky depositors recoiled.[52]

Suddenly unable to refinance by issuing commercial paper, banks became fearful both for themselves and their counterparties. They frantically hoarded reserves at central banks instead of lending them out. In the five days after Lehman collapsed, bank reserves held at the Fed more than doubled (Jones 2009), while bank borrowing from the Fed surged.[53] Perhaps the most striking indicator of the crisis, however, was the behavior of the London Inter-Bank Offered Rate (LIBOR), the rates banks in London charge each other. Interest rates charged on the shortest maturities, which should be the safest, doubled, while the LIBOR yield curve inverted, as bank willingness to lend at longer maturities appears to have withered.[54]

Most of the world, however, only dimly appreciated the meaning of the reports in the financial press that interbank lending was grinding to a halt. Instead, for most observers, the most arresting effects of the bankruptcy came in stock markets, as market operators realized that even the greatest Wall Street houses and banks now could not be worth much more than Lehman.

They immediately started shorting the stocks, as other investors fled. Within hours, one of the most famous and characteristic features of American financial life—the powerful, indeed, often dominant role of a handful of famous investment banks—came to a sudden, terrifying end. Seeing the handwriting on the wall, Merrill Lynch consented to a shotgun wedding with Bank of America just hours before Lehman became history. Beset by wave after wave of short sellers, Goldman Sachs briefly flirted with buying Wachovia (whose CEO was a former Goldman executive) before emulating Morgan Stanley and transforming itself into a bank holding company, able to tap the Fed forever.

In the meantime, a wave of bankruptcies and defensive mergers rippled

---

54) Taylor relies on the spread between three-month LIBOR and the three-month overnight index swap as his measure of disruption. The latter records the market's guess about what the Fed funds rate will be over the same period, so the difference between the two rates should reflect banks' anxieties about lending to each other. That measure did not move much until roughly the time when Paulson and Bernanke went to Congress. Taylor, accordingly, argues that it must have been the political intervention rather than Lehman's bankruptcy that disrupted world markets.

Economic historians will be familiar with previous economic crises in which published rates failed to reflect market realities. Such appears to be the case here. Let us set put aside, for now, suspicions voiced earlier in the year that LIBOR rates had gradually become extensively fictional (cf. Carrick Mollenkamp, "Bankers Cast Doubt On Key Rate Amid Crisis," *Wall Street Journal*, April 16 2008). Jones, "Why," well describes problems in interpreting LIBOR quotations even in normal times. In the Lehman crisis, special force attaches to all his reservations. Our Figure 6 indicates a tremendous demand for the shortest term LIBOR borrowings; it is inconsistent with any notion that money was easily available for longer periods. This conclusion also coheres with the evidence of the Fed's H.4.1 statistical release discussed above, which indicates sharply increasing demand for official short-term credits, even if they carry a stigma, and with Jones's analysis of the behavior of money market funds and bankers' reserve balances at the Fed. Additional evidence that banks were desperately seeking short-term funds because money for the longer term was unavailable is found in Phillip Swagel, "The Financial Crisis: An Inside View," Brookings Papers on Economic Activity (March 30, 2009), in press; see especially his remarks on commercial paper borrowings.

We also think that the "event analysis" approach Taylor uses is more problematic than he allows. He is, of course, aware that, in principle, complex, lagged causal effects could muddy the distinction he wants to draw between market reactions to the bankruptcy as opposed to the government's subsequent interventions. But his paper appears to underestimate the market turmoil. For example, American brokerage houses with operations in London only slowly awoke to the dangers that English bankruptcy laws posed to their ability to gain access to funds they had deposited with Lehman; see, e.g., Mackintosh and Hughes, "New York." The Fed just as clearly misjudged its ability to fund the UK part of Lehman's broker-dealer business (cf. John Gapper, "We Need to Share the Burden on Bailouts, *Financial Times*, March 25, 2009). Such confusions took some time to sort out, or even to be recognized. They imply that neat distinctions between the periods are likely to be very misleading.

through the commercial banking system. Fears of already nervous investors turned to sheer terror, however, when the FDIC's terms became public for JPMorgan Chase's takeover of Washington Mutual (WaMu), the largest savings and loan in the United States. The FDIC insisted that WaMu actually go bankrupt first, then approved sale of the deposits to Morgan for $2 billion. (Sender et al. 2008). This reduced strain on the FDIC's straitened insurance fund but wiped out both stockholders and unsecured creditors of WaMu. On the heels of Lehman's bankruptcy and the GSE restructurings, the message seemed clear: Neither bank debt nor preferred stock in financial institutions was safe; deposits alone were a stable source of bank funds (Lex 2008). Investors responded by stampeding out of bank stocks and dumping debt.[55]

The first step to a new, born-again Paulson Put took place as AIG, the giant insurer, came under attack. AIG was nominally in the insurance business, but the day after Lehman went down the world awoke to discover that the firm had been running a massive, now disastrously money-losing, division that wrote credit default swaps (insurance contracts against defaults on bonds). Though details of the rescue decision remain murky, certain key facts have slipped out. First, AIG had written credit default swaps for a broad cross section of the leading financial houses of New York and Europe. It had also overextended its securities lending with many of the same firms. Bankruptcy of AIG would leave these firms exposed just as financial companies were going down like nine pins. AIG's biggest domestic counterparty (customer) just happened to be giant Goldman Sachs, the firm Paulson had formerly headed. As officials deliberated on how to respond, only one private bank chief executive was in the room: Goldman CEO Lloyd Blankfein.[56]

Reeling from the Lehman shock, Paulson and Co. made a dramatic

---

55) Henry Sender et al., "WaMu Seized and Sold to J P Morgan," *Financial Times*, September 25 2008.; Lex, "Washington Mutual," *Financial Times*, September 26, 2008.
56) Cf. For Blankfein, cf. Gretchen Morgenson, "Behind Insurer's Crisis, Blind Eye To A Web of Risk," *New York Times*, September 27, 2008, including the "Correction" that ran two days later. For Goldman and AIG, see Mary Williams Walsh, "A.I.G. Lists Banks It Paid With US Bailout Funds," *New York Times* (March 15, 2009). AIG also appears to have overextended itself in the repo market. See Michael Mackenzie, "Deleveraging Leads Repo Market into Mire," *Financial Times*, April 8, 2009.

about-face back to single payer: Law or no law, they effectively nationalized AIG by taking warrants for the Treasury worth 79.9 percent of AIG's stock in exchange for an $85 billion loan from the Fed (Karnitschnig et al. 2008).[57] In fact, however, the $85 billion was just a down payment; AIG soon claimed many billions of dollars more.

The nationalization aroused outrage, not only from McCain but also from many others who could not understand why AIG was being granted what Lehman had been denied. In succeeding weeks, their outrage turned to perplexity, as Treasury and the Fed kept pouring money into the firm with no real explanation. Eventually, the deal's true nature became dimly visible. It only appeared to be about AIG. In fact, Treasury and the Fed were subsidizing the giants—including Goldman, Citigroup, Bank of America, Morgan Stanley, and other large European firms—that were its counterparties on credit default swaps and securities lending. At a time when no one else in the market was getting a hundred cents on the dollar, these fortunate concerns were having their credit default swaps paid off at par by the people of the United States (Morgenson 2009). It was big government corporatism in almost laboratory pure form, public—private partnership in the tradition of Mussolini's Istituto per la Ricostruzione Industriale (Institute for Industrial Reconstruction).[58]

---

57) Had Treasury taken 80 percent of the stock, AIG would have had to be carried on its books. In August, 2009, incomplete records of Paulson's phone calls during the crisis leaked into the media (Morgenson and Van Natta 2009). These showed the Treasury Secretary making far more calls to the head of his old firm than to other leading figures on Wall Street and raised searching questions about possible conflicts of interest. The article quotes a range of views; some claims put forward are obviously far from the truth. The Treasury, for example, had to play a major role in the takeover of AIG; the Fed may have provided the financing, but by law it cannot hold the warrants. The Treasury has control of those, which is surely why it was Paulson himself who informed AIG's chief that he was out, as the story records. The evidence we present in this paper on the price of credit defaults swaps on Goldman Sachs confirms the implication of the phone records – presented in a web link to the electronic version of the *Times* story at http://www.nytimes.com/imagepages/2009/08/09/business/09paulson_graphic_ready.htm—that Tuesday and Wednesday, not the weekend before, were crucial decision days for the AIG rescue.

58) Gretchen Morgenson, "At A.I.G., Good Luck Following the Money," *New York Times*, March 14, 2009; Paulson tapped Edward Liddy to be the new head of AIG. Liddy resigned from the board of Goldman Sachs when he took the job but continued to hold over $3 million worth of stock in Goldman. As of April 2009, he had not divested himself. See Timothy P. Carney, "AIG Head's $3M in Goldman Stock Raises Apparent Conflict of Interest," *Washington Examine*, April 10, 2009).

But with world markets raging out of control, Wall Street and the banks now had more problems than just credit default swaps. Short sellers were still having a field day with Goldman and Morgan Stanley, while Citigroup was turning into the Incredible Hulk. There was not a moment to be lost. In a stunning display of money politics in action, Morgan Stanley's John Mack telephoned Senator Charles Schumer (D-NY) (Nocera 2008a). Schumer in turn pressed the Treasury, the Fed, and the SEC to temporarily ban short sales (New York Times 2008c). Barely months before, regulators had stonewalled desperate pleas for regulatory relief from consumers as oil prices spiraled upward (Cho 2008a). This time the SEC unceremoniously tossed free market ideology overboard and honored Schumer's request (New York Times 2008c).[59]

The Fed and the Treasury had been discussing the limits of their authority for weeks. For the Treasury, the priority was "to avoid Congress." It "maintained that the Fed had broad legal authority and could possibly take on distressed assets from banks directly, without congressional approval." But the hammer blows of Lehman, AIG, and the worldwide market downturn appear to have crystallized the doubts of Bernanke and senior Fed staff. On September 17, after consulting at least some other Fed governors, Bernanke informed Paulson that the time for bazookas was over. It was time to go to Congress and ask for the economic equivalent of nuclear weapons—a gigantic on-budget bailout fund. Initially noncommittal, Paulson watched world markets plummet. The next morning he agreed.[60]

There is no doubt that the Fed understood how this should be done, at least in broad outline. Economic history is littered with examples of bursting asset bubbles. Best practices for coping are not secret. The government, operating preferably through a specially dedicated, on-budget entity, such as the New Deal's Reconstruction Finance Corporation rather

---

59) For Schumer, cf. "Schumer's Stands," *New York Times*, December 12 2008 and Joe Nocera, "As Credit Crisis Spiraled, Alarm Led To Action," *New York Times*, October 1 2008; for the earlier oil futures case, see David Cho, "Investors' Growing Appetite For Oil Evades Market Limits," *Washington Post* (June 6, 2008). Then Senator Hillary Clinton and others joined in the pleas.
60) Hilsenrath, Solomon, and Paletta, "Paulson.", including the quoted passage.

than the central bank (which can be tempted to monetize its way out of problems) or the Treasury (which has other things to do), surveys the condition of the banking system. It closes banks that only St. Jude, the patron of hopeless cases, could love — a step that although wildly unpopular with financiers, saves vast sums for taxpayers. Then the government sweeps all the toxic waste into a "bad bank" and gets it out of circulation. Finally, the state recapitalizes the banking system to a level higher than the minimum capital adequacy requirement after marking down bank assets to realistic levels, not banker fictions. Counterparty risk vanishes, as the new equity gives the banks the cushion they require to take risks and make loans again.[61]

Done properly, as in Sweden or Norway in the early 1990s or the United States in the New Deal, such schemes do not necessarily saddle the public with large losses. They can even show a modest profit in the long run. At least some bad assets can eventually be sold at reasonable prices. The critical step, however, is for the government to take equity (common or preferred stock) or warrants (rights to stock at a set, low price) in banks it recapitalizes. After the banks revive, the shares can be sold, recouping most or all the expense. There is a catch and it is a big one: The new public shares dilute holdings of existing shareholders because the public has first claim on future earnings and the government shares normally also pay a dividend.

The Swedish bailout of the early 1990s is perhaps the most widely acclaimed contemporary example of a rescue along these lines. In the late spring of 2008, after Bear Stearns failed, Federal Reserve vice chair Donald Kohn was reported to be closely studying that experience. But there were no hints of Kohn's advance work in the plan Paulson and Bernanke presented to Congress: Their insultingly brief two and a half page sketch made no mention of inspection or recapitalization. It proposed only a publicly financed version of the superfund that Paulson had tried to interest the banks in without success in the fall of 2007. The maximum

---

61) Readable summaries of the traditional approach are J. Stiglitz, "A Bank Bailout That Works," *The Nation*, March 23 2009 or Thomas Ferguson and Robert Johnson, "Bridge Loan To Nowhere," in *Meltdown*, ed. Katrian vanden Heuvel (New York, 2008); on the RFC, see Todd, "History," and Epstein and Ferguson, "Monetary Policy."

size of this superfund was set at $700 billion (a so-called balance sheet limit, implying that over time the Treasury could replenish it by selling assets it acquired and recycling the proceeds into new purchases). What and how to buy were left entirely to Paulson: There was to be no review or accountability; language borrowed from the Gold Reserve Act of 1934 banned even court reviews.

The concept was breathtakingly flimsy. Paulson subsequently admitted that even he no longer believed in it by the time the bill passed. Buying $700 billion worth of assets might have made a difference in the earliest days of the Shadow Bailout. But the delay arising from the Shadow Bailout was fatal: There was way too much junk out there. After the Lehman bankruptcy, all $700 billion could buy was relief for a few lucky financial houses, not a serious bailout for the U.S. banking system.

Realizing this point, critics asked how Paulson and Bernanke planned to determine the prices at which the Treasury bought the assets. Despite heady talk of "reverse auctions" in which the Treasury would select the house that offered the lowest price (which would force would-be sellers to offer only assets they urgently needed to get off their books), under questioning Bernanke proved uncharacteristically elusive. Setting aside his prepared text, he indicated a preference for the Treasury to buy at prices "close to the hold-to-maturity price," that is, well above anything shattered markets were likely to offer. A leaked Treasury conference call revealed that the Treasury was clearly hoping to pay above market

---

62) For Bernanke, see Scott Lanman and Craig Torres, "Bernanke Says Normal Markets Needed or Growth to Halt (Update 3)," *Bloomberg.com* (September 23, 2008); for the leaked telephone call, Yves Smith, "Mussolini-Style Corporatism in Action: Treasury Conference Call on Bailout Bill To Analysts (Updated)," *Naked Capitalism*, September 29 2008; on Treasury and dilution, see Deborah Solomon and Damian Paletta, "Treasury Hones Next Rescue Tool -- Direct Investment in Bank Likely Would Be Designed To Spare Existing Shareholders," *Wall Street Journal*, October 13 2008; for Treasury's objections to government ownership, cf. Krishna Guha and James Politi, "US Shift As UK Takes Path To Recapitalize," *Financial Times*, October 9 2008.

63) One very special case of Treasury's adherence to this dictum merits separate notice. In October, after declines in Morgan Stanley's stock value threatened a previously negotiated investment by Mitubishi UFJ Financial Group, Treasury smoothed agreement to complete the deal by helping to work out an agreement that protected the Japanese investors from dilution in the event of later capital injections by Treasury. This deal had obvious foreign policy implications, but they must wait for another paper. Cf. Andrew Ross Sorkin, "U.S. Said To Offer Mitsubishi Protection on Morgan Deal," *New York Times Dealbook*, October 13, 2008.

prices. And, as the Treasury eventually acknowledged, it opposed diluting existing shareholders and thus wanted to avoid injecting capital into banks. Treasury was also averse to the whole idea of government becoming involved with running private businesses.[62]

"Thou shalt not dilute shareholders" was, indeed, the first commandment enshrined in the new Paulson Put and key to the disaster that engulfed the United States and the world afterward.[63] The new, truncated Put's second commandment was equally predictable: "Thou shalt not constrain bankers' compensation." In the face of white hot public indignation, members of Congress called—in public—for restrictions on executive compensation. Treasury responded with proposals that it privately ensured financial houses would be unenforceable.[64]

After his much ridiculed testimony to Congress about asset prices, Bernanke lowered his profil, whereas Paulson raised his. Under withering criticism from George Soros and many others, the notion of just buying assets lost steam in favor of capital injections. These would support many times their value in new lending and thus held promise of halting the deadly process of "deleveraging" that was now shrinking the supply of credit.[65] (Soros 2008).

But capital injections proved a hard sell. Many Democratic congressional representatives, labor, and liberal interest groups did not understand what was at stake. They had little to say about the bailout and concentrated on agitating for an economic stimulus program or mortgage relief. The first version of the bailout legislation contained language authorizing capital injections, though it still afforded pride of place to asset purchases. As the much amended second incarnation of the bill emerged, Representative Barney Frank, chair of the House Financial Services Committee, insisted

---

64) Treasury made a small change in the final bill limiting its application only to firms that actually sold assets to the Treasury—precisely the plan that Paulson has since confessed he did not believe in by the time the bill passed. None of the banks that subsequently received capital injections were affected by this clause, though heads of several leading houses talked about voluntarily foregoing bonuses and, in the end, sometimes did. Note that the bonus pool for six large Wall Street houses for 2007 was estimated to amount to 10 percent of the value of the entire TARP. At some moments in fall 2008, indeed, Morgan Stanley's bonus pool was worth more than the firm's entire value on the stock market.
65) George Soros, "Paulson Cannot Be Allowed A Blank Check," *Financial Times*, September 25, 2008.

on taking out the language authorizing capital injections. Eventually, after Soros spoke to Speaker of the House Nancy Pelosi (D-CA), Frank and the Democratic leadership agreed to accept an "intent of Congress" statement from the House floor by Representative Jim Moran (D-VA) in conjunction with Frank that would provide legal cover for capital injections. By then Democratic leaders were claiming that the intervention was in accord with the Treasury's program; this is consistent with Paulson's later confession that he changed his mind before the bill passed.[66] But this backdoor authorization ensured that there were minimal safeguards against frittering the money away.

Path To Disaster

The worldwide market meltdown that greeted passage of the bill and the creation of the Troubled Assets Relief Program (TARP) shocked the American establishment.

It should not have. As soon as the bill passed, Paulson and Bernanke should have followed with a series of rapid-fire announcements of actions taken under its auspices. Instead, they laid low, while the Treasury put out word that a thirty-something former Goldman Sachs executive who had previously served as Paulson's special assistant would start figuring out how to implement TARP.

World markets could see clearly what neither the Democrats nor the Republicans, for different reasons, could admit. That even if TARP worked perfectly, it could at best only unclog the arteries of the financial system. But getting blood flowing through the patient's arteries again would not make her healthy; it would just keep her from dying. Private investment and consumption were collapsing in both the United States and the rest of

---

66) The best existing account of the legislative maneuvering is Nouriel Roubini, "How Authorization to Recapitalize Banks Via Public Capital Injections ('Partial Nationalization') Was Introduced -- Indirectly Through the Back Door -- Into the TARP Legislation," *RGE Monitor*, October 9 2008. We had excellent vantage points to observe what happened, and we draw on this experience for other details here. Jeffrey Toobin, "Barney's Great Adventure," *New Yorker*, January 9, 2009, portrays Barney Frank as a strong supporter of equity injections; in fact, he came late to that position and remained very friendly to asset buying. Note that Frank represents a Boston area district; the city is a center for money market funds, which, in sharp contrast to investment houses, have no easy way to permit government equity ownership in the funds themselves.

the world; only large and immediate government fiscal stimulus packages (which included major housing relief) held any prospect of checking this. Republicans, in the main, were opposed to stimulus for the usual ideological reasons. Democrats were divided, with even many friends of a stimulus preferring to hold off until a new Democratic president took office. The United States and some other countries were also reluctant to negotiate internationally coordinated packages for various reasons, including the prospect that the United States veto over the International Monetary Fund would eventually come up for discussion. As a result, leaders of both parties agreed that the bailout would not include a fiscal stimulus. Senator Obama also urged Democratic congressional leaders not to try to include provisions in the bill giving bankruptcy judges power to alter mortgage terms.[67] (Edsall 2008).

The TARP, in short, was a failure from its first day. Nothing Paulson did later improved the situation. When, under international pressure, he saw the light and abandoned his emphasis on asset buying, he (and Bernanke) did not insist on rigorous bank examinations to find out who was solvent and who was not. The Fed and Treasury did not try to estimate whether and how much money it would take to get solvent banks to normal lending. Instead Paulson conferred with heads of nine leading financial institutions. Then he simply awarded them sizeable sums, on terms that contrasted glaring with, for example, those Warren Buffett received for his much ballyhooed investment in Goldman Sachs.

Although TARP money was formally a capital injection, it soon became clear that much of the money would, practically speaking, offset funds committed to banks' bonus pools, so that taxpayers were in effect financing bonuses for the people who had created the mess.[68] (Bowers 2008). Paulson also pointedly declined to set any targets for lending; indeed, it quickly became clear that the Treasury was deliberately encouraging the lucky

---

67) For Obama, see Thomas Edsall, "Obama Says Bailout Bill Should Not Include Bankruptcy Reform," *Huffington Post*, September 26 2008.
68) Simon Bowers, "Wall Street Banks in 70 Bn Staff Payout -- Pay and Bonus Deals Equivalent To 10 Percent of US Government Bail-out Package," *Guardian*, October 18, 2008.
69) For the bonuses, see Bowers, "Wall Street"; for buying other banks, cf. Joe Nocera, "So When Will Banks Make Loans?," *New York Times*, October 24 2008; for the tax breaks, cf. Amit R. Paley, "A Quiet Windfall For US Banks," *Washington Post*, November 10 2008.

banks that received money to consider buying other banks (Nocera 2008b). When no one was looking, the Treasury also issued a ruling giving massive tax breaks to banks—perhaps as much as $140 billion worth (Paley 2008b). The FDIC also guaranteed new bank debt, allowing banks to raise funds when almost no one else could.[69]

Nonbanks could see the handwriting on the wall. Not surprisingly, they stampeded to the trough. American Express, many insurers (Patterson et al. 2009), and even General Motors Acceptance Corporation (GMAC) started turning themselves into banks or buying banks or thrifts. The Fed also obligingly changed the rules to make it easier for private equity groups —by now desperate for financing—to buy into banks. Other industries began building cases for bailouts too.

But the financial system showed few signs of returning to normalcy. As a result, the Federal Reserve increasingly moved to fill the vacuum. It cut rates virtually to zero and proliferated special facilities for lending. It lent directly to large corporations. Some of these efforts showed results: With the Federal Reserve buying commercial paper of the fifty largest issuers, that market thawed out. Effectively, however, the Fed no longer was supporting private financial markets. It was extensively replacing them. There seemed little to do but wait for the new U.S. president and hope for the best.

第12章 エピローグ―世界経済危機が日中印に与える衝撃

Chapter 12　Epilogue—Impacts of the Global Economic Crisis on Japan, China and India

Lim Hua Sing [*]

　A financial crisis erupted in the United States on 15th September 2008 and immediately spread to the rest of the world, and created the world-wide financial crisis soon after. Mr Alan Greenspan, the former Chairman of the Federal Reserve Board, in his recent publication entitled "The Age of Turbulence", warned the world that we are in fact facing a world-wide financial turmoil. He also described this crisis as a financial tsunami or a financial crisis which happens once every one hundred years!

　When Mr Greenspan was summoned by the Congress in the United States, he admitted frankly that he was partially responsible for the financial crisis. It had hit literally everybody, the whole planet, at the same time. The world-wide financial crisis seems to have calmed down now. However, the following problems have remained unchanged. Namely, high unemployment rates in both developed and developing countries, sluggish economies in most countries, economic and financial reforms not carried out smoothly, and protectionist tendencies in most countries restricting international trade and economic cooperation etc. The after effects of the financial crisis are going to drag on for years.

　Our first main concern here is the financial crisis in Japan. Firstly, the financial sector in Japan is less affected compared to those in the United States and Europe. Japan has been conducting financial reform, together with political and social reforms, over the last 20 years since the collapse of the bubble economy in April 1991. The financial sector in Japan is therefore comparatively healthier compared to those in Western nations.

　Secondly, Japan's economic fundamentals in terms of international trade surpluses, unemployment rate, foreign assets, savings rate and

---

[*]　Professor, Graduate School of Asia-Pacific Studies, Waseda University.
　　Professor, Institute of Asia-Pacific Studies, Waseda Unversity.
　　Director, Institute of Chinese Economies, Waseda University.

foreign currency reserves, is much better than her Western counterparts. Unfortunately, Japan has been investing heavily in stock markets in the United States and has therefore suffered significant losses in recent weeks. Besides, since Japan has been a typical export-led growth country, with the United States being Japan's most important market, Japan's exporting industries have since suffered seriously from the down-turn in the American economy.

Our second main concern is the financial crisis in China. It can be argued that the Chinese economy has not been seriously affected by the crisis due to the following reasons:

Firstly, the Chinese financial sector is not widely linked to the rest of the world. In other words, Chinese financial sector is, to a certain extent, controlled by the Chinese Central Government.

Secondly, banking corporations, financial institutions and securities companies in China are rather healthy compared to those in the United States and Europe.

Thirdly, China has international trade surpluses, financial surpluses, high savings rates and sufficient foreign currency reserves. These sound economic fundamentals have enabled China to tackle the financial crisis.

However, due to China's heavy reliance on international markets, especially the American market for her exports, Chinese manufacturing industries have started to feel the hit from the sluggish American economy. Furthermore, share prices and property prices started falling soon after the financial crisis.

After several bailout policies implemented by the Chinese Government, public funds have flowed into the property and stock markets in China, which has created the property bubble in the country now.

Our third main concern is the financial crisis in India. It can be argued that the Indian economy has also not been seriously affected by the crisis due to the following reasons:

Firstly, compared to Japan and China, the Indian economy (the financial sector in India in particular) is less developed and is less linked to the global financial sectors, especially that of the United States. Thus, the financial crisis affected the Indian economy less.

Secondly, compared to Japan and China, India is a less export-led growth country in nature, and therefore Indian economic development is less reliant on international markets and especially that of the United States. Indian economic development relies more on domestic consumption and the domestic market.

Thirdly, despite the fact that India is still a poor country, it has been developing quite smoothly and continuously over the years as a newly emerging economy. India's economic fundamentals are not as sound as Japan and China, but they have improved quite stably.

What should Japan, China and India do, or what have these three countries done in the face of the financial crisis?

For Japan, she has done the following:

Firstly, in order to stimulate the domestic economy, she acted promptly to reduce interest rates, from 0.5% to 0.3% and then to 0.1%.

Secondly, Japan set aside 23 trillion yen (much smaller than that of China in terms of GNP) to stimulate and to expand her domestic economy. (For example, to assist the small and medium-sized enterprises, to increase the purchasing power of the Japanese, etc.)

Thirdly, she continued to carry out her reform policies under the new Democratic Party of Japan, in order to get rid of her gloomy economy lasting for 20 years since the bubble economy burst in April 1991.

For China, she has so far done the following:

Firstly, in order to activate domestic consumption, she has reduced interest rates to a third since the American financial crisis erupted in September 2008.

Secondly, in order to stimulate domestic economy and expand the domestic market, China set aside 4 trillion Renminbi (approximately 57 trillion Japanese yen then) on the 5th November 2008, to improve social and industrial infrastructure, to improve the environment, to upgrade its welfare system, to assist the small and medium-sized enterprises, to reconstruct Sichuan province after the earthquake etc within 2 years. These measures, in my opinion, were very timely and constructive.

In addition, various ministries and provincial/local governments had also allocated huge budgets to stimulate the domestic economy. For example, Ministry of Railways: 7 trillion Renminbi; Ministry of Transportation: 5 trillion Renminbi; Civil Aviation 450 billion Renminbi. Furthermore, Shanghai and Ji'nan allocated investment budgets amounting to 500 billion Renminbi and 800 billion Renminbi respectively. Sichuan Province and Yun'nan Province also announced that they would each invest 3 trillion Renminbi to reconstruct their provincial economies.

For India, she has done the following:
Firstly, continue to carry out political, economic and social reforms in order to obtain continuous political stability, economic development and social equalities under the same government. All these efforts are aimed to immunize against the financial crisis and the world-wide economic downturn.

Secondly, continue to carry out her long term and immense social and industrial infrastructures. Infrastructural construction and development have lagged behind rapid economic development in India. India has been keen to mobilize domestic capital and overseas assistance to upgrade her domestic infrastructural networks.

Thirdly, continue to increase domestic demand and to enlarge her domestic economy, as world-wide economic development slows down and protectionist tendencies are rising in both developed and developing countries.

All in all, Japan, China and India have not poured in money to rescue (bail out) banking corporations, financial institutions and securities companies, unlike the Western nations.

Besides, China has managed to keep the Renminbi stable and cut taxes in order to stimulate export trade. Japan, on the other hand, has made full use of her strong currency to increase foreign investments. India refrained from taking drastic actions in the face of the global financial crisis.

The Chinese government set up two investment corporations, namely China Investment Ltd. Co. and China Central Huijin Investment Company, which have been actively making some overseas investments. These investment corporations are expecting high returns, but are of course, bearing high risks as well.

As for Japan, the Japanese Government has so far not set up any Government Fund (or Sovereign Wealth Fund), despite the fact that Japan has accumulated a substantial amount of foreign currency reserves, and more importantly Japanese national financial assets, cash, shares and properties amounting to 1,600 trillion yen. Japan made her overseas investments through banks, finance and securities companies. Up till the 29th November 2008, 692 financial institutions suffered from 3 trillion 273 billion in losses. It was also estimated that Japanese national financial assets were reduced by 128 trillion yen in November 2008.

Both Japan and China, and to a much lesser extent India, were big buyers of American national bonds and corporate shares. Soon after 15th September 2008, the American government announced a 700 billion bailout plan for banks, finance and securities companies. The Bush Administration also announced a 230 billion US dollar (2-3 trillion yen) plan to rescue the three big automobile companies (GM, Ford and Chrysler).

Where can America get the money from? The final solution was to issue more national bonds, printing notes and selling corporate shares.

America's foreign currency reserves is only 83.3 billion dollars (as of the end of July 2009) while that of China, Japan and India are 2 trillion 273 billion dollars (as of the end of September 2009), 1 trillion 74 billion dollars (as of the end of November 2009) and 287.3 billion (as of the end of December 2009) respectively. China and Japan, and to a lesser extent India, are important buyers of American debt. China has become an increasingly important purchaser of American debt. It is estimated that China utilized 30%-40% of her foreign currency reserves to purchase bonds issued by the American government. During the last American presidential period, Mr McCaine suggested that "the American people owed Chinese people 500 billion dollars" and Mr Obama surprised the world by saying that "China has purchased 1 trillion dollars of national bonds issued by the American government". Recent records showed that China, Japan and India purchased national bond issues by the American government to the tune of 776.4 billion dollars (as of the end of June 2009), 711.8 billion dollars (as of the end of June 2009) and 38.8 billion dollars (as of the end of May 2009) respectively.

Should Japan, China and India assist the United States to solve her financial crisis problem? If the answer is "Yes", then how and to what extent should these three countries assist the United States and the world? By doing so, what can Japan, China and India benefit from their contributions?

The G8, G20 and the APEC meetings are held periodically. Share prices continue to drop incessantly. World currencies (except Japanese yen) continue to depreciate drastically. Presidents of France and Russia have publicly suggested that the world should consider whether the American currency should continue to be the major currency in the world? If not, can Euro, Chinese Renminbi or Japanese Yen replace it? The answer again is "no".

The world economy is now in a very messy and awkward situation. The global financial crisis has somehow calmed down but the aftereffects are going to drag on for years. Every country has to give priority to develop her national and domestic economy. As for the Asia-Pacific region, economic co-operation and integration between China and ASEAN, Japan and ASEAN, and Korea and ASEAN should be further strengthened. Economic cooperation and integration among the ASEAN 10+3 should be further encouraged and prompted. The global financial crisis will definitely stimulate economic co-operation and regional economic development among the countries involved and expedite the formation and establishment of the East Asian Economic Community.

主な略語一覧

ACU	→	Asian Currency Unit アジア通貨単位
ACU	→	Asian Clearing Union アジア決済同盟
ADB	→	Asian Development Bank アジア開発銀行
AFTA	→	ASEAN Free Trade Area ASEAN自由貿易地域
AMF	→	Asian Monetary Fund アジア通貨基金
APEC	→	Asia-Pacific Economic Cooperation アジア太平洋経済協力
APP	→	ASIA-PACIFIC PARTNERSHIP ON CLEAN DEVELOPMENT AND CLIMATE クリーン開発と気候に関するアジア太平洋パートナーシップ
ARF	→	ASEAN Regional Forum ASEAN地域フォーラム
ASEAN	→	Association of South-East Asian Nations 東南アジア諸国連合
ASEAN + 3	→	ASEAN plus Three 東南アジア諸国連合＋日中韓
ASEM	→	Asia-Europe Meeting アジア欧州会合
BIS	→	Bank for International Settlements 国際決済銀行
BRICs	→	Brazil, Russia, India and China ブラジル（Brazil），ロシア（Russia），インド（India），中国（China）の頭文字を合わせた4ヶ国の総称
CAFTA	→	China-ASEAN Free Trade Area 中国・ASEAN自由貿易地域
COP15	→	United Nations Framework Convention on Climate Change 国連気候変動枠組条約第15回締約国会議（COP15）
CSCAP	→	The Council for Security Cooperation in the Asia Pacific アジア太平洋安全保障協力会議
DAC	→	Development Assistance Committee （OECDの）開発援助委員会
EAS	→	The East Asia Summit 東アジア首脳会議

EPA	→	Economic Partnership Agreement 経済連携協定
ERIA	→	Economic Research Institute for ASEAN and East Asia 東アジア・ASEAN経済研究センター
ESCAP	→	Economic and Social Commission for Asia and the Pacific 国連アジア太平洋経済社会委員会
FTA	→	Free Trade Agreement 自由貿易協定
EMS	→	Electronics Manufacturing Service 電子機器の生産委託サービス
EU	→	European Union 欧州連合
FDI	→	Foreign Direct Investment 外国直接投資
GAP	→	Green Aid Plan グリーン・エイド・プラン（環境問題に取り組むための支援プログラム）
GDP	→	Gross Domestic Products 国民総生産
IAEA	→	International Atomic Energy Agency 国際原子力機関
IMB	→	International Maritime Bureau 国際海事局
IEA	→	International Energy Agency 国際エネルギー機関
IMF	→	International Monetary Fund 国際通貨基金
JI	→	Joint Implementation 共同実施
KEDO	→	Korean Peninsula Energy Development Organization 朝鮮半島エネルギー開発機構
MDGs	→	Millennium Development Goals ミレニアム開発目標
NEACD	→	NorthEast Asia Cooperation Dialogue 北東アジア協力対話
NGO	→	Non-Governmental Organization 非政府組織
NIEs	→	Newly Industrializing Economies 新興工業経済群あるいは新興工業経済地域

NPT	→	Treaty on the Non-Proliferation of Nuclear Weapons 核兵器不拡散条約
ODA	→	Official Development Assistance 政府開発援助
OECD	→	Organization for Economic Cooperation and Development 経済協力開発機構
OEM/ODM	→	Original Equipment Manufacturing/Original Design Manufacturing 委託元のブランドで製品を生産する（OEM）。委託先ブランドで製品を設計，生産する（ODM）。
PPP	→	Public-Private Partnership 政府民間パートナーシップ
PECC	→	Pacific Economic Cooperation Council 太平洋経済協力会議
ReCAAP	→	Regional Cooperation Agreement on Combating Piracy and Armed Robbery against Ships in Asia アジア海賊対策地域協力協定
RMSI	→	Regional Maritime Security Initiative 地域海洋安全保障構想
SAARC	→	South Asian Association for Regional Cooperation 南アジア地域協力連合
SCO	→	The Shanghai Cooperation Organization 上海協力機構
SDR	→	Special Drawing Rights 特別引出権
TFP	→	Total Factor Productivity 全要素生産性
UNDP	→	United Nations Development Programme 国連開発計画
UNFCC	→	United Nations Framework Convention on Climate Change 気候変動に関する国際連合枠組条約
WTO	→	World Trade Organization 世界貿易機関

執筆者略歴

林華生（りむ・ほぁしん）

早稲田大学大学院アジア太平洋研究科教授（早稲田大学中華経済研究所所長兼任）。一橋大学経済学部・経済修士課程修了。ロンドン大学博士号取得。シンガポール国立東南アジア研究所，シンガポール国立大学，中京大学などを経て早稲田大学教授。南開大学，同済大学，上海交通大学，北京師範大学，北京大学，中山大学，復旦大学，ヘルシンキ大学，南洋工科大学などの顧問・客員教授を兼務。主な著書に，「ASEAN経済の地殻変動」（同文館・東京），「アジア四極経済」（ダイヤモンド社・東京），「東盟，日本与中国人地区経貿合作」（編著・世界科技出版社・シンガポール），「東亜経済圏」（世界知識出版社・北京），「剖析東亜経済」（編著・世界科技出版社・シンガポール），「Japan and China in East Asian Integration」（Institute of Southeast Asian Studies, Singapore），「アジア経済のアキレス腱」（編著・文真堂・東京），など。

谷口　誠（たにぐち・まこと）

桜美林大学北東アジア総合研究所特別顧問，北東アジア研究交流ネットワーク（NEASE-Net）代表幹事。中国の上海同済大学，武漢大学客員教授。一橋大学経済学部修士課程終了。英国ケンブリッジ大学卒業。外務省入省。在ＮＹ日本政府国連代表部特命全権大使，OECD事務次長，早稲田大学アジア太平洋研究センター教授などを経て岩手県立大学学長，日立金属株式会社社外監査役，天津外国語学院客員教授などを務めた。主な著書に「南北問題　解決への道」（サイマル出版），「21世紀の南北問題　グローバル時代の挑戦」（早稲田大学出版），「東アジア共同体　経済統合のゆくえと日本」（岩波新書）など多数。

王少普（おう・しょうふ）

復旦大学歴史学部，華東師範大学歴史学研究所卒業。歴史学博士。
上海社会科学院アジア太平洋研究所研究員，副所長。早稲田大学社研所客座研究員などを歴任。現在は，上海交通大学環太平洋研究センター，日本研究センター主任教授，中華日本学会常務理事，中華アジア太平洋学会理事（副秘書長），上海国際関係学会常務理事，上海日本学会副会長，上海世界経済学会理事，上海台湾研究会理事，上海統一戦線理論研究会理事；復旦大学日本研究センター，韓国研究センター，中国国台弁海峡両岸研究センター特邀研究員；早稲田大学アジア太平洋研究センター特別研究員。

木下　俊彦（きのした・としひこ）

早稲田大学アジア太平洋研究科教授（客員）。慶應義塾大学経済学部卒業。1963年，日本輸出入銀行入行，営業第一部長，財務部長，海外投資研究所長などを経て，1996年退職。A.T.カーニーアジア担当特別顧問，早稲田大学商学部・大学院商学研究科，国際教養学部教授を経て，現職。主要著作に，『21世紀のアジア経済　危機から復活へ』（共編著，東洋経済新報社，1999年），『アジア経済：リスクへの挑戦』（共編著，勁草書房，2000年），「日本企業のビジネスモデルと日中経済」（浦田秀次郎他編著『経済共同体への展望』，早稲田

大学 COE プロジェクト，岩波書店，2007 年，第 2 章）。"Changes of Japanese Corporate Business Model Under Global Pressure: Evidence Justifying KPM" & "Examples of Changes of Japanese Corporate Business Model: Why is KPM Essentially Important Now?, (Shigenobu Ohara & Takayuki Asada ed.,) Japanese Project Management, KPM－Innovation, Development and Improvement, World Scientific, London & Singapore, 2008, pp83-110 & pp.403-424. などがある。

澁谷　祐（しぶたに・ゆう）
早稲田大学アジア太平洋研究センター特別研究員。慶応義塾大学商学部卒（国際経営）。石油連盟，外務省（在クエイト日本大使館書記官），ジェトロ・ロンドンセンター石油資源部長，アジア太平洋・エネルギーフォーラム設立幹事研究主幹を経て，（有）エナジー・ジオポリティクス代表。英国ミドルイーストコンサルタント・インターナショナル（MEC）シニア・コンサルタント（兼務）。著書（共著）「とことんやさしい『石油の本』」（日刊工業新聞社），「アジア経済のアキレス腱」（編著・文真堂・東京）。

美根　慶樹（みね・よしき）
キヤノングローバル戦略研究所特別研究員。東京大学教養学部非常勤講師。東京大学法学部卒業。ハーバード大学で修士号取得（地域研究）。外務省勤務。防衛庁（当時）国際参事官，在ユーゴスラビア連邦共和国（当時）大使，地球環境問題担当大使，在軍縮代表部大使，アフガニスタン支援調整担当大使，日朝国交正常化交渉日本政府代表を歴任。著書に『スイス歴史が生んだ異色の憲法』。

浜　勝彦（はま・かつひこ）
創価大学名誉教授。社団法人中国研究所理事長。東京大学大学院（農業経済学）修士。アジア経済研究所で香港とシンガポールに海外派遣員。外務省出向（在北京日本国大使館経済部特別研究員）などを経て，動向分析部長。1991 年創価大学文学部教授。（有）アジア・マクロシステム研究所取締役・所長（兼務）。中国研究所理事として「21 世紀シルクロード研究会」を主宰。日本現代中国学会員，日本アジア政経学会員。主な著作に『中国－トウ小平の近代化戦略』（アジア経済研究所），『トウ小平時代の中国経済』（亜紀書房），「アジア経済のアキレス腱」（編著・文真堂・東京）など。

清水　学（しみず・まなぶ）
帝京大学経済学部教授。東大教養学部卒。アジア経済研究所（南アジア，中東，旧ソ連中央アジア）のほか，インド・ターター社会科学研究所，エジプト・社会調査犯罪学研究所で研究に従事。宇都宮大学，一橋大学経済学研究科教授を経て，現在上智大学・法政大学等で非常勤講師。（有）ユーラシア・コンサルタント社代表。主要編著書は『中東新秩序の模索―ソ連崩壊と和平プロセス―』（アジア経済研究所），『中央アジア―市場化の現段階と課題―』（アジア経済研究所），共著『中東政治経済論』（国際書院），共著『ロシア・東欧経済論』（ミネルヴァ書房），「アジア経済のアキレス腱」（編著・文真堂・東京）など。

Hans C. Blomqvist

Hans C. Blomqvist is Professor of Economics at the Hanken School of Economics and Business Administration in Helsinki and Vasa, Finland. He has also worked as a Visiting Professor and/or Visiting Fellow at Stanford University, the Institute of Southeast Asian Studies, the Australian National University, the University of Queensland, Waseda University and the Stockholm School of Economics. His research interests include development economics, international economics and political economy, all with a focus on Southeast Asia.

H.S. Prabhakar

Associate Professor in Japanese Studies, School of International Studies, New Delhi.

H.S.Prabhakar obtained his Ph.D from Jawaharlal Nehru University and has been teaching there since 1985. He was a visiting foreign researcher at the Institute of Social Sciences, University of Tokyo from 1983-85 and 1995, and at Waseda University in 2006 with fellowships from the Japan Foundation. He was also a foreign researcher and project participant in 1995 at Osaka International University, Osaka Japan.

He has several publications to his credit, including topics on India-Japan relations. He is also a regular commentator in the Indian media.

Thomas Ferguson

Thomas Ferguson is Professor of Political Science at the University of Massachusetts, Boston and a Senior Fellow of the Roosevelt Institute. He received his Ph.D. from Princeton University and taught formerly at MIT and the University of Texas, Austin. He is the author or coauthor of several books, including Golden Rule (University of Chicago Press, 1995) and Right Turn (Hill & Wang, 1986) . He is a long time Contributing Editor to The Nation and a member of the editorial boards of the Journal of the Historical Society and the International Journal of Political Economy. He also serves on the advisory board of the Institute for New Economic Thinking.

Robert Johnson

Robert Johnson is Executive Director of the Institute for New Economic Thinking and Director of Financial Regulatory Policy at the Roosevelt Institute. He received his Ph.D. in Economics from Princeton University and then worked for the Board of Governors of the U.S. Federal Reserve before becoming the Chief Economist of the Banking Committee of the United States Senate and then Managing Director at Soros Funds Management. In 2008-9 he served on the United Nations Commission of Experts on International Monetary and Financial Reform, chaired by Joseph Stiglitz.

日中印の真価を問う──世界経済危機をめぐって
Asia Giants in the Face of the Global Economic Crisis

2010年3月12日 初版発行

編著者	林　華生
	浜　勝彦
	澁谷　祐
発行者	佐藤康夫
発行所	白帝社

〒171-0014　東京都豊島区池袋2-65-1
電話 03-3986-3271　FAX 03-3986-3272
info@hakuteisha.co.jp
http://www.hakuteisha.co.jp/

組版・印刷　(株)東神堂　　製本　カナメブックス

Printed Japan　〈検印省略〉6914　ISBN978-4-86398-012-9
落丁乱丁の際はお取り替えいたします。